P9-BZY-707

A LIFE OF
IMPACT

LEADERSHIP PRINCIPLES OF JESUS

A LIFE OF
IMPACT

LEADERSHIP PRINCIPLES OF JESUS

Tom Hedman

NEW LIFE PUBLICATIONS
Toronto, Los Angeles

NEW LIFE PUBLICATIONS
P.O. Box 220152, Santa Clarita, California 91322-0152

COPYRIGHT © 1992, TOM HEDMAN

All rights reserved. No part of this book may be reproduced or transmitted in any form or by any means, electronic or mechanical, including photocopying, recording, or any information storage and retrieval system, without permission in writing from the Publisher.

Scripture taken from the HOLY BIBLE, NEW INTERNATIONAL VERSION. Copyright © 1973, 1978, 1984 by International Bible Society. Used by permission of Zondervan Publishing House. All rights reserved.

The "NIV" and "New International Version" trademarks are registered in the United States Patent and Trademark Office by International Bible Society. Use of either trademark requires permission of International Bible Society.

Canadian Cataloguing in Publication Data
Hedman, Thomas P. (Thomas Paul), 1961—
    A life of impact

Includes bibliographical references and index.
ISBN 0-9696031-0-X

1. Jesus Christ — Character. I. Title.

BT304.H44 1992   232.9'03   C92-094506-6

PRINTED IN CANADA
First Printing: 1993

For my wife, Sow-Foong,
You are my joy

ACKNOWLEDGMENTS

One man dreams, but an army conquers. My deepest gratitude is due to those without whose help the dream for this book would not have materialized. First of all I thank Darrell Johnson, my editor and good friend. Darrell took my thoughts, my concepts and my ramblings and sifted and clarified them until they spoke clearly. In answer to prayer we've produced something that neither one of us could possibly have done without the other. Like Darrell, Jeff Solway has done much more for me than provide the illustration for the cover of this book. In fact, Jeff has been my very best encourager. It is great to work with best friends.

Thanks to all of the members of Carpe Diem, the writers group to which I belong. Their positive and constructive criticisms have made a great impact on this book. Special thanks to Douglas Jacoby, Paul Finlayson, Greg Taylor, Peter Bovin and Jeff Carlton for their editorial comments. Thanks also to Henry Kreite, Mark Mancini, and Dave Eastman for teaching me about Jesus. There are many others to whom I am indebted: Barry Wilson and Greg Nicholas for their production assistance, Carl and Sharon, Yvonne Solway, Robert and Diana, Ron and Cheryl and my mom and dad.

Last and most of all, I would like to thank my wife, Sow-Foong. Your patience and support have been invaluable. You trusted me while I chased a dream. I love you with all my heart, and I always will.

Tom Hedman

Contents

INTRODUCTION

impact (im'-pakt) *n*. **1.** The striking of one body against another; a collision. **2.** The effect of one thing upon another.[†] **3.** The force of impression of one thing on another : an impelling or compelling effect.[‡]

If we were to analyze its current usage, we would discover that the word "impact" has captured some new and exciting meanings. It's such a catchy, energetic little word that it has stolen the limelight from competing synonyms. My first serious encounter with this word was in a physics class, where I found it to have a very precise definition; in the field of dynamics, "impact" refers to a measurable quantity which describes the energy transfer resulting from a collision. But this word has many other common uses. For example, some bombs are designed to explode "on impact." In a more positive sense, one may discuss the "impact" of a painting, or of a piece of music. "Impact" is also used frequently in other sciences and engineering, in medicine and dentistry (ie. an "impacted" tooth), in publishing, in economics and the military.

But what exactly is meant by "a life of impact"? Does this imply becoming a human bowling ball, with the goal of

[†]New American Heritage Dictionary
[‡]Webster's New Collegiate Dictionary

striking, knocking down and scattering those we come in contact with? Maybe you're not so sure that you want to live an impacting life.

In this book we will examine how our own personal impact may be increased. Personal impact is more than mere influence, more than an after-effect of leadership. **For the purposes of this study we will define *personal impact* as the difference individuals can make in their world by the way they live their lives.** Such a difference can endure long after their departure.

How can we become men and women of impact? Over two hundred specific and practical answers to this question can be found in the Gospel of Mark. It may be surprising to some that out of all the world's literature the work with the richest insights into how to become more influential would be the story of a man whose only crown was made of thorns, and whose closest friends abandoned him in his last days. What could we possibly learn from a man who was publicly beaten, spat on, and whipped? Why would we want to follow the example of a man who, because of his ways and his words, was condemned to die before the eyes of the multitude as a hideous object of scorn—nailed to a cross? After all, wasn't he defeated? Didn't he fail in his mission? Haven't his followers since then always been a weak-willed and unimpressive lot of hypocrites who have never quite been able to live up to the ideals professed by their master?

On the contrary, Jesus of Nazareth is debatably the most influential man who has ever lived. In merely three years he began a movement that has influenced nearly everyone on the planet over the past twenty centuries. Consider his impact: almost all of his closest friends died violent deaths proclaiming his divinity. The church, despite its humble beginnings, eventually conquered Rome itself. Missionary zeal became the force spurring the exploration of the New World. Social reform began in Jesus' name; hospitals, orphanages, homes for unwed mothers, were motivated by his words. A vast number of great works of art and music—Handel's "Messiah," DaVinci's "The Last Supper"—have found their inspiration in him. A great number of books, "more than the world can hold,"† have been written about him.

His present day disciples believe that he is the only Son of God, that he was raised from the dead. Most everyone agrees that he was an actual historical figure who walked the earth twenty centuries ago in Palestine. Just what was there in the life and character of this simple carpenter that produced such a phenomenal impact on the lives of the people around him? Why was he always front page news, always the talk of the town, always surrounded by throngs of people—some wanting to kill him, others willing to die for him? How did he inspire people to radically change their lives and ultimately turn the whole world upside-down? And for those of us today who aspire to do great things with our lives, to have an impact on our world, what can we learn from this man, Jesus of Nazareth?

The inspiration for writing this book came from a personal desire to make a difference in this world. At the time I began my research, I was relatively unaware of the vast array of books available on the subject of personal effectiveness. I had not yet discovered the work of Stephen Covey; I hadn't even heard of Anthony Robbins. I had read *In Search of Excellence*,‡ and I understood what it meant to have a Positive Mental Attitude. Yet what I yearned for was a flesh-and-blood example, someone who not only understood the principles of personal effectiveness, but who was also a master of them. From my life as a Christian, I knew that Mark's gospel revealed many insights into the ways of Jesus of Nazareth. I was also convinced through much study and observation that this planet has never been quite the same since Jesus appeared on the scene.

†John 21:25
‡Thomas J. Peters, Robert H. Waterman, Jr., Warner Books

Therefore I embarked on a journey *into* the Gospel of Mark to see what I could learn from Jesus. To my surprise, I discovered that Mark's gospel was a gold mine of simple and authoritative lessons on how to live a life of impact, lessons that had the ring of truth. Having completed the first leg of my journey, I am now even more excited; my study has radically changed the way I live my life.

Likewise, I believe that the observations compiled in this book, because they are insights from God's inspired word, can transform the reader—if he or she is willing to be transformed. This book is intended for those who want their lives to count! It aims to help those who want to change the world, to leave their mark on it. It is a study for people who want to excel in their careers and their marriages, those who want life-changing relationships. It is intended to assist people who aspire to be movers and shakers, world leaders, trend-setters, and pioneers. It should serve to complement the many available texts in the realm of personal effectiveness.

Most of all, this book is for the disciple of Jesus who wants to have an incredible impact on this world for Jesus' sake. It is for the person who has been impacted by the cross: cut to the heart, inspired, and forever changed. Jesus commissioned all of his disciples to duplicate his purposes in their lives. He called all that would come after him to lay down their lives for him. They were not given leave to modify or water down his message in order to better adapt to an irreverent age. Rather, disciples need to be ever changing to become more like him—the ultimate messenger of God.

And if the primary aspiration of all people claiming to be Christians is to become like Jesus,† then doesn't it stand to reason that they, like him, should also become catalysts for change? If God does multiply the talents of those who utilize

---

†Mark 1:16-18, Luke 9:23-26, 57-62, John 12:23-26, 14:12, I John 2:3-6

what they have,† should not all Christians have a significantly greater impact on this world than one would think possible, given their talent, their upbringing, their drive and their circumstances? Should they not be attaining, even surpassing, their potential?

Don't put this book down, however, just because you are not a Christian, you have no desire to become one, and you have little tolerance for religious thought. Though the biblical references are many (including the entire Gospel of Mark), and a few of the sections may have no direct application for someone who is not a Christian, **the lessons are straightforward and intended to help anyone who desires to increase his or her own personal impact.** You have nothing to fear from reading this book. I assure you of this: you will grow in your admiration and respect for Jesus. He has set an impressive example, by anyone's standards. Yet what you do with this information will be completely up to you. My hope is that this book will provide you with the practical knowledge that you need to gain a sense of purpose and to live a life of greater significance.

I am convinced that each one of us was created to live a life of impact. We want to do something great and memorable with our lives. So let us now begin to examine the life of a master "impacter." We will frequently interrupt Mark as he tells Jesus' story in order to discuss how and why Jesus was able to have such an unique impact, and how we might imitate his example.

†Matthew 25:14-30, Luke 19:11-27

1
INITIAL IMPACT

Expectation

Mark 1:1 The beginning of the gospel about Jesus Christ, the Son of God.

Mark begins his book with a succinct introduction of his real-life character: Jesus, the Christ (meaning Messiah or Savior), and Jesus, the Son of God. The validity of these claims about Jesus is an extremely important, yet contentious issue. Therefore, let us not endeavor to defend or refute claims about Jesus here, in order that we may focus our attention on how he made an impact.

Imagine yourself emerging into a new life as the only son or daughter of a wealthy, influential man. To what would you aspire? And what would you expect to accomplish in your lifetime? People of royalty, position, or great wealth tend to lead lives of influence and notoriety. It is often expected that they live extraordinary lives in keeping with the high expectations of their position. Although Jesus was born into extremely humble circumstances, his heritage was of the most noble kind. He was and knew he was the only son of God. Therefore, he expected a lot from himself. He never accepted that he was born to simply be a good carpenter, to be kind to his neighbor and to grow old and die. Such a thought while he was growing up would have made him laugh. He knew he was born to save the world.

The expectations we have for our lives will dramatically affect how we live our lives. They will dictate what we try to do, how hard we try to do it, and ultimately, whether or not we will succeed. I remember a conversation I had with the mother of my best friend near the end of my undergraduate studies in engineering. Although I had done rather well in my program, I had decided not to apply to schools the likes of MIT or Stanford for my graduate studies. In my thinking, an application to one of these premier schools would be inappropriate for a common person like myself, regardless of my past performance. I simply wouldn't fit in there.

My family was eager to respect and support whatever decision I made about my education, so I decided to apply to my state university and some comparable schools. It was at this point that I spoke to my best friend's mother, Babs. She was astounded that I wasn't even going to apply to either of these great schools. Her oldest son had sent his applications to the very best law schools in the country and had been accepted by one of them. Babs was beside herself when I told her that I hadn't even considered applying to MIT because I didn't consider myself MIT "caliber." One thing she said I think I will never forget. She asked me how I thought I would feel when I was her age looking back at my life. Would I regret not even attempting to get into one of the very best schools when I had the chance? Would I feel good about not shooting for the stars when I was younger? She eventually won me over. I applied, was accepted, and completed my Master's Degree in Mechanical Engineering at MIT. Not only did I receive an excellent education, but in those two years I caught a new vision for my life. I had considered entering the Peace Corps but opted instead to become a disciple of Christ. I met many men and women bent on changing the world. Best of all, I met my wife on the campus of MIT. Thanks Babs!

Jesus had high expectations of himself because he knew that he was the only son of God. In the same way, are not all Christians members of God's family?[†] As John the apostle wrote: "How great is the love the Father has lavished on us, that we should be called children of God! And that is what we are!"[‡]

If we are baptized disciples of Jesus, then we are people of *royal second birth.* **We must therefore expect ourselves to live** *extraordinary* **lives.** We must expect that we will be the ones to persevere through difficult situations in our work places with never a complaint, that we will be those brimming with confidence, those who are strong and courageous.[§] To act in any other way is to act in a way not befitting our birth. To wallow in self pity, to cower in fear, to simply give up when the going gets tough, is inappropriate behavior for a son or daughter of the Lord God Almighty, the Lord of lords and the King of kings!

Announcement

Mark 1:2-8 It is written in Isaiah the prophet: "I will send my messenger ahead of you, who will prepare your way—a voice of one calling in the desert, 'Prepare the way for the Lord, make straight paths for him.'" And so John came, baptizing in the desert region and preaching a baptism of repentance for the forgiveness of sins. The whole Judean countryside and all the people of Jerusalem went out to him. Confessing their sins, they were baptized by him in the Jordan River. John wore clothing made of camel's hair, with a leather belt around his waist, and he ate locusts and wild honey. And this was his message: "After me will come one more powerful than I, the thongs of whose sandals I am not worthy to stoop down and

[†]Ephesians 2:19
[‡]1 John 3:1
[§]Joshua 1

untie. I baptize you with water, but he will baptize you with the Holy Spirit."

Jesus was announced. He was introduced as a "high-powered" man of God. The people around Jesus knew they would have to repent, to get their lives in order, before they even talked with him. John's announcement gave Jesus an impressive reputation before he even started his ministry.

We can put this principle to work in our workplaces: "Aside from being an excellent engineer, Wayne's my right hand man. He really moves this laboratory and he's continually suggesting better ways of doing things. I couldn't get by without him." Likewise, if we are leaders in the church, we should announce our men and women: "Jeff is a man who truly loves God. His life has radically changed because of his relationship with God." Wouldn't Wayne do his best work for the boss who had announced him in such a complimentary way? And wouldn't Jeff walk into the next group Bible discussion with his head held high if he knew he was talked about in this way? **People consistently live up to the perceptions others have of them.** I remember so well how this was practiced by Scott, a Christian who walked with me and discipled my spiritual life for years. Several times Scott introduced me as an accomplished scientist to friends of his who wanted to study the Bible with us. He would then describe how God had worked powerfully in my life. It always amazed me how earnestly Scott's friend would listen to what I had to say, and how easy I found it to boldly share my faith with him, after having received such a glowing introduction.

John believed in Jesus and gave him a head start. Jesus didn't begin his ministry as a nobody, alone, desperately trying to gain people's attention. On the contrary, **a noted "somebody" spoke very well of him and urged everyone to listen to him.** In a way it's surprising that Jesus would even need someone to go before him to prepare people to meet him. John himself didn't have this luxury; he had to make a name for himself.

Perhaps Jesus didn't actually need the help, but the Father decided that his son deserved an introduction. If we ourselves have had the privilege of having a "somebody" believe in us and announce us, we know how much an announcement helps create a strong first impression. We can implement this principle by announcing the people we believe in to others in our circle of influence.

Encouragement

Mark 1:9-11 At that time Jesus came from Nazareth in Galilee and was baptized by John in the Jordan. As Jesus was coming up out of the water, he saw heaven being torn open and the Spirit descending on him like a dove. And a voice came from heaven: "You are my Son, whom I love; with you I am well pleased."

Jesus was personally encouraged by his father immediately after his baptism. He was told that he was very special, that he was the Son of God, loved by the Father and pleasing to Him. I can easily imagine that Jesus was *ready to take on the world* at this point in his life! Imagine how excited he must have been with this affirmation of love and support from his Father. Surely he was inspired to do incredible things! But how can we relate to this? It's exciting when our own fathers do the same kind of thing for us, but how much more exhilarating it must be to be personally encouraged by the Almighty God! Yet we needn't be envious. The Bible teaches that those who are born again in baptism come into the family of God.[†] Therefore we too can be encouraged and excited by the fact that the Father loves us even as he has loved Jesus.[‡] God is a god who initiates love. The Bible provides this definition: "This is love: not that we loved God, but that he loved us and sent his Son as an atoning sacrifice for our sins."[§]

[†]Galatians 3:26-27
[‡]John 17:23,26
[§]1 John 4:10

When a person understands and accepts how deeply and personally he is loved by God, it will undoubtedly change his life. On one of my trips to Boston a few years back, I made a point of having lunch with a Christian friend who lived there. I had grown a bit stale in my walk with God, and I knew Don would be able to encourage me; after years of being a disciple who had little or no impact on others, he was now a very dynamic and productive leader in the church. After spending a few minutes getting to know each other over Whoppers and fries, I asked him what had inspired him, after years of relatively unproductive Christianity, to dramatically change his life. The answer was very quick in coming. It wasn't prayer and fasting; it wasn't a life-changing talk with someone; it wasn't a powerful Sunday morning lesson. On a trip to Japan a year or so earlier, Don had simply come to realize that God loved him. He was not merely one of many sons of God through Christ. God knew him personally, God liked him and God loved him! From that point on, Don was a new man. And after talking with him, I was also encouraged. I too had begun to intellectualize the love of God. I needed to listen to the encouraging voice of God in the Bible, and I had to learn how to take God's affirmations of love personally. Don's life demonstrated to me the impact of God's encouragement.

Preparation

Mark 1:12-13 At once the Spirit sent him out into the desert, and he was in the desert forty days, being tempted by Satan. He was with the wild animals, and angels attended him.

Jesus went through forty days of spiritual boot camp. He was led by the Spirit into the desert to toughen up. Mark's gospel doesn't even mention that he was fasting for these forty days. Instead, Mark focuses on the fact that Jesus was strengthened for his mission by resisting various temptations for forty days all alone in the desert. **Many of us lack the toughness to be forceful in our relationships, the inner drive to make things happen.** Perhaps we have lived cushy lives where we've never had to push against apparently immovable objects. We haven't strengthened the inner self and consequently our character remains timid and we are easily overwhelmed. **Jesus overcame himself first so that he could then overcome the world.** His body and his own desires for comfort and temporary pleasures were not going to get in the way of his destiny. He dealt with them first, head on. Many of us would lead dramatically different lives if we toughened up through focussed self-denial. Fasting is one tremendous biblical method of focussing the mind and soul on the more important issues of life. It is also an effective way of toughening up by mastering the desires of the body. Another way to grow stronger is to deal with difficult challenges. For example, when we face six weeks of very difficult work on our jobs or at our studies we should rejoice because our inner self will be strengthened. James wrote: "Consider it pure joy, my brothers, whenever you face trials of many kinds, because you know that the testing of your faith develops perseverance. Perseverance must finish its work so that you may be mature and complete, not lacking anything."†

How reasonable would it be to expect someone to make a significant contribution to an athletic team without first participating in the preseason practices? Or how likely would it be for a soldier who somehow skipped boot camp to be any good to his commanding officer in a time of war? And wouldn't we question the sanity of a lawyer who decided to embark on a career without first sweating it out through a reputable law program? We understand that these **times of preparation are essential if an individual is going to have any impact in his or her chosen field.** Why then do we sometimes begin major campaigns for our bosses, or for God, with little or no special

†James 1:2-4

preparation? Certainly, too many of us in the present-day movement of God have taken lightly the concept of preparation. Perhaps some of us have completely overlooked this crucial stage in Jesus' ministry. If Jesus needed to be prepared through focussed self-denial in order to perform his ministry, **can we expect to reach our goals, spiritual or otherwise, without preparation?** We may think that we are "lean mean fighting machines," when in truth we are fat, flabby and out of shape spiritually. No wonder some people fall flat on their faces when they begin to lead a group of Christians for the first time, or when they go to a new city to help start a new church. Let us not be deceived. The road is not covered with rose petals, and our enemy is not unaware of our efforts. If we merely "play church" like so many around us, we will have as little true impact for God as they are having. We must toughen up; we must spend time in preparation. In the words of Juma Ikanga, a long-distance runner whose weekly regimen includes 140 miles of high-altitude training: **"The will to win is nothing without the will to prepare."**

The Message

Mark 1:14-15 After John was put in prison, Jesus went into Galilee, proclaiming the good news of God. "The time has come," he said. "The kingdom of God is near. Repent and believe the good news!"

Jesus was a bearer of Good News. He wasn't negative or doomsdayish. **His message was *attractive*** because he proclaimed that an intimate involvement with God was now available to the people; a divine relationship was now within reach. Clearly, Jesus was convinced that he was bringing to the people what they really needed. He wasn't like the dishonest fruit vendor who candy coated a bitter fruit; Jesus knew that what he was offering people tasted good all the way to the core. Yet it wasn't without cost; he let them know the price upfront.

Jesus laid out in two words what it was going to take to become a part of this new spiritual kingdom: repentance and belief. But his message was overwhelmingly positive. He didn't go around proclaiming the "bad news": "At this point none of you are going to heaven, the kingdom of God is near but none of you are in it because you all have sin, doubt and cynicism in your life." No, Jesus' message inspired people to look more deeply into what he was saying.

Jesus urged people to "seize the day." **He proclaimed an *urgent* message, and he called for an immediate response.** He spoke as if he expected people to jump at his invitation. Indeed, those who responded did tend to respond without delay because of *his* urgency, *his* faith and *his* convictions.

In the same way, if we want people to join quickly and wholeheartedly with us in our campaigns—whether they be job projects, athletic contests, or efforts to further the work of God—we must be fully convinced of their importance. We shouldn't ram our message down anyone's throat; instead, we should inspire others to take a step in the same direction where we ourselves are headed. We must be urgent with people if we want them to act urgently. We must give people a vision of what is before them, well within their reach. Of course, they will not see everything clearly at first, and the obstacles to be overcome will loom before them. Therefore, they will need assurance that their goal is achievable; it can be obtained, but not without initiative and concentrated effort. We must inspire people to investigate more deeply into what we are proposing. We must believe and proclaim that this may be their only opportunity to respond.

The Call ...

Mark 1:16-18 As Jesus walked beside the Sea of Galilee, he saw Simon and his brother Andrew casting a net into the lake, for they were fishermen. "Come, follow me," Jesus said, "and I will make you fishers of men." At once they left their nets and followed him.

... To a Purpose

It is interesting that Jesus first of all called these disciples to be men of impact. His initial invitation did not promise them forgiveness, or salvation, or the excitement of watching many miracles, even though he could and would provide all of these. Instead, he called them to a life of purpose. He vowed to give their lives meaning: they would influence other men for God. It's just as interesting that Jesus' last command to them was also to influence others for God.† In fact, all the way through Jesus' ministry on earth he was concerned with raising up men and women who would impact others for God.

... To Imitate Him

Many leaders in industry today call their people to emulate successful people, past and present. However, **Jesus had a bit of a different slant on the use of imitation as a training technique.** From the very beginning, Jesus called his men to imitate *his* lifestyle. When he said: "Come, follow me," those who followed knew that he wasn't inviting them to a picnic. He wanted them to be with him and to become like him. He wanted to show them a lifestyle which they could imitate and then pass on to others. It is a good thing to encourage people to mimic the ways of other great people. But how much of the lives of distant superstars will be exposed to our people? **We need to become what we want our people to become. Then we can call them to imitate the good in our lives.**

†Mark 16:15-19, Matthew 28:16-20

In this very act of calling his disciples, Jesus sets an example for those who were to accept his invitation, an example illustrating the very purpose to which he was calling them. In effect, he himself was fishing ("trolling," to be more precise) for men who would also become fishers of men who would also become fishers of men.... He demonstrated a passion for his purpose, and he showed that he had deep convictions about what he was doing. And as his men spent time with him and followed his lead, they too would share his purpose. They would also share his passion for that purpose. They would become men who could also inspire other men to lead lives of impact.[†]

... *To a Mutual Commitment*

Jesus moved people to action by issuing a call to a relationship in which he promised that he would first be committed to them (ie. "I will make you..."). He did not expect them to leave all behind to follow him with no reciprocal commitment on his part. He didn't say that he would do his best to help them but in the end their success or failure would be their own responsibility. Instead **he committed himself to their ultimate success**. Insofar as it was within his power, he would bring them to victory. If they would indeed follow him, he would ensure their success.

The best relationships are those in which both parties are completely committed both to the cause and to their partner. Marriage is an excellent example of this principle. Unfortunately, we live in an age of selfish independence where most people entering marriage are committed only to the pursuit of their own happiness. Because of this, one is almost as likely to make it big in a lottery as to have a fulfilling and lasting

[†]II Timothy 2:12

marriage. Except, of course, in the case where both husband and wife are committed to each other in the way that God directs. God, after all, created marriage. **If a marriage is structured the way God designed it to be, it will flourish.** The Bible teaches that the husband is to lovingly lead in the marriage much as Jesus led his devoted followers. It also teaches that the husband must be committed to the spiritual, physical and emotional well-being of his wife, to the extent of daily laying down his life for her.[†]

As another example of the need for mutual commitment in relationships consider the realm of national or international organizations. Aspiring leaders in business, politics or other domains often make the colossal mistake of expecting people to be completely committed to them while offering only fairness and an opportunity to succeed in return. Consider how long-lasting leaders in industry and innovation such as IBM, Proctor and Gamble, 3M and others share a common commitment to their employees. People are eager to get a job with one of these companies because they are committed to treating their employees well, they believe in promoting from within, and they look to develop and groom every one of their employees for greater roles within the company. **Mutual commitment is the foundation for good employer-employee relations.** Consequently, it's also a key to maintaining long-term financial success of a company.

A Good Judge of Character

The disciples in Mark 1:16-20 display sincere humility and respect for this man of God by responding to his call immediately, even to the extent of leaving their families and

---

[†]Ephesians 5:23-30

livelihoods behind. Jesus must have been able to recognize their humility before God. Incredibly, Jesus had only met these men a short time earlier, and had probably spent but one day with them.[†] This shows that Jesus was a quick and accurate judge of men's characters and hearts. In fact, the Bible states that Jesus knew people's thoughts and their lives.[‡] Jesus "knew what was in a man."[§] But how can we even dare to think that we can imitate the Son of God's divine insight into human hearts? We are after all mere men and women. However, if we are spiritual people we can have great insight into other people's lives. Examine the following scriptures:

> Your commands make me wiser than my enemies, for they are ever with me. I have more insight than all my teachers, for I meditate on your statutes. I have more understanding than the elders, for I obey your precepts. (Psalm 119:98-100)

> The proverbs of Solomon son of David, king of Israel: for giving prudence to the simple, knowledge and discretion to the young—let the wise listen and add to their learning, and let the discerning get guidance. (Proverbs 1:1,4-5)

> The purposes of a man's heart are deep waters, but a man of understanding draws them out. (Proverbs 20:5)

> For the word of God is living and active. Sharper than any double-edged sword, it penetrates even to dividing soul and spirit, joints and marrow; it judges the thoughts and attitudes of the heart. Nothing in all creation is hidden from God's sight. Everything is uncovered and laid bare before the eyes of him to whom we must give account. (Hebrews 4:12-13)

The Bible is useful in teaching us to be wise and insightful. It shows us how to identify the proud, mockers, the lazy ("sluggards"), fools and the wicked. It also affirms that the purposes of a man's heart can be drawn out. It exposes even the attitudes of the heart. Those of us who have deliberated long

[†]John 1:35-51
[‡]Matthew 9:1-4, 12:22-28, Luke 9:46-48, 11:16-17, John 2:24-25, 4:3-19, 13:11
[§]John 2:25

and hard to choose the right person to work for us know all too well the value of these insights. We don't want to hire people who are mockers, those who have no respect for authorities or leaders in their lives. We also don't want to hire someone who would be lazy, someone who might give up when the going gets tough, or someone too proud to listen to correction or receive direction. **We would love to be able to recognize the team player, the person with the "all for one and one for all" spirit, and the person who is teachable.** Very often these characteristics of the heart are not obvious from the outside. Can the Bible really teach us to know, like Jesus did, what is in a man? Paul had something interesting to say about the uniqueness of our inner struggles: "No temptation has seized you except what is common to man."†

Any temptation that a person may experience, he shares in common with the rest of us. We've either personally been tempted in the same way or we know someone who has. This truth can give us tremendous insight into the inner struggles that people experience, and thus, into their strengths and weaknesses of character. *No one has unique struggles, although most of us think we do.* To know our own sinful nature is to know the workings of all human hearts. Jesus adds this directive: "...first take the plank out of your own eye, and then you will see clearly to remove the speck from your brother's eye."‡ **If we have seen and dealt with the sin in our own heart we are able to see more clearly into other people's hearts.** A man who has been deeply convicted of the selfishness in his own life can more easily detect selfishness in someone else. Conversely, the man who is not able to admit and face up to the selfishness in his own life will be in no position to appreciate the gravity of the same sin in another man's life.

†I Corinthians 10:13
‡Matthew 7:5

By utilizing the Bible's insight into our own hearts and our own characters, **we can be better equipped not to** *condemn* **but to** *detect* **the attitudes and the characteristics of other people's hearts.** This insight will help us in many areas: for example, in choosing who we may want to work for, or who to hire, or who to enter into partnerships with, or who to marry.

Relatability

When Jesus initiated conversation with these men by the sea of Galilee, he did so with **language that piqued their curiosity.** Their motive in following him at first may have been partly to figure out exactly what a "fisher of men" was. He "baited" them (in a good way) by making this invitation. He didn't prey on their greed or their pride, but on their desire to do something great for God. At the same time, **he spoke to them in terms they could understand.** They certainly knew and understood what fishing was all about. Thus, Jesus made himself relatable to them. And by so doing **he showed them that he was thinking about them,** considering the purpose of their lives. He was very serious and deliberate about asking them. Calling them to be his disciples and co-workers was obviously not an afterthought. He appeared to be passionate and determined about this decision. He most certainly got their attention.

Consider what kind of impact this type of language would have on you. Ineffectual leaders typically fail to get others excited about their projects. They tend to describe a project in a very dry and boring way, as if they didn't want to do the work themselves. They describe the project in the same terms to everyone, terms that make sense to themselves. They also tend to describe the project in excessive detail before the prospective follower has been able to grasp the big picture. It is significant that Jesus did not say to these men, "Come follow me and we will cover two or three thousand miles of Judean countryside.

We will get up very early every morning to pray before setting out to meet people's needs all day long and late into the night. And I will send you out to proclaim my message to strangers, many of whom will reject you.''

People who effectively move the masses relate to and concentrate on the individuals. Few of us will commit ourselves in a big way to someone who doesn't care enough about us to find out who we are. But **when someone goes out of her way to consider us as individuals we feel** *important.* **And we** *excel* **when we feel important.** The assembly line worker who has been told personally by the president of the company that his spot welding function is vital not only to the manufacture of a quality product, but also to the reputation of the company, can be inspired for life. If the president also lets him know personally that she depends on him as much as on her vice-presidents, then he will feel important. On the other hand, the corporate leader who is not approachable and addresses the employees only in large groups will not move the individuals or the company. **The ultimate form of unrelatability is no communication at all, which conveys a subtle message that the employee is not worth knowing.**

Some of us who are leaders have found out the hard way that we cannot inspire and motivate those we lead by speaking to them only in groups. If we do not give our people individual attention they will not feel valuable. Sometimes leaders of large groups feel that their people will gain all the encouragement they need from the people immediately over them in the organization. This is simply not true. Even people who intellectually understand and appreciate the time constraints of their leader's leader will likely feel less important if they never have one-on-one time with him or her. Therefore, we must not neglect individual attention, even as we strive to move large groups of people. **"For when we change the individual, we have begun to change the world."**†

---

†Kip McKean: "Discipleship Study" on tape

The Challenge

Mark 1:19-20 When he had gone a little farther, he saw James son of Zebedee
             and his brother John in a boat, preparing their nets. Without delay he
             called them, and they left their father Zebedee in the boat with the
             hired men and followed him.

**Jesus didn't hesitate to call people to a significant level of
commitment.** He was urgent and not at all embarrassed. He
expected them to respond radically and immediately! He didn't
seem to care what their friends, family or co-workers would
think or say about it. By his expectation of a radical and
immediate response, he gathered men who were decisive and
not weak-willed. **Someone who is strongly affected by the
opinions of others is not going to be able to have a great
impact on others.** Often people claim that they need more time
to reach such a decision. This is often an indicator of
indecisiveness, of an unwillingness to take a risk or to make
mistakes. Such people are debilitated by their pride. Either they
are afraid of what others might think or say about them or they
are unwilling to chance spoiling their self-perceived perfection.
Jesus wanted to focus his time and energies on people who
would continue to respond to his challenges. They would prove
themselves to be malleable and he would transform them into
men of impact.

In all likelihood, we don't tend to hire employees, to put
together a sports team or a band, or to select those we will
disciple to maturity in Christ with this same perspective in
mind. Talent and experience are usually our primary selection
criteria. **An openness to making rapid and radical changes
will, however, out-impact talent and experience in most
situations.** After all, how many Pharisees or teachers of the
Law did Jesus call to be his most intimate disciples? These men
knew the Old Testament better than anyone else and they were
experienced speakers and leaders. Yet not many of them were

open to relearning a great deal, except perhaps Joseph of Arimathea and Nicodemus. In fact, most of these religious leaders weren't willing to be taught anything! **People who are already satisfied with their level of achievement will rarely grow to achieve more than they already have.** People who think they know it all are not open to correction. They will not be easily influenced and they will be unable to pass on new teachings with any personal conviction. Because they are holding on to their past achievements, they will not be able to change and become like their teacher. Consequently, they will have nowhere near the impact of their teacher. Jesus said, "A student is not above his teacher, but everyone who is fully trained will be like his teacher."† Peter, Andrew, James and John, who were open to making radical changes, all became like their teacher. Even their enemies would recognize this; as we read in Acts 4:13, "When they saw the courage of Peter and John and realized that they were unschooled, ordinary men, they were astonished and they took note that these men had been with Jesus."

Vision

Although this passage teaches us about the calling of the first disciples, it was not the first or only time Jesus would call these men to follow him. In the gospel of John, chapters one and two, we read about the time when these men first met Jesus. He invited them to follow him, and they did.‡ Then they went with him to a wedding at Cana in Galilee a couple of days later. There Jesus performed his first miracle, "and his disciples put their faith in him."§ After this they went down to Capernaum

†Luke 6:40
‡John 1:37-39,43
§John 2:11

with him and eventually up to Jerusalem for the Passover. While on this trip to Jerusalem they watched Jesus clear the temple. It appears that these were contiguous events and Jesus' new disciples were with him the whole time. It also appears, though, that after this episode they all went back to their nets. With this understanding of the order of events we can see another powerful leadership quality in Jesus: he had vision for his followers. He believed in them. He continued to give them opportunities even after they had parted company with him. In fact, he had to call them back to following him again and again.[†]

How many second and third chances do we give to people? Do we continue to believe in them even after they make a mistake, even if they are "clued out" about what we are trying to do? Suppose an employee of yours has let you down or disappointed you. Do you continue to have a vision for how he could change and what he could accomplish? Typically I feel somewhat discouraged after I have had to correct someone or call him back to his commitment or responsibilities. I tend to share his doubt that he can and will change. But it's at these times that he needs to be believed in more than ever. He needs to be shown that I still believe in him and that I will give him another chance. An ineffective leader frequently expresses doubt in his people's abilities. **People will tend to not surpass our expectations or our vision for them. We need to believe in people, like Jesus did, and in so doing, give them hope.**

It is mind-boggling to think that Jesus planned to turn the world upside down through twelve plain ordinary men. No one would have believed him if he had announced it in advance. **Jesus not only had an *unrelenting vision* for these men; he also had a *radical vision*, for them to become men who would change the world.** He didn't limit his vision for these men due to their low ratings on all the conventional measures. They lacked

[†]Luke 5:1-11, John 21:1-19

formal education. They didn't have long resumes stating that they were talented or that they could lead effectively. They may not have had natural speaking ability or people skills. One thing that anyone could see, however, was that they were tough and could work long and hard. They weren't "wimps"—fishing back then wasn't the cushy hobby that it has become today. But other than this one quality they weren't all that impressive. **Jesus didn't let their existing qualities or lack thereof affect his dream for what they could become.**

Do we dare to dream the incredible? **Do we fight for our dreams and refuse to live ordinary lives?** If we truly want to be like Jesus and to be men and women of impact, we must dream great dreams. We need to look and see the bigger picture. We must accept that all great projects begin with a humble infancy stage. **Greatness does not suddenly appear. It is the end product of a process which begins with a dream.** As an example of this, consider the developmental process of a human being. In a purely physical sense a human being starts out as one cell with a spectacular plan. This one cell multiplies itself and copies the same plan into each new cell. Cells with discordant plans (ie. viruses and cancers) are destructive to the whole body and must be eliminated. Eventually these new cells carrying the original plan mature and associate themselves with other cells to do what they are best at doing, and together they successfully achieve their goal. This very familiar process is commonly referred to as the miracle of life. The developmental process reveals a paradigm illustrating what it takes to make an impact in this world. What an amazing concept, that a single cell could develop into a mature, diversified, multifunctional, adaptable and intelligent being! In the same way, **each of us is destined for greatness, but we must first dream great dreams.** We are, after all, created in the image of the God who envisioned this universe and then said, "Let there be light...."†

†Genesis 1:3

Initiative

Mark 1:21 They went to Capernaum, and when the Sabbath came, Jesus went
    into the synagogue and began to teach.

Jesus was a self-starter. He not only knew what to do but he got
up and did it without any other person to motivate him or hold
him accountable. **How many great plans fail and how much
great talent is wasted because of a lack of initiative?**
Likewise, consider how many mediocre plans succeed very well
and how often an average talent goes a long way because the
man or woman who possesses it has a lot of initiative. By
definition, world changers do not succeed through the superb
application of already well established methods and because of
the encouragement and prodding of someone else. **Men and
women of impact do not simply envision a changed world;
without hesitating, they get out and pursue their dreams.**

Authority

Mark 1:22-28 The people were amazed at his teaching, because he taught
    them as one who had authority, not as the teachers of the law. Just
    then a man in their synagogue who was possessed by an evil spirit
    cried out, "What do you want with us, Jesus of Nazareth? Have you
    come to destroy us? I know who you are—the Holy One of God!"
    "Be quiet!" said Jesus sternly. "Come out of him!" The evil spirit
    shook the man violently and came out of him with a shriek. The
    people were all so amazed that they asked each other, "What is this?
    A new teaching—and with authority! He even gives orders to evil
    spirits and they obey him." News about him spread quickly over the
    whole region of Galilee.

Jesus was an amazing teacher because he taught as one who had
authority. So what does that mean? One in authority gives
orders and commands the people. Consider how often Jesus
used these phrases: "do...," "do not...," "I tell you...,"

"don't think...." **People in authority issue policy, guidelines and truths as the final word on the subject. They are fully convinced that they have every right to say what they say, and to do what they do, and to expect what they expect.** This is not to say that they will never be wrong or never make mistakes; those under their authority must simply live with their errors. (Thank God that Jesus never made mistakes, and that he appeared, even to his enemies, to be without fault.[†]) But can someone in authority actually expect to have an impact on this world? Don't we all resist and feel uncomfortable around authorities? An important distinction must be made here. Jesus spoke as one who had authority—he was *authoritative*—but he did not act like the authorities the Jews were familiar with, who were *authoritarian.* **Jesus allowed people to decide for themselves whether they would obey him or not.** Yet he made it clear that if they wanted what only he could give them—"No one comes to the Father except through me." (John 14:6)—they would have to completely obey him as their Lord. Jesus did not force people to conform to his example any more than God forces people today to love, worship and obey him. Jesus gave people a choice.

Similarly, Paul, the disciple of Christ who arguably made a greater impact than any other, knew that he had the authority he needed to carry out his work. But he also knew, from following the example of Jesus, how to use his authority properly.[‡]

But how can we apply this? **First of all, we need to understand just what authority we do have.** Let us first consider our working environments. Most of us possess different types of authority on the job. In a few areas we may have *absolute authority*, where our decisions are not subject to anyone else, but in most areas we have only *limited authority*.

[†]John 8:46
[‡]II Corinthians 13:10

Some of us work in environments where the authority structures have not been made known to us, or have been left rather vague. These environments tend to be chaotic and can be full of crippling bad attitudes and unresolved conflicts. Limited authority usually presents itself in the form of *delegated authority*; that is, our superiors declare that the decisions and directives that we ourselves make and give are to be fully obeyed by those under us, who may nevertheless appeal our decisions by going directly to a higher authority (our boss).

Once we understand the authority that we've been delegated, we can be assertive leaders. We can confidently call those under our authority to follow our directions. **We shouldn't have to demand that they submit to us; instead, we should explain that if they follow our directions they will personally benefit, and the whole group will function more smoothly and efficiently.** Supposedly, we've been put in authority because those over us believe that we know best how to accomplish certain tasks. It stands to reason, then, that each member of the group and the group as a whole will be most productive when each individual reliably follows the directions he has been given. This seems so obvious that one might wonder why there are so very few effective leaders in our work places. This dearth of effective leadership may be due to the fact that most leaders are unwilling to call their subordinates to carefully follow their exact directions. Also, it may be that too many leaders lord it over their employees, expecting homage and reverence on top of submission. Chances are they get none of the above. In contrast, it's fascinating to observe those who properly and aggressively use their authority for the good of the group. They are the ones who bring projects to completion. They knock down obstacles. They command respect from everyone. They act as those fully persuaded that they have all the authority they need to do what is good for the organization. Let us follow their example, and Jesus' example, and not fail to speak with authority just because it's abused or misused by some.

This may all be well and good in the work setting, but by what authority does a Christian carry out the ministry of Christ? The answer is: the delegated authority of God. We have "all authority in heaven and on earth."† It is true that some people have wrongly claimed the delegated authority of God, and have used it for evil. But again, can we allow the misuse of authority by others to hinder or eliminate our proper use of it? Jesus spoke and taught with authority even though the Jews were a people oppressed by the heavy-handed practices of the Roman ruling authorities. He did not temper his speech around the Jewish religious leaders who were jealous of his influence. And because of this, the common people were amazed, and news about him spread quickly. This is a good thing for a person trying to impact the world.

Gentleness

Mark 1:29-34 As soon as they left the synagogue, they went with James and John to the home of Simon and Andrew. Simon's mother-in-law was in bed with a fever, and they told Jesus about her. So he went to her, took her hand and helped her up. The fever left her and she began to wait on them. That evening after sunset the people brought to Jesus all the sick and demon-possessed. The whole town gathered at the door, and Jesus healed many who had various diseases. He also drove out many demons, but he would not let the demons speak because they knew who he was.

Jesus was gentle. He went in to Simon's mother-in-law, took her hand and helped her up. He didn't call from the other room, "Woman, be healed, and get out of bed." We should picture Jesus speaking softly, bending over and smiling as he took her hand. We should see him gently helping her to sit up, and then steadying her as she stood.

There can be no doubt but that Simon's mother-in-law would

†Matthew 28:18-20

adore Jesus from this point onward. Here was the man who had caused some rifts in her family, who had pulled Simon out of his respectable and financially secure occupation to be part of a roving band of preachers, a change in life-style which had the potential of hurting his wife—*her daughter.* But now here he was, in her own home, treating her with such gentleness and respect that she must have felt like crying. Indeed, emotions well up in our hearts some twenty centuries later as we read about this tender episode.

> "He will not quarrel or cry out; no one will hear his voice in the streets.
> A bruised reed he will not break, and a smouldering wick he will not
> snuff out . . ." (Matthew 12:19-20)

Often it is not the loud voice that will truly move people, but the soft whisper. We all appreciate being treated with gentleness; how many of us try to practice it toward others? At times we may need to raise our voices and push in order for things to get done. But often, using a gentle tone and pitching in to help will accomplish far more good.

What a great example for us! Just one paragraph ago, we saw Jesus amazing the people with his authoritative speech. Now we see the emphasis placed upon his gentleness and tenderness. Jesus combined in his character a perfect balance of power and gentleness: man of steel, man of velvet. Who could fail to be impressed?

Fueling

Mark 1:35-39 Very early in the morning, while it was still dark, Jesus got up, left the house and went off to a solitary place, where he prayed. Simon and his companions went to look for him, and when they found him, they exclaimed: "Everyone is looking for you!" Jesus replied, "Let us go somewhere else—to the nearby villages—so I can preach there also. That is why I have come." So he traveled throughout Galilee, preaching in their synagogues and driving out demons.

Jesus got up early in the morning. **People who love sleep don't usually change the world.** If we can't even drag ourselves out of bed, how can we expect to move anyone else? Jesus didn't walk with the Father when he "had the time," or preach when he "had the time." Instead, Jesus slept when he "had the time." He knew he needed sleep, so he slept. But Jesus pushed himself hard. He was consumed with his purpose, and here he shows us his serious commitment to relying on and praying to the Father. Jesus was extremely eager for prayer, and he came out of his prayer times deeply convicted, focussed and ready for action. He came out with specific plans for his day and for the future.

Jesus saw his purpose very clearly. He knew that he was on earth to preach to the people of Israel. He also knew that he could not wander far from Jerusalem for he would eventually die in that city. **Most of us live with only a vague idea of our purpose.** Even those of us who are disciples of Jesus tend to accept a rather general description of our purpose—"to seek and to save what was lost"†—without bothering to focus in on the more specific and personal purposes to which God may have called us. For example, what types of people has God best prepared us to share our faith with? What talents or experience do we have that can be developed and used for the good of the kingdom of God?

To best appreciate the significance of the outcome of this prayer of Jesus, we need to look carefully at the context. In contrast to the persecution he had met with elsewhere, Jesus had been well received in Capernaum. In fact, he was downright popular. He even had a house to stay in when he visited. It would have been very comfortable for Jesus to settle down in Capernaum and make disciples there. He could alter his original plan and base his operations in this more hospitable northern city rather than roaming around the countryside with frequent stops in Jerusa-

†Luke 19:10

lem, the city where they stone the prophets.† But Jesus, in prayer, deepened the conviction that he had to stick to his original plan.

In the same way, in different areas of our lives such as our marriages, our jobs, and our personal ministries, **we can be tempted to "lose the fire," to settle down and get comfortable.** Often as we grow older we begin to achieve some of our goals and we are able to attain some of the niceties that were always out of reach in the past. But these niceties, whether they be a spouse, children, financial independence, or the opportunity to invest our money, always bring complications. They tend to make focussing our hearts and minds on our ideals and goals more and more difficult. **We come to laugh patronizingly at friends younger than us who are yet idealists, zealots and radicals.** We amuse ourselves with the knowledge that they too will mellow with age, they too will become more balanced and level-headed, "sobered by the realities of life"—or perhaps, more accurately, discouraged by the cost of change.

We, like Jesus, need time to refocus—preferably every day. For those of us who have a relationship with God, to whom could we rather choose to go for advice and wisdom, comfort and conviction? Jesus didn't have a legalistic, putting-in-his-time relationship with his father. His relationship with God fueled his life.

Compassion

Mark 1:40-45 A man with leprosy came to him and begged him on his knees, "If you are willing, you can make me clean." Filled with compassion, Jesus reached out his hand and touched the man. "I am willing," he said. "Be clean!" Immediately the leprosy left him and

†Luke 13:33-34

he was cured. Jesus sent him away at once with a strong warning: "See that you don't tell this to anyone. But go, show yourself to the priest and offer the sacrifices that Moses commanded for your cleansing, as a testimony to them." Instead he went out and began to talk freely, spreading the news. As a result, Jesus could no longer enter a town openly but stayed outside in lonely places. Yet the people still came to him from everywhere.

Jesus was willing to get radically and unconventionally involved with people. He didn't minister from a safe distance; instead, he came close to people and got his hands dirty—literally. We all know what it means to have problems and to be embarrassed about certain aspects of our lives. Someone who gives us pat answers when we are in need or who pays little or no attention to our deeply-felt concerns will certainly never win us over. Conversely, Jesus demonstrates that **we can have a powerful and lasting impact on someone else if we are willing to go deep.**

Mark describes Jesus' emotional state as he is confronted by this man with leprosy. In order to understand his reaction, it's important to try to imagine what it must be like to be "filled with compassion." There was absolutely no room left in Jesus for fear, disgust or apprehension. Most of us would probably have a significant portion of these other emotions in a similar situation. Perhaps the only time we experience the undiluted emotion of compassion is at the movies when the hero or heroine suffers grief at the death of a loved one. Because we are observing from a safe distance, there is no need for fear. But how can we, with our fear and suspicion and self-interest, relate to Jesus in a real-life situation that demands compassion? And what does compassion have to do with having an impact?

Jesus demonstrates that it is sometimes good to go along with the overflow of our emotions—when these emotions cause us to do something good for the other person and not something bad against him. Jesus knew that his emotional state was righteous, and because of this he did not hesitate to reach out and touch this diseased man. He didn't try to "control himself," to act only on the basis of reason; instead, he let his emotions move him. How many other people may have felt compassion for this same man without ever acting on their feelings? How many may have even caught themselves reaching out with a loving touch and then had abruptly pulled back, realizing the personal danger inherent in such an act? Surely the well-meaning people who walked by with their compassion bottled up inside them had only a negative impact on the leper.

Some of us are so afraid of being too emotional that we go through life all bottled up inside. We are so disciplined and calculating that our touch turns cold, soon to be followed by our hearts. The world is in dire need of people who don't withhold their love. It's sad that in many circles it's considered a strength to "control" or suppress emotions and a weakness to act on them. **Real strength is displayed in a man like Jesus who was able to deny himself when his emotions were against what is good[†] and who acted without hesitation on emotions that produced good.**

Humility

Jesus sent this leper away immediately after healing him. Mark tells us that Jesus gave the man a strong warning not to tell anyone about what he had done for him. At first glance this warning seems contrary to Jesus' expressed purpose for his life, but upon further investigation we learn that Jesus was purposefully avoiding seeking glory for himself. He was strong in his warning in order to avoid being seen as an attention-seeking miracle worker. Jesus foresaw that his popularity would eventually curtail his ability to freely move around to carry out his ministry. He was thinking ahead. Imagine what his "strong warning" might have sounded like: perhaps he raised his voice,

[†]Matthew 26:36-46

looked the man straight in the eye and pointed his finger at him.

People who succumb to their desire for personal glory or adulation don't usually get very far in enlisting others to their cause. Personal glory becomes their goal and their original program is subverted. A friend of mine worked for a man who openly stated that he was primarily motivated by the glory he would personally receive if their project were successful. (He even gave this statement in writing!) Needless to say, the rest of the people on the project did not share his motivation. They were more excited about the possibility of developing a device that could help relieve pain and increase the productivity of individuals suffering from a particular malady. They also simply wanted to do well on their jobs in order to earn an honest wage. Because they weren't all seeking their boss's personal glory, numerous skirmishes and disagreements occurred throughout the course of the project. Ultimately, in my opinion, this conflict of motivations led to the eventual break-up of the team and ended up stalling the whole project. The boss's headlong pursuit of glory affected how he wanted the projects to be done and in what order they were to be completed. Those on the research team found themselves engaged in an ongoing fight to maintain their professional integrity without losing their jobs for insubordination. The boss viewed any constructive criticism of their work by other professionals as a personal attack. Unfortunately, by the time of the break-up, six years and over a million dollars had been spent on the project.

Opportunism

Mark 2:1-2 A few days later, when Jesus again entered Capernaum, the people heard that he had come home. So many gathered that there was no room left, not even outside the door, and he preached the word to them.

Jesus made the most of every opportunity. He was alert and single-minded. In this case, he didn't allow the opportunity to slip away, but instead took charge and preached to them. Perhaps these people were gathered around him to see another miracle like the ones he had performed on his previous visit. Perhaps they just wanted to see what all the commotion was about concerning this wandering prophet. Whatever their motivation, Jesus had their attention and he preached the Word of God.

Jesus was always ready to make the most of an opportunity because he was always eager to be productive. He longed for fruitful labor; he didn't dread his work and he didn't procrastinate. In fact, he seemed to make no distinction between time spent working and the rest of his life. His "work switch" was always in the "on" position because he was not content to merely exist. **To Jesus, life itself was an opportunity, so every event in life was a "once in a lifetime opportunity."** Most of us fail to realize how fleeting and how unique the episodes of our lives are until after the majority of these episodes have passed. Perhaps it was because Jesus knew he only had a few months to live that he milked the most out of each hour. **If today were your last day, would you be pleased with how you lived it?** The challenge from Jesus' example is to live life to the full,[†] every hour of every day, with no regrets. Let us make "carpe diem" our motto, making the most of every opportunity!

Commendation

Mark 2:3-5 Some men came, bringing to him a paralytic, carried by four of
        them. Since they could not get him to Jesus because of the crowd,
        they made an opening in the roof above Jesus and, after digging

---

†John 10:10

through it, lowered the mat the paralyzed man was lying on. When Jesus saw their faith, he said to the paralytic, "Son, your sins are forgiven."

In a room full of people who believed in him, Jesus was able to discern the extraordinary faith of four men who went to great trouble to get their friend to meet Jesus. Jesus noticed and rewarded the aggressive faith of these men. He wasn't offended by this disruption of his meeting, nor did he think these people were trying to steal the focus away from him. Instead, Jesus showed that he was hungrily looking for people with faith, and he knew that exceptional actions always accompany great faith.

How consistently do we commend the noteworthy actions of our peers or of those we lead? **Too often we are only quick to note the failures of those around us, and we get so caught up in the many minor crises and disruptions that fill our days that we fail to notice worthy deeds.** Positive contributions and even great accomplishments can easily go unnoticed if we are not actively watching out for them.

Forgiveness

Interestingly, Jesus does not first tell this man to get up and walk. Instead, he says to him, "your sins are forgiven." To most of us, this doesn't make immediate sense. We see only the tremendous physical need that the man presented. But Jesus saw the greater need—indeed, the root problem in this man's life: he needed forgiveness. This applies to the rest of us as well. The Bible, if the reader will consider it, makes this very clear. Consider the following passages:

A heart at peace gives life to the body, but envy rots the bones. (Proverbs 14:30)

Blessed is he whose transgressions are forgiven, whose sins are covered. Blessed is the man whose sin the LORD does not count against him and in whose spirit is no deceit. When I kept silent, my bones wasted away through my groaning all day long. For day and night your hand was heavy upon me; my strength was sapped as in the heat of summer. Then I acknowledged my sin to you and did not cover up my iniquity. I said, "I will confess my transgressions to the LORD"—and you forgave the guilt of my sin. Therefore let everyone who is godly pray to you while you may be found; surely when the mighty waters rise, they will not reach him. (Psalms 32:1-6)

O LORD, do not rebuke me in your anger or discipline me in your wrath. For your arrows have pierced me, and your hand has come down upon me. Because of your wrath there is no health in my body; my bones have no soundness because of my sin. My guilt has overwhelmed me like a burden too heavy to bear. My wounds fester and are loathsome because of my sinful folly. I am bowed down and brought very low; all day long I go about mourning. My back is filled with searing pain; there is no health in my body. I am feeble and utterly crushed; I groan in anguish of heart. All my longings lie open before you, O Lord; my sighing is not hidden from you. My heart pounds, my strength fails me; even the light has gone from my eyes. . . . For I am about to fall, and my pain is ever with me. I confess my iniquity; I am troubled by my sin. (Psalms 38:1-10,17-18)

The Bible's teaching on the matter of sin and forgiveness is very clear. **The guilt of sin can have a crippling or debilitating effect on even our physical bodies.** It is well accepted that our emotional well being is a key factor in determining our physical health; we see here that the Bible goes one step further, linking our spiritual and physical health. It is also evident from the above passages that physical suffering may often be God's means of alerting people to their spiritual depravity. This, of course, is not to say that all disease and illness is the result of sin or the heavy hand of God (ie. see John 9:2-3). But on the other hand, to completely disregard the possible spiritual causes of some of mankind's sufferings would be a serious oversight.

Abandon

Mark 2:6-12 Now some teachers of the law were sitting there, thinking to themselves, "Why does this fellow talk like that? He's blaspheming! Who can forgive sins but God alone?" Immediately Jesus knew in his spirit that this was what they were thinking in their hearts, and he said to them, "Why are you thinking these things? Which is easier: to say to the paralytic, 'Your sins are forgiven,' or to say, 'Get up, take your mat and walk'? But that you may know that the Son of Man has authority on earth to forgive sins. . . ." He said to the paralytic, "I tell you, get up, take your mat and go home." He got up, took his mat and walked out in full view of them all. This amazed everyone and they praised God, saying, "We have never seen anything like this!"

Jesus didn't walk on eggshells when he was around those who opposed him. He didn't bother to change his wording or his teaching style to please the religious leaders of his day. He called it like he saw it, by the authority of God, and with no fear of the potential opposition that he could stir up. In contrast, **we are often so careful not to offend anyone that no frankness and no power is left in our speech.** Jesus said: "Woe to you when all men speak well of you. . ."[†] **If we try hard to please everybody, the odds are good that we will have little or no impact on anybody.** We need instead to be constantly ready to withstand opposition, and we should not try to avoid the confrontations that will certainly occur as we make our stand.[‡]

Intuition

Another amazing ability that Jesus possessed is evidenced in this passage. Mark tells us that Jesus "knew in his spirit" what the teachers of the law were thinking; he was actually able to respond to what they were thinking in their hearts. Most of us possess this ability in a limited quantity. We refer to it as our "gut feeling" or our "intuition" about a situation. I believe

[†]Luke 6:26
[‡]Ephesians 6:10-12, II Timothy 3:12

Mark's expression means that a spiritual man or woman could potentially be more alert and sensitive to the unspoken than could an unspiritual person. The challenge then, for those of us who are baptized disciples of Jesus, is to play our hunches. In effect, this means for us to trust that we are truly led by the Spirit of God.†

Selfless Authority

Let us once again examine Jesus' attitude towards authority. In Mark 2:6-12, Jesus says clearly that he was aware of and unembarrassed about his authority. People who seem apologetic about the authority they have, or who hesitate to exercise it, are not very impressive. The reason they act the way they do is likely the same reason that other people might abuse authority: they see it as a means of gaining something for themselves rather than a means of achieving a goal for the one who delegated the authority to them. **In order to be men and women who make a difference, we need to boldly use the authority we've been given—not for ourselves, but for others and ultimately for God** who reigns over all powers, rulers and authorities. Consider again Jesus' attitude toward and use of his own authority, as seen in one of his last prayers:

> After Jesus said this, he looked toward heaven and prayed: "Father, the time has come. Glorify your Son, that your Son may glorify you. For you granted him authority over all people that he might give eternal life to all those you have given him. . . . I have brought you glory on earth by completing the work you gave me to do. (John 17:1-2,4)

Compare Jesus' attitude with that of Pontius Pilate, governor of Judea. Pilate was not unlike other rulers in that he failed to understand why he was in a position of power. He eventually learned about the origin of his own power from Jesus:

†Romans 8:6-9,14

"Do you refuse to speak to me?" Pilate said. "Don't you realize I have power either to free you or to crucify you?" Jesus answered, "You would have no power over me if it were not given to you from above." (John 19:10-11)

As we've mentioned earlier, Paul imitated Jesus' attitudes toward authority. Read what Paul writes about the authority God has delegated to human governments:

"Everyone must submit himself to the governing authorities, for there is no authority except that which God has established. The authorities that exist have been established by God. Consequently, he who rebels against the authority is rebelling against what God has instituted, and those who do so will bring judgment on themselves . . . . Do you want to be free from fear of the one in authority? Then do what is right and he will commend you. For he is God's servant to do you good. But if you do wrong, be afraid, for he does not bear the sword for nothing. He is God's servant, an agent of wrath to bring punishment on the wrongdoer." (Romans 13:1-4)

Jesus, at the end of his personal mission on earth, very clearly spelled out to his followers the authority he was transferring to them. He tells them, and through them all disciples: "All authority in heaven and on earth has been given to me. Therefore go and make disciples of all nations, baptizing them in the name of the Father and of the Son and of the Holy Spirit, and teaching them to obey everything I have commanded you. And surely I am with you always, to the very end of the age."[†] We, like Jesus, should not hesitate to make use of this authority, and we should be unashamed. Paul writes, "For even if I boast somewhat freely about the authority the Lord gave us for building you up rather than pulling you down, I will not be ashamed of it."[‡] Paul also says that Jesus has been given sovereign power for the sake of his church.

. . . and he [God, the Father] seated him [Jesus] at his right hand in the heavenly realms, far above all rule and authority, power and dominion, and every title that can be given, not only in the present age but also in

[†]Matthew 28:18-20
[‡]II Corinthians 10:8

the one to come. And God placed all things under his feet and appointed
him to be head over everything for the church, which is his body, the
fullness of him who fills everything in every way. (Ephesians 1:20-23)

With absolute authority over us and exercised on our behalf,
and with even a measure of heavenly authority given to us, how
can disciples of Jesus not be bold and assertive? We must be
forceful people.

Focus on the Individual

Mark 2:13-14 Once again Jesus went out beside the lake. A large crowd came
to him, and he began to teach them. As he walked along, he saw Levi
son of Alphaeus sitting at the tax collector's booth. "Follow me,"
Jesus told him, and Levi got up and followed him.

It is interesting how Mark notes that Jesus was teaching a large
crowd when he met and called Levi, also known as Matthew.
Although Jesus was frequently swarmed by people, he was most
interested in the individual faces in the crowd. We don't know
exactly what inspired Jesus to call Levi. Perhaps he saw a
certain look on this tax collector's face, one of humility or awe.
More likely, he simply knew in his spirit that Levi would be a
faithful man. Whatever the case, this mention of Levi shows us
that when Jesus was surrounded by crowds of people, he didn't
"miss the trees for the forest," so to speak. He recognized the
individual. He looked beyond the sea of faces and saw people,
one by one. Each with his or her own character, maturity, trials,
accomplishments and potential. **He was always searching for
the diamond in the rough.** Although Jesus was committed to
teaching the crowds, he was equally committed to singling out
individuals within those crowds and giving them a personal
invitation to follow him.

For us, it can be very easy to lose sight of the individuals who
work in our offices and who live in our neighborhoods, to blur
them together into one conglomeration of "others." It can be

overwhelming, especially while crammed on the subway, attending a hockey game or a movie, or shopping in a big mall, to try to imagine that the countless people we encounter every day are people just like us and are just as important as we are. As our responsibilities in life increase, we tend to deal with more and more people—and each appointment can seem less important and less deserving of our full attention. Unfortunately, people know when we are preoccupied; they can see quite clearly when we begin to treat them as just another "problem" or "detail" in a long day. **If we are to imitate Jesus' attitude towards people, we cannot allow ourselves to grow dull to the preciousness of each individual. Each person is unique, and all people share the same human experiences, the joys and the trials of life.** To make each encounter one of consequence, we must be like Jesus and give each person we interact with all the personal attention we can muster. We must not allow ourselves to lose them in the crowd.

Acceptance of Others

Mark 2:15-17 While Jesus was having dinner at Levi's house, many tax
collectors and "sinners" were eating with him and his disciples, for
there were many who followed him. When the teachers of the law
who were Pharisees saw him eating with the "sinners" and tax
collectors, they asked his disciples: "Why does he eat with tax
collectors and 'sinners'?" On hearing this, Jesus said to them, "It is
not the healthy who need a doctor, but the sick. I have not come to
call the righteous, but sinners."

In even stopping to invite Levi to follow him, Jesus was doing a radical thing. Jesus was willing to associate with absolutely every type of people, from prostitutes to traitorous tax collectors, from religious hypocrites to religious zealots. In fact, Jesus appeared very eager to get close to all these people, to spend time with them. He accepted them even though some were probably quite rough, materialistic and foul-mouthed. And they accepted him, which indicates that he must not have talked down to them or acted in a self-righteous way as did the Pharisees, who made these "sinners" feel extremely uncomfortable. He didn't seem to worry about ruining his reputation. Similarly, if we want to have an impact on the world we need to break out of our limited, socially acceptable circle of acquaintances, and take a chance by getting to know people from all levels of our workplaces, neighborhoods, and communities. **What would be wrong, after all, about a "suit" having lunch with a "blue collar"? And how could an employee fall for the old line about how everyone in the company is equally important when the president only associates with other executives?** How will people of different races, religions, or age groups in our neighborhood be able to put away their suspicions and insecurities if we only invite a select group of neighbors into our home?

Nonconformist

Mark 2:18-22 Now John's disciples and the Pharisees were fasting. Some people came and asked Jesus, "How is it that John's disciples and the disciples of the Pharisees are fasting, but yours are not?" Jesus answered, "How can the guests of the bridegroom fast while he is with them? They cannot, so long as they have him with them. But the time will come when the bridegroom will be taken from them, and on that day they will fast. "No one sews a patch of unshrunk cloth on an old garment. If he does, the new piece will pull away from the old, making the tear worse. And no one pours new wine into old wineskins. If he does, the wine will burst the skins, and both the wine and the wineskins will be ruined. No, he pours new wine into new wineskins."

Jesus did not feel obligated to fulfill religious traditions and live up to conventional expectations. He was not bound to currently accepted practices; indeed, he was willing to radically depart from well-established ways. He insisted that those following him should not try to fit his bold new teaching into their old understandings. He encouraged them to be open to a fresh approach (which incidently did not condemn the old teachings, but rather fulfilled them). Jesus was not afraid of being labeled a radical or a revolutionary. He challenged popular notions of what to live for and gave people enough of a shake-up to inspire them to think again about what they were doing and why they were doing it.

Are we willing to rock the boat? **Do we challenge the comfortable customs of our generation and put our own traditions on trial? Do we scrutinize the well-accepted but timeworn policies in our company and look for better, more appropriate, or more timely ways of reaching our goals?** Men and women who make an impact during their lifetime may not have any more creative juices flowing through their veins than anyone else, but they will necessarily be people who won't accept "because we've always done things that way" as a valid defense for outmoded ways of doing things. Ralph Waldo Emerson wrote: "I am ashamed to think how easily we capitulate to badge and names, to large societies and dead institutions."[†] The non-conformist will consistently stir things up and cause others to rethink their positions. **Only the person who refuses to automatically conform to generally accepted practices can expect to find a better way.** According to Ben Shahn: **"Every great historic change has been based upon non-conformity, has been bought either with the blood or with the reputation of non-conformists."**[‡]

Jesus also understood that truly radical changes do not come about by merely adding on to or making minor adjustments to the existing framework. Trying to combine the old with the new is like pouring new wine into an old wineskin: it will ruin them both. Therefore Jesus demanded that people rid themselves of

[†]Ralph Waldo Emerson: Self Reliance
[‡]Ben Shahn: Atlantic Monthly, September, 1957

their preconceived ideas. A radical change requires a brand new perspective, a clean slate, a fresh approach, and a willingness to start building again from the very foundation. **Familiarity produces a sense of security, but people who are unwilling to let go of the old and venture into new and unfamiliar territory over and over again will never be men and women of impact.** They are afraid of change. They value their own security more than the good that might be achieved by a change. This is why it's impossible to become a citizen of the kingdom of God without starting all over again. This is more difficult for people who feel they have already achieved a great deal and who compare their achievements against what others have achieved, and not against the standard of perfection. A man named Nicodemus learned this lesson from Jesus: you can't enter the kingdom of God by just adding something good to what you already have.†

In addition to being willing to start all over again ourselves, we need to look for other people who are willing to completely forsake their old ways if need be to make room for new ways. Such people are not stuck in mediocrity. They are open to making whatever changes are necessary in order to achieve their goals.

Protector

Mark 2:23-28 One Sabbath Jesus was going through the grainfields, and as his disciples walked along, they began to pick some heads of grain. The Pharisees said to him, "Look, why are they doing what is unlawful on the Sabbath?" He answered, "Have you never read what David did when he and his companions were hungry and in need? In the days of Abiathar the high priest, he entered the house of God and ate the consecrated bread, which is lawful only for priests to eat. And he also gave some to his companions."

†John 3:1-5,7,9,10

Jesus was not given to legalism. Rather, he was gracious, bent on mercy. Legalistic people can be extremely frustrating. Most of us can probably remember a bureaucrat we may have had dealings with who was not willing to lift one finger or involve one neuron in his brain to go beyond the letter of the instructions he was asked to follow. Obviously such people do not believe they are paid to think or to care about or empathize with others. **Legalism occurs when one values an easy decision over true justice. Legalism appears to preserve the rights of all, but on the contrary, reduces the rights of all and adds power only to the law itself, and not to those the law was intended to serve.** The difference between a good administrator and a "paper-pusher" often boils down to this one trait. Because it is easier to be legalistic, we are all prone to legalism. Therefore we must guard against it. **Like Jesus, we must take into consideration the immediate circumstances, the intended purpose of the "law," and the people whose interests it is designed to protect, each time there is a conflict.**

Jesus protected his followers. Since he was giving them direction, he assumed responsibility for their actions. It is difficult to envision Jesus saying to these accusers, "Go ask them! They are the ones eating grain, not me!" or, "Am I my brother's keeper?" Instead, Jesus stood up for them. Consider how this must have made the disciples feel. They must have felt very safe when Jesus was around, and they must have felt very loved. The Bible teaches that "love always protects."[†] In fact, one of the most visible and compelling acts of love in a parent-child or a marriage relationship is the offering of protection from harm, accusations, or the threats of others. Employees who see their boss "go to bat" for them will feel secure and will be more eager to produce. **It's no wonder that the "Me Decade" has given birth to greater amounts and depths of insecurity than have ever been seen before.** We

[†]I Corinthians 13:7

need to protect those around us and to feel their protection.

"But," the skeptic will say, "Jesus died and left his disciples to fend for themselves." In response to this, consider the confidence that Jesus instilled in his disciples that they would be able to follow his example and stand up to their opponents. In Luke 21:15, Jesus is recorded as saying, "For I will give you words and wisdom that none of your adversaries will be able to resist or contradict." Jesus also said, "I have told you these things, so that in me you may have peace. In this world you will have trouble. But take heart! I have overcome the world."† And, even better, Jesus assured them (and us) that God would continue to provide them with protection after his departure:

> "And surely I am with you always, to the very end of the age." (Matthew 28:20)

> "But I tell you the truth: It is for your good that I am going away. Unless I go away, the Counselor will not come to you; but if I go, I will send him to you." (John 16:7)

Challenger

It is hard for us to appreciate how the Pharisees must have felt when Jesus asked them, "Have you never read . . ?" These men prided themselves on their knowledge of the Hebrew scriptures. They probably had most of the scriptures memorized. They were the teachers and spiritual leaders of the nation of Israel. And here was this radical young man who had been stirring up trouble all over Israel daring to challenge them, all but calling them ignorant of the Word of God to which they had dedicated their lives. He was practically treating them like spiritual idiots, not like the high and holy men that they were. What an outrage! To say that Jesus quietly and humbly pointed out their wrongs would be quite inaccurate. Jesus knew their

†John 16:33

prideful hearts and he purposely used words designed to deflate their over-inflated self-images and stir them up.

Jesus was an unabashedly challenging man. He didn't try to bruise their egos; he went straight for the heart. Could you picture yourself challenging the top executives in your workplace in this way, even if you were totally in the right? Would you be willing to humble the religious establishment of your day, to make the high and mighty look stupid? Could you picture yourself standing defiantly before a denominational minister, asking him (or her), "Have you never read?" Is this how you picture Jesus?

Conciseness

Mark 2:27-28 Then he said to them, "The Sabbath was made for man, not man for the Sabbath. So the Son of Man is Lord even of the Sabbath."

After Jesus finished challenging the Pharisees, he did something that had become a trademark of his teaching: he made a clear and direct statement that, in only a few words, completely cleared up an issue of contention. This is one mark of an excellent teacher.

Boldness

Mark 3:1-6 Another time he went into the synagogue, and a man with a shriveled hand was there. Some of them were looking for a reason to accuse Jesus, so they watched him closely to see if he would heal him on the Sabbath. Jesus said to the man with the shriveled hand, "Stand up in front of everyone." Then Jesus asked them, "Which is lawful on the Sabbath: to do good or to do evil, to save life or to kill?" But they remained silent. He looked around at them in anger and, deeply distressed at their stubborn hearts, said to the man, "Stretch out your hand." He stretched it out, and his hand was

> completely restored. Then the Pharisees went out and began to plot
> with the Herodians how they might kill Jesus.

Apparently Jesus could smell the trap that his opponents had
laid for him. It is significant that Jesus didn't quietly go about
his business. Instead, he made sure that everyone could see
what he was about to do. Jesus, knowing that they were trying
to accuse him, took the offensive and exposed the evil
intentions of their hearts.

Anger

By asking the question he asked, Jesus gave his would-be
accusers every opportunity to see for themselves their error in
opposing him. Yet when they would not respond, Jesus became
angry and deeply distressed. He healed the man at that moment
in order to publicly condemn their stubborn hearts. He had
clarified and simplified the issue of what should and shouldn't
be done on the Sabbath in such a way that even a child could
understand. And yet out of sheer stubbornness and an
unwillingness to be corrected, the Pharisees refused to listen to
him. **It is a relief for many of us to see that Jesus did get
angry in this situation, and that he expressed his anger on
the spot.** It's a relief because we know that we ourselves get
angry when we are faced with stubborn people who don't
respect us and who refuse to be corrected. Some of us may
"stuff" our anger, only to blow up later when it gets out of our
control. Some of us may blow up on the spot with no self
control. Others of us may feel guilty for getting angry in the
first place, thinking that we should be totally cool and that
nothing should make us angry. It's exciting to observe Jesus'
example here and to realize that we can express our anger on
the spot and still not wrong the people we are angry with. In his
letter to the Ephesians, Paul reiterates this message: "In your
anger do not sin: Do not let the sun go down while you are still

angry, and do not give the devil a foothold."[†]

Jesus was so confident, so determined, so strong and forceful, that his opponents saw no other way to stop him than to kill him. Diplomacy and bargaining would not work. They were just beginning to see that he could not be trapped or outwitted. He appeared to be intent on reforming their religion, taking away their followers, and challenging, convicting and humiliating them on every turn. Jesus was quite an impressive adversary. Yet he was only one man. Surely they could stop this one man, and contain or even obliterate his message. What they didn't realize was that his death would only be the beginning, and he knew it.

We need to ask ourselves: how does my boldness, my confidence, and my determination compare with that of Jesus? In light of this episode in Jesus' life, this is a humbling and revealing question. We must not cool off or back down when our message or the stand we have taken causes us to become less popular; we must grow even hotter and face up to our opponents. This is as true for the person aiming to rise up the corporate ladder as it is for disciples of Jesus today who are striving to make other disciples. **We simply cannot achieve something great without facing up to and overcoming our opposition. To use the vernacular, we've got to be *gutsy*.**

Simplification

Jesus' ability to simplify a complicated issue that had often drawn heated debate is another mark of an influential leader. Men and women of impact do not try to complicate things, which could have the effect of both impressing and losing their audience. On the contrary, their objective is to make the issue clear. **Truth usually rings out when it is revealed.** It is

[†]Ephesians 4:26,27

intrinsically brilliant and glorious. Robert G. Ingersoll said that **"the man who finds a truth lights a torch."** Jesus claimed to do more than light a torch; he claimed himself to be the light of the world. He also claimed, if you can accept it, to be the very embodiment of truth.[†]

_____

Up to this point we have been examining the initial impact of Jesus' ministry. It would seem, with his enemies already determined to kill him, that Jesus was on his way out. But **opposition always follows impact.** Try to think of a leader in the world today who doesn't experience threats or even assassination attempts. Jesus was just on the verge of entering his glory days.

[†]John 14:6

2
GLORY DAYS

Effective with Crowds

Mark 3:7-12 Jesus withdrew with his disciples to the lake, and a large
crowd from Galilee followed. When they heard all he was doing,
many people came to him from Judea, Jerusalem, Idumea, and the
regions across the Jordan and around Tyre and Sidon. Because of
the crowd he told his disciples to have a small boat ready for him,
to keep the people from crowding him. For he had healed many,
so that those with diseases were pushing forward to touch him.
Whenever the evil spirits saw him, they fell down before him and
cried out, "You are the Son of God." But he gave them strict
orders not to tell who he was.

Jesus had incredible drawing power. Because he was approachable and because he was known as a man who met people's
needs, people flocked to him from great distances. It had
probably cost many in this crowd a few days of travel time to
come see this Galilean with their own eyes. Jesus didn't seem
surprised at the size of the crowd. He was cool, collected and
on top of the situation. He was clear-thinking enough to instruct
his disciples to ready a boat in case he was crowded by the
people.

What are we like in front of a crowd? Do we become so self conscious and concerned about how people will perceive us that we completely freeze up and lose our ability to think or speak clearly and passionately? Are we so lacking in confidence that we think everyone will notice every wrong thing we say or do? Or do we speak on and on, thoroughly enjoying the "power trip" and the sound of our own voices? Jesus, as we see here, went about his business just as he always had. Evidently, being in front of crowds did not cause Jesus to be anxious, afraid or insecure. Nor did he begin to play up to the crowds, to try to please them.

Tolerance Of Disorder

As we look at Jesus in this situation, we also see that he tolerated the chaos and disorder of the crowd while he met needs. It was more important to Jesus to communicate his message than to organize the people into straight lines. He probably wasn't even planning on preaching to the crowds that day—they just showed up.

Sometimes we value order and proper manners more than resolution of conflict or need-meeting. We may lack tolerance for calamity, confusion and everybody wanting something from us at the same time. We may even have a breaking point where we say, "Enough! Leave me alone!" People in leadership positions who are approachable and who have a reputation of listening to and meeting needs often find themselves in similar situations. Jesus apparently had no limit to his ability to tolerate a very demanding crowd. On this and other occasions, he was even in danger of being crushed by the pressing multitudes. Surely none of us have ever been in that much demand. Few of us have had our lives endangered by the demands others have placed on us.

His Ch•ice

Mark 3:13-19 Jesus went up on a mountainside and called to him those he
wanted, and they came to him. He appointed twelve—designating
them apostles—that they might be with him and that he might
send them out to preach and to have authority to drive out
demons. These are the twelve he appointed: Simon (to whom he
gave the name Peter); James son of Zebedee and his brother John
(to them he gave the name Boanerges, which means Sons of
Thunder); Andrew, Philip, Bartholomew, Matthew, Thomas,
James son of Alphaeus, Thaddaeus, Simon the Zealot and Judas
Iscariot, who betrayed him.

Jesus chose those on whom he wanted to focus most of his
time. He didn't leave his choice to fate, chance, or another's
decision. He wasn't haphazard, letting things fall together and
reacting to situations as they came along. Jesus formed and
carried out a deliberate plan. He called to himself those he
wanted. Similarly, it is preferable to allow responsible leaders to
personally choose those from among their "followers" (employees, students, disciples) to whom they will give their best
time and effort. One advantage of this is that it will give the
leader added incentive to make sure that these particular
followers benefit from his or her leadership. True, Jesus was in
a unique position; he had started up his own movement and
could therefore do whatever he thought best, including the
selection of the people on whom he would focus. Often,
whether in business or in the Lord's church, it is not entirely up
to us who will be working with us or for us: we either have to
answer to a superior or we should seek the advice of someone
superior to us. To some extent, however, we do have a degree
of input on decisions of that kind. Even when we don't, we can
still choose what type of focus we will have on the people who
happen to be around us.

It would be impossible and ineffective to distribute our time and
efforts equally among all the people surrounding us. We must

choose the people through whom we can most effectively work and we must give them the best of our time. Even Jesus, while he was on earth, was limited by space and time. We cannot allow ourselves to be spread too thin. If we do, nobody will benefit, and our movement will stall.

It was clearly Jesus' intention to multiply his impact by personally training these twelve men to be able to do the same thing that he was doing (ie. preaching the word and driving out demons). Not only did Jesus' plan ensure the most rapid growth of impact possible, it also provided a means for his impact to continue even after his time on the earth was over. This is especially good news to us who were born many centuries after his death. We can experience the same call to action as those who received Jesus' word-of-mouth invitation. It is exciting to consider that our lives could similarly produce an impact that would affect more people than we would ever personally meet and that would carry on long after we are gone.

The key to multiplying impact is *replication*. **It takes a relatively short amount of time to persuade one person to do something. It takes much longer to convince them that they also need to persuade other people to do the same thing.** The person with the talent and determination to persuade three hundred people a year to follow him may seem impressive. But the person who invests himself in one other person for a full year to fully convince that person and to teach that person everything that he himself knows can out-produce the talented person one hundred-thousand fold in the long run. "How can that be so?", you may ask. Mathematically, it is relatively simple: a geometric progression can grow much more rapidly than an arithmetic progression. Here's how it works: after thirty years the talented persuader will have nine thousand followers (30x300), while the person who duplicates himself in others will have personally won over thirty people (30x1). However, those thirty people will be able to win over an average of thirty people each in their own lifetimes (30x30=900), if they stick to the plan. Each of those nine hundred people can win over thirty more people, and so on. On paper this would work out to over *one billion* people being won in those first thirty years, and there would be no reason for this movement to stop just because the one original person passes on. Of course this is a simplified theoretical example, but it is useful in demonstrating the effectiveness of Jesus' plan. Many businesses in our day choose to pursue financial gain in this manner. But in Jesus' day, there was probably no precedent for this type of multiplying ministry. Once again Jesus amazes us with his keen insights into effective leadership.

When he chose the Twelve, Jesus very clearly let them know that they were his special focus. Everyone else in Jesus' company also knew on whom he was focussing his energies. Perhaps he had to deal with some petty jealousies and some bad attitudes because of this, but they were not insurmountable. On the other hand, imagine the exuberation of the Twelve when they realized they had been hand picked by Jesus. What an honor, to share his daily life and to be personally trained by him! We can only imagine how often they must have reflected back on the honor of this day later in their lives. It must have been a valuable memory for them when they were leading the charge into the very city that had publicly assassinated Jesus, and while they were preaching in other equally hostile places. Other followers may well have been inspired by this day also, to aspire to leadership and to show themselves worthy of greater responsibility. Then they too could be personally selected by the Master for some good work. **Publicly honoring the few who have been selected for some special responsibility is good for the whole group.**

Those of us who are disciples of Christ have also been *personally* selected by Jesus to do his good work. Therefore we need not quietly envy the Twelve. Consider the following passages:

So too, at the present time there is a remnant [a relatively small group which has remained faithful to the call of Jesus] chosen... (Romans 11:5)

For he chose us in him before the creation of the world to be holy and blameless in his sight. In love he predestined us to be adopted as his sons through Jesus Christ, in accordance with his pleasure and will... (Ephesians 1:4-5)

For we are God's workmanship, created in Christ Jesus to do good works, which God prepared in advance for us to do. (Ephesians 2:10)

Therefore, as God's chosen people, holy and dearly loved, clothe yourselves with compassion, kindness, humility, gentleness and patience. (Colossians 3:12)

For we know, brothers loved by God, that he has chosen you,... (I Thessalonians 1:4)

But we ought always to thank God for you, brothers loved by the Lord, because from the beginning God chose you to be saved through the sanctifying work of the Spirit and through belief in the truth. (II Thessalonians 2:13)

He chose to give us birth through the word of truth, that we might be a kind of firstfruits of all he created. (James 1:18)

Peter, an apostle of Jesus Christ, To God's elect, strangers in the world, scattered throughout Pontus, Galatia, Cappadocia, Asia and Bithynia, who have been chosen according to the foreknowledge of God the Father, through the sanctifying work of the Spirit, for obedience to Jesus Christ and sprinkling by his blood: Grace and peace be yours in abundance. (I Peter 1:1-2)

But you are a chosen people, a royal priesthood, a holy nation, a people belonging to God, that you may declare the praises of him who called you out of darkness into his wonderful light. (I Pet 2:9)

They will make war against the Lamb, but the Lamb will overcome them because he is Lord of lords and King of kings—and with him will be his called, chosen and faithful followers.'' (Revelation 17:14)

Living the life of a Christian is even more exciting when you understand that you are one of the chosen few. Each and every disciple who has come out of the world and into the kingdom of God has been hand picked by the Lord. And the Lord has specific tasks ready and waiting for us to do. Probably most of us have experienced the potentially humiliating situation of being chosen to be on a team for an athletic event, say a soccer game. Usually two "superstar" athletes are chosen by the group to be the captains of their respective teams, and then proceed to alternately choose people out of the group to be on their teams. It is good for one's self-esteem to be selected early. I was usually taken second to last. Perhaps this was because I wore glasses, or because I was labeled a "brain," or possibly because I was about as fast as a dog on its hind legs. In any case, there was something more important than the order in which we were selected. To win the game was everything. **The phrase "it doesn't matter whether you win or lose, its how you play the game" is meant to comfort the losers. Winning teams do not huddle up and recite it.** In the great game of life, Captain Jesus will never have to consider the possibility of losing. He, and all those he has chosen to be on his team, will win a great victory over this world. That is why I am glad he chose me, and that is why I have chosen to be on Jesus' team.

Jesus further distinguished three of the Twelve by giving them nicknames. To James and John he gave the name Sons of Thunder, because he saw them becoming powerful men of God. To Simon, who had an impetuous temperament, he gave the name Peter, which means rock. These three, not by coincidence, were his closest companions and became strong pillars in his church. The nicknames that he gave them were not demeaning, but rather positive and visionary, and they served to promote a close yet informal camaraderie. To advise the budding leader to assign nicknames to his or her closest co-workers would not by itself make him or her a more effective leader. Instead, **we need to be devoted to the type of open and vulnerable relationships where nicknames come very naturally. And then we need to be sure to give inspiring nicknames, ones that people will want to grow into.**

Radical

> Mark 3:20-22 Then Jesus entered a house, and again a crowd gathered, so
> that he and his disciples were not even able to eat. When his
> family heard about this, they went to take charge of him, for they
> said, "He is out of his mind." And the teachers of the law who
> came down from Jerusalem said, "He is possessed by Beelzebub!
> By the prince of demons he is driving out demons."

**Jesus was so radical and so consumed with his purpose that
his own family thought that he had "gone off the deep
end."** Jesus' mother, his younger brothers (James, Joseph,
Judas and Simon)† and his sisters were so concerned by the
news of what Jesus was doing and how he was "making a
spectacle of himself" that they felt compelled to come and
forcibly take him home. What could have led them to such a
wrong assessment of the situation? First of all, they weren't
following Jesus or even listening to his teachings themselves;
they only heard things second hand. Secondly, they truly loved
him and were convinced that he was hurting himself. Imagine
how you would feel if your son or brother was so consumed
with some activity that he wasn't even eating.

Similarly, when the teachers of the law saw how Jesus was
acting and observed the furor that he caused among the people,
they thought he must have been filled with the most evil of evil
spirits. Jesus was completely uninhibited, and he lived his life
and pursued his goals with such intensity that people were taken
aback. **Jesus didn't conform to socially acceptable levels of
zeal, enthusiasm, and single-mindedness.** His intensity they
could only compare with the driven quality of those who were
out of their mind or those who were possessed by evil spirits.

**Extraordinary levels of intensity and commitment in an
individual's life are commonly perceived by the general
public as characteristic of *fanaticism* or an *obsession*.**

†Mark 6:3

Fanaticism seems to be *politically correct* only when the person is involved in athletics, the military or making money. In the same way, groups of people who are extremely committed to a particular cause are often shunned by the mainstream of today's society. A religious organization which expects a high level of commitment from each of its members is often called a cult. **Consequently, people who are trying to have an impact should not be surprised if they are called fanatics, if other people think they are obsessed with their purpose, or if their group is labeled a cult.** These are all *good* signs that they are achieving something unique; they should be encouraged to press onward.

Jesus told people to: "Enter through the narrow gate. For wide is the gate and broad the road that leads to destruction, and many enter through it. But small is the gate and narrow the road that leads to life, and only a few find it."[†] **Throughout the Bible, God makes it clear that he only accepts those who leave the broad path of socially acceptable religion and choose the narrow path of exceptional faith.** And yet from before Jesus' day until now societies which have accepted the Bible in some sense have also actively discouraged and condemned those who dare to break free from the pack. Surely this is because the lives of the truly-committed followers of God expose the mediocrity and complacency of those who are a part of the religious establishment.

The business establishment similarly renounces many of its mavericks who brashly attempt to better or change the status quo—at least until they succeed, at which point a new broad path is trampled down by hordes of imitators, envious of the maverick's achievements.

Are we willing to throw off our inhibitions, to care less about what people think of us, to break out of the mold and radically and single-mindedly pursue our goals? Such is one

[†]Matthew 7:13-14

mark of a man or woman of impact.

Reasonability

Mark 3:23-30 So Jesus called them and spoke to them in parables: "How
can Satan drive out Satan? If a kingdom is divided against itself,
that kingdom cannot stand. If a house is divided against itself, that
house cannot stand. And if Satan opposes himself and is divided,
he cannot stand; his end has come. In fact, no one can enter a
strong man's house and carry off his possessions unless he first
ties up the strong man. Then he can rob his house. I tell you the
truth, all the sins and blasphemies of men will be forgiven them.
But whoever blasphemes against the Holy Spirit will never be
forgiven; he is guilty of an eternal sin." He said this because they
were saying, "He has an evil spirit."

In the face of accusations about his state of mind and his
possession by Satan, Jesus calmly reasoned with his accusers.
His self control and his sensible and logical thinking made him
the victor in this confrontation. The people had arrived at an
unwarranted conclusion from the information available to them.
Jesus helped them interpret their observations in a different
way. An insane man could not reason so clearly. In contrast,
**many of us find it difficult to reason with people about
anything without getting argumentative or emotionally
stirred up.** If we want to be convincing to people, we need to
be much slower to take offense and much quicker to calmly
explain why an accusation is false.

Jesus used this situation to prove that not only was he not
Satan, but he clearly had access to more power than Satan did
because he was able to counteract Satan's work. He didn't boast
of his power and authority nor did he make any unsupported
claims. He also did not retaliate by accusing his accusers.
Instead he left it up to the listener to consider the evidence and
arrive at a logical conclusion.

Discipliner

Mark 3:31-35 Then Jesus' mother and brothers arrived. Standing outside,
they sent someone in to call him. A crowd was sitting around
him, and they told him, "Your mother and brothers are outside
looking for you." "Who are my mother and my brothers?" he
asked. Then he looked at those seated in a circle around him and
said, "Here are my mother and my brothers! Whoever does God's
will is my brother and sister and mother."

**Jesus refused to allow his personal feelings to interfere with
achieving the best outcome for everyone concerned.** Perhaps
he knew that his family had come to take charge of him because
they thought he was going overboard with his preaching (verses
20-22: *Radical*). Certainly he did know that they weren't
supportive of what he was starting to do. On the contrary, if
they could they would pull him away from this crowd of people
who were eager for his message, eager to hear about and obey
God's will. Consequently, on this occasion he literally left his
family standing outside in the cold. This may seem surprising to
us; even if they were in the wrong, was it really necessary for
him to hurt his own mother's feelings in that way? Mary may
have felt embarrassed, offended, and more concerned than ever
about what her son was doing. Yet Jesus could not have done
otherwise if he truly wanted them to begin to listen to him as
their *savior* and not simply as their son and brother. Jesus cared
more about their souls than about their feelings. **Feelings mend,
misunderstandings can be cleared up, and love can be
reaffirmed. But if Jesus had tried to appease his family, they
would not have clearly understood how wrong he perceived
their actions to be.** They would probably have continued trying
to dissuade him from pursuing his goals. They would certainly
never have joined him in his mission, as indeed they eventually
did.[†]

[†]Acts 1:14, James 1:1, Jude 1 [Tradition claims that this James and Jude were
Jesus' brothers.]

The Bible teaches that God is willing that people suffer in order to learn something for their own greater good. After all, ''No discipline seems pleasant at the time, but painful. Later on, however, it produces a harvest of righteousness and peace for those who have been trained by it.''[†] God disciplines those he loves.[‡] Jesus handled this situation with his family exactly as his Father would have him handle it.

If God is willing to allow those he loves to hurt and suffer in order to change for their greater good in the long term, then what about us? Are we willing to put relationships with our family and friends on the line in order to influence them in a powerful way? **Do we allow sentimentality to rule in our relationships in such a way that we cannot win over those we are closest to?**

Sentimentality can also be a factor on the job. If we are unwilling to allow people's feelings to get hurt because of our administrative decisions then we are politicians and not true leaders. If we always side with our closest colleagues on the job then we are being unduly influenced by our relationship with them. We should always give responsibilities and promotions to those who deserve them and not necessarily to those we have known the longest or those with whom we have the most in common.

Partiality will destroy the unity of any group. I can remember the disrespect I felt for past hockey coaches who showed favoritism to their sons who were playing on the team. This disrespect is in sharp contrast with the admiration I had for those other coaches who were noticeably a little bit tougher on their own sons than on the other boys. Jesus' tough love, his uncompromising stance on who was for God and who was not, is similarly admirable. Jesus never failed to love his mother and brothers; eventually, he won them over. If we love but do not

[†]Hebrews 12:11
[‡]Hebrews 12:5-10

give in to sentimentality, then we too will have a powerful impact.

Discernment

One more question begs to be asked of those of us who are disciples. Are we willing to differentiate and prioritize our relationships according to a single parameter: is this particular person also a part of the Movement of God? **Jesus saw people as being either for him or against him. They were either movers for God, or still needing to be moved by God.** They were either obedient believers or not true believers at all. Jesus considered those who were doing God's will to be his family. If we are not willing to take a stand like Jesus did to his own family then we will never win our families for Christ. If we succumb to our friends concerns about our new life-style, and try to appease them through compromise, they will never be convinced that they are in the wrong before God Almighty.

Storyteller

Mark 4:1-12 Again Jesus began to teach by the lake. The crowd that gathered around him was so large that he got into a boat and sat in it out on the lake, while all the people were along the shore at the water's edge. He taught them many things by parables, and in his teaching said: "Listen! A farmer went out to sow his seed. As he was scattering the seed, some fell along the path, and the birds came and ate it up. Some fell on rocky places, where it did not have much soil. It sprang up quickly, because the soil was shallow. But when the sun came up, the plants were scorched, and they withered because they had no root. Other seed fell among thorns, which grew up and choked the plants, so that they did not bear grain. Still other seed fell on good soil. It came up, grew and produced a crop, multiplying thirty, sixty, or even a hundred times." Then Jesus said, "He who has ears to hear, let him hear."

> When he was alone, the Twelve and the others around him asked him about the parables. He told them, "The secret of the kingdom of God has been given to you. But to those on the outside everything is said in parables so that, 'they may be ever seeing but never perceiving, and ever hearing but never understanding; otherwise they might turn and be forgiven!'"

If a picture is worth a thousand words, then a parable—an illustrated truth—is worth a thousand statements. Jesus taught by using parables. Similarly, we can teach and communicate our ideas more effectively by using illustrations, analogies, allegories, metaphors, similes and the like.

You may be thinking, "I already know that!" True, most of us are well aware of the necessity of using simple illustrations in order to communicate effectively. Yet so few of us consistently practice this valuable technique. And, consequently, fewer still are proficient teachers. I recall the frustration that I have experienced on numerous occasions while trying to describe a technical engineering concept to colleagues who speak English as a second or third language. Similarly I have often felt frustrated while teaching the basics of the gospel of Christ to my friends, many of whom come from drastically different cultural, economic, educational and religious backgrounds than my own. My solution has been the copious use of illustrations which make use of situations, relationships and things common to us. I have frequently been asked how the Father, the Son and the Holy Spirit could all be the same God.[†] To friends of mine familiar with the sciences, I have used the analogy of the tri-phasic quality of water: one container of water can simultaneously contain H_2O in its liquid, solid and gaseous states. With my non-scientific friends I might discuss the three sides of a coin. With children I like to talk about the three leaflets on a clover leaf.

But why do illustrations and parables work so well in communicating concepts and principles? One reason is that they

[†]John 1:1

inspire visualization and mental creativity. A simple outpouring of facts may leave the listener burdened with the task of memorizing a list of important information, as well as figuring out the structure of the information and how the concepts are interrelated. Contrast that with a story that a six-year-old could remember which also communicates sophisticated concepts, and which uses the structure of the story to place the main teaching in context with related concepts. Such is the beauty of an illustration.

Another reason that parables and illustrations work so well is that they force people to think about what is said in order to reach a full understanding. They are like riddles with a hidden meaning intended to pique the curiosity of the listener. The one who pays close attention and strives to understand is richly rewarded with wisdom. On the other hand, the person who doesn't care enough to apply himself to understand is left out in the dark. Jesus was very eager for people to be enlightened. His expression "He who has ears to hear, let him hear," was meant to bait the people, even dare them to listen carefully and contemplate what he said. Jesus realized that his teachings would work to sift the people. Some of them would turn so that they could be forgiven; others would reject the message. Those of us who follow Jesus today have the same goal: that men and women be awakened to the state of their relationship with their Creator, repent, and share in the forgiveness of sins. As we see in the following passages, **God has always expected those who desire a relationship with him to search for understanding.**

And you, my son Solomon, acknowledge the God of your father, and serve him with wholehearted devotion and with a willing mind, for the LORD searches every heart and understands every motive behind the thoughts. If you seek him, he will be found by you; but if you forsake him, he will reject you forever. (1 Chronicles 28:9)

The Spirit of God came upon Azariah son of Oded. He went out to meet Asa and said to him, "Listen to me, Asa and all Judah and Benjamin. The LORD is with you when you are with him. If you seek him, he will be found by you, but if you forsake him, he will forsake you. (2

Chronicles 15:1-2)

My son, if you accept my words and store up my commands within you, turning your ear to wisdom and applying your heart to understanding, and if you call out for insight and cry aloud for understanding, and if you look for it as for silver and search for it as for hidden treasure, then you will understand the fear of the LORD and find the knowledge of God. For the LORD gives wisdom, and from his mouth come knowledge and understanding. (Proverbs 2:1-6)

You will seek me and find me when you seek me with all your heart. (Jeremiah 29:13)

Ask and it will be given to you; seek and you will find; knock and the door will be opened to you. (Matthew 7:7)

Therefore consider carefully how you listen. Whoever has will be given more; whoever does not have, even what he thinks he has will be taken from him. (Luke 8:18)

From one man he made every nation of men, that they should inhabit the whole earth; and he determined the times set for them and the exact places where they should live. God did this so that men would seek him and perhaps reach out for him and find him, though he is not far from each one of us. (Acts 17:26-27)

Chastening

Mark 4:13 Then Jesus said to them, "Don't you understand this parable? How then will you understand any parable?

When explaining some matter, we often tell people they shouldn't be afraid of asking a "stupid question." Yet we see in this instance that Jesus chastened his most devoted followers for not understanding a simple parable. While he took note of and appreciated their humble and seeking hearts, he was also willing to express his disappointment in their lack of insight. Even while allowing their feelings to be hurt he encouraged them to use their heads. By convicting them of their spiritual dullness, he successfully motivated them to seek understanding with greater diligence.

While some of us are too hard on people we are teaching or leading, most of us are too soft, and too unwilling to hurt people's feelings: "What if their pride kicks in and they get defensive and won't listen? What if they get angry with me?" If we give in to such fears, they can drastically reduce the impact we make on other people. **Bearing in mind that heart and character changes do not come easily, we need to be ready to challenge and convict those we lead when necessary.**

Discernment

Mark 4:14-20 The farmer sows the word. Some people are like seed along the path, where the word is sown. As soon as they hear it, Satan comes and takes away the word that was sown in them. Others, like seed sown on rocky places, hear the word and at once receive it with joy. But since they have no root, they last only a short time. When trouble or persecution comes because of the word, they quickly fall away. Still others, like seed sown among thorns, hear the word; but the worries of this life, the deceitfulness of wealth and the desires for other things come in and choke the word, making it unfruitful. Others, like seed sown on good soil, hear the word, accept it, and produce a crop—thirty, sixty or even a hundred times what was sown.

Jesus categorized people by how they responded to God's Word. **Because of dark shadows in the recent past, many of us recoil at the thought of categorizing, grouping or labeling people at all.** We think it is wrong to "judge" other people. It is true that we have no authority to sit in judgement over someone else, to "*pronounce* judgement" on them (ie., to condemn). However, if we have heard the verdict, proclaimed by God himself, we can and should *announce* his judgement. In another sense, we make formal or informal "judgements" of people all the time—"judgement" meaning to assess their abilities, to appraise their performance, to evaluate their accomplishments, to differentiate them from others, to review or measure what they have or haven't done, to compare them with others or with ourselves, to rate or rank them with respect to a standard or with each other. This function of judgement will be a part of human society as long as there are differences in people. However if we make these judgements in order to exalt ourselves or our group over another, or in order to decrease the "value" of another person, we have used our God-given ability to differentiate for evil purposes.

Following Jesus' example, **we need not be afraid to identify the different types of people around us and to categorize them when this will help us to respond to them in ways that will meet their different needs.** For example, in any work place one can find different "types" of people. Some employees are strictly interested in putting in their time, staying out of trouble, and receiving their paycheck. They are punctual and reliable and willing to do what they must do to keep their job—but they have few or no aspirations to move ahead, and they are not very concerned about the overall condition of the company for which they work. A wise manager wouldn't give such a person increased responsibility or allow him to manage others no matter how much seniority he might have. In contrast to this non-ambitious type, some other people are overly ambitious. For them, their present position is merely a stepping stone on their path to where they think they really belong. They are also putting in their time, but the difference is that they can't wait to move on. They are not easily convinced that they have a lot to learn in their present position or that they could benefit from listening to their present peers or supervisors. They are on the fast track, after all, and are merely pausing on this rung to catch their breath before continuing their ascent up the ladder. Such people usually try to look good in front of the "higher ups," especially those that are several rungs higher on the ladder. They would also have little concern or loyalty for the company, and they would gladly "jump ship" as soon as it began to sink. Again, a wise manager would consider this type of employee to be a poor choice for advancement. Unfortunately, people like this are often perceived as being "high-achievers," and are the first to be promoted. At some point it will be clearly seen that they are aggressive only in order to advance themselves, not the company.

Many employees simply want to do an excellent job on whatever assignment they are given. They feel obligated to do their level best to help the company to be successful. That's what they are paid for, after all. Some of these people, however, though they may start out with high ideals, may be corrupted by the bad attitudes around them. They may turn cynical, critical and bitter. It is right for them to feel guilty, because they have consciously given up their ideals and forsaken the right way. They begin to doubt everyone else's motivations and are eager to stir up controversy and find fault. They can even become like a deadly virus, and should be encouraged to leave before they infect others in turn. The fourth category of people, those who hold to their ideals and maintain an "all for one and one for all" attitude, will usually produce well beyond their own or anyone else's expectations. Such people should form the heart and soul of the organization. A wise manager will promote them and help them to successfully accomplish their responsibilities No matter what they are paid, they will always give much more back to the company. They might not have the greatest ability, but the value of their smile among frowns, their respect in the midst of scoffing, their offer of help to a peer in distress at the sacrifice of their own visible productivity, cannot be measured. Such a spirit is invaluable to the company. A good manager will recognize this.

Productivity

Jesus was clearly concerned with people's "spiritual productivity." He taught that a good heart toward God's Word always produces an amazing outcome. Jesus also described what he considered to be the appropriate outcome of the life of a man or woman of God: an amazing, multiplying impact.[†] If you planted one apple seed and carefully supplied the seed with all the nourishment it requires to become a mature tree, would you expect only one apple in return? Of course not! You would expect hundreds of apples. An apple tree that produced only one or two apples would be cut down and used for firewood. The very commonplace nature of this miracle does not diminish the incredible wonder of the transformation of a small, dull and tasteless speck into a great number of delicious, juicy and nutritious apples. Such a miracle of nature mirrors God's expectation of the man or woman who lives by faith. **Spirituality and productivity are related.** Whether the multiplication is thirty fold or one-hundred fold doesn't matter as much as the fact that the quantity of fruit born from our lives can only be explained by the power of God. "From everyone who has been given much, much will be demanded; and from the one who has been entrusted with much, much more will be asked."[‡] What is there in your life that can only be explained by the power of God?

Disclosure

Mark 4:21-23 He said to them, "Do you bring in a lamp to put it under a bowl or a bed? Instead, don't you put it on its stand? For whatever is hidden is meant to be disclosed, and whatever is concealed is meant to be brought out into the open. If anyone has ears to hear, let him hear."

Jesus encouraged his listeners to speak openly of the impact the Word of God was having on their lives. He didn't want them to keep the benefits of his teaching to themselves. Instead they were to let these benefits shine brightly to all the people around

---

†Mark 4:8
‡Luke 12:48

them. The Word of God is a treasure which was never meant to be hidden or privately shared with only a select group. On the contrary it was meant to be proclaimed to and shared with everyone. Widening its exposure does not diminish its value. The proclaimer does not suffer loss, but rather increases in riches.

Let us consider another illustration. In the region where Jesus taught can be found a body of water called the Sea of Galilee. This so-called "Sea" is actually a fresh water lake teeming with fish. To this day, many of the inhabitants of the surrounding cities derive their livelihood from fishing its waters. The Sea of Galilee has one principal tributary and one river flowing out from it, the Jordan River. The Jordan runs a seventy-mile course and then empties into the forty-five mile long Dead Sea. The Dead Sea is the end of the line for the Jordan waterway and for two other tributaries. In fact, it is the lowest point on Earth, almost 3000 feet below sea level. Because of this, nothing flows out of it. Consequently, it is smelly and lifeless, surrounded by a flat scorching desert and barren hills. Mark Twain said of it, "It makes one think of funerals and death."

We don't want to be "Dead Sea Christians" or "Dead Sea Employees": terminal instead of germinal, unable to enrich other people's lives through what we have learned. Nor do we want those in whom we invest our lives, by teaching, training, loving and serving them, to be the end of the line.

This principle became more real for me this past year when one of my heroes in the faith, Ken Guidroz, began to invest more of his life in me. I felt privileged and honored to receive his personal attention. He clearly believed in me and sought to deepen our friendship and to raise me up as a leader in the church. I can remember how obligated I felt to do my very best in passing on what I was learning to my peers and to those I was teaching. Ken couldn't possibly give to each of the others what he was giving to me—and I knew it. I was a key part in his life as a man of impact, and I wanted to prove faithful.

The Challenge to Listen

Mark 4:24-25 "Consider carefully what you hear," he continued. "With
         the measure you use, it will be measured to you—and even more.
         Whoever has will be given more; whoever does not have, even
         what he has will be taken from him."

Teachers, supervisors and parents, among others, have the
responsibility of effective communication of information to
others. However, **once the words are spoken, responsibility
for the information rests upon the shoulders of the listener.**
Jesus challenged people to listen well, and to carefully consider
what they heard. He taught that we will receive understanding
to the extent that we earnestly seek it, and along with it, we will
receive an unexpected bonus of wisdom for trying so hard.
Conversely, if we are casual about what we hear and do not
truly apply ourselves to understand the message, we will even
lose what understanding we have. We will become more
confused and less convinced. My own experience leads me to
believe that this principle holds true not only in the realm of
spiritual truths, but in any realm of learning. When I resolve to
fully understand some obscure scientific principle or master the
technical jargon of my research peers in order to decipher their
writings, I discover, along the way, deep and fresh insights into
many other related and unrelated topics.

In today's information-rich environment, good note-taking is a
requisite for thorough understanding of most verbal, visual and
even written communication. The very practice of taking notes
usually indicates that one is earnestly seeking understanding.
The arrogant sit smugly, confident of their ability to retain oral
information. The humble augment their oral retention by taking
notes and later meditating on them. By reviewing the main
points, they are able to inquire about anything in particular they

find to be unclear.

As leaders in any domain, we need to follow Jesus' lead by admonishing our subordinates to pay careful attention to what we say. We should expect those we lead to routinely take notes when appropriate. We should ask them if they have considered or reflected upon what we discussed. In this way, we will help them to benefit from our experience and teaching. Otherwise, we may be wasting our breath.

A Dream Shared

Mark 4:26-32 He also said, "This is what the kingdom of God is like. A man scatters seed on the ground. Night and day, whether he sleeps or gets up, the seed sprouts and grows, though he does not know how. All by itself the soil produces grain—first the stalk, then the head, then the full kernel in the head. As soon as the grain is ripe, he puts the sickle to it, because the harvest has come." Again he said, "What shall we say the kingdom of God is like, or what parable shall we use to describe it? It is like a mustard seed, which is the smallest seed you plant in the ground. Yet when planted, it grows and becomes the largest of all garden plants, with such big branches that the birds of the air can perch in its shade."

When Jesus taught about the Kingdom of God, he highlighted its amazing and unexplainable yet inevitable growth and maturation. He wasn't conservative in his hopes for the kingdom he was building. He didn't say, "I hope some day it might be like this...." **His expectations for the Kingdom were high and lofty, and he didn't hesitate to express his vision to those around him. How unlike most of us, who "hedge our bets" in order not to look too foolish if we fail.** Our fear of failure predisposes us to fall short of our dreams. We must be confident and act accordingly. Especially if our goal is related to advancing the Kingdom of God, we have no reason to express our dreams in a conservative or timid way—God's

Kingdom will prevail. Let me give a personal example. Before
learning this lesson, I would never have dared to go out on a
limb to produce a book like this one. How could I ever
convince others to join me on this risky adventure? What helped
me to overcome my many fearful thoughts was a mental picture
of Jesus holding a tiny mustard seed in the palm of his hand
and pointing toward an immense tree as he described the
Kingdom of God to his few simple followers. I also gained
courage by remembering that I only have one chance in this
journey called "life." I was then able to communicate my
vision of what this publishing company would accomplish to
prospective coworkers. You now hold in your hands the
firstfruits of a dream.

**Jesus' confidence that the Father would keep his promises
fostered faith in his followers.** And our faith that God will
come through for his obedient followers will help to generate
faith and confidence in those we lead. We don't have to be
there at every moment to ensure their success. Night and day,
whether we sleep or get up, God will continue to do his work to
raise them to maturity.

Choice Words

Mark 4:33-34 With many similar parables Jesus spoke the word to them,
           as much as they could understand. He did not say anything to
           them without using a parable. But when he was alone with his
           own disciples, he explained everything.

Jesus didn't teach over his listeners' heads nor did he
overwhelm them with information. By speaking in parables he
insisted that they listen with inquisitive and active minds. But
when he was with those who were already committed to
following him, "he explained everything." We begin to see
here that Jesus was very deliberate in how he taught those
around him. He wasn't haphazard, blabbing everything to

everyone. **Most of us don't think enough before we speak.** We may sometimes think about *what* should be said, but we rarely think about *how to say it* or *to whom* it should be said. **The way we speak has almost as much to do with determining our impact as what we say.**

Actions Speak Louder

Mark 4:35-41 That day when evening came, he said to his disciples, "Let us go over to the other side." Leaving the crowd behind, they took him along, just as he was, in the boat. There were also other boats with him. A furious squall came up, and the waves broke over the boat, so that it was nearly swamped. Jesus was in the stern, sleeping on a cushion. The disciples woke him and said to him, "Teacher, don't you care if we drown?" He got up, rebuked the wind and said to the waves, "Quiet! Be still!" Then the wind died down and it was completely calm. He said to his disciples, "Why are you so afraid? Do you still have no faith?" They were terrified and asked each other, "Who is this? Even the wind and the waves obey him!"

Personally I wouldn't like to be woken up with a negative, insinuating complaint. In this instance, that is exactly how Jesus was woken up by his disciples. They didn't come to him saying, "help us Lord, we are about to drown." Instead they assumed that he couldn't help and they wondered if he even cared. They woke him questioning his love for them. The first thing Jesus did was to rebuke the wind and the waves, and then he rebuked his disciples. By doing things in that order he showed them both that he cared, and that he could handle the situation. My natural reaction would have been to rebuke the disciples first for doubting me and for doubting my concern for them. Let them stew in their distress a little while longer before I saved them. It would serve them right! But they wouldn't have heard me; they were, after all, fearing for their lives. There can be no doubt that they did hear Jesus. He got their full attention. I'm sure they never forgot this little conversation.

Likewise, it is very effective to respond to an employee's complaint about a task which he perceives to be impossible by doing it yourself immediately *and then* rebuking the employee for not being resourceful. Conversely, we would have very little impact on the employee if we only rebuked him or if we did the job for him and then failed to give him a strong correction.

Power

Mark 5:1-17 They went across the lake to the region of the Gerasenes. When Jesus got out of the boat, a man with an evil spirit came from the tombs to meet him. This man lived in the tombs, and no one could bind him any more, not even with a chain. For he had often been chained hand and foot, but he tore the chains apart and broke the irons on his feet. No one was strong enough to subdue him. Night and day among the tombs and in the hills he would cry out and cut himself with stones. When he saw Jesus from a distance, he ran and fell on his knees in front of him. He shouted at the top of his voice, "What do you want with me, Jesus, Son of the Most High God? Swear to God that you won't torture me!" For Jesus had said to him, "Come out of this man, you evil spirit!" Then Jesus asked him, "What is your name?" "My name is Legion," he replied, "for we are many." And he begged Jesus again and again not to send them out of the area. A large herd of pigs was feeding on the nearby hillside. The demons begged Jesus, "Send us among the pigs; allow us to go into them." He gave them permission, and the evil spirits came out and went into the pigs. The herd, about two thousand in number, rushed down the steep bank into the lake and were drowned. Those tending the pigs ran off and reported this in the town and countryside, and the people went out to see what had happened. When they came to Jesus, they saw the man who had been possessed by the legion of demons, sitting there, dressed and in his right mind; and they were afraid. Those who had seen it told the people what had happened to the demon-possessed man—and told about the pigs as well. Then the people began to plead with Jesus to leave their region.

When Jesus wielded power that no one had ever witnessed

before, his disciples were terrified[†] and the Gerasenes were so afraid that they pleaded with him to leave their region. Jesus, to put it mildly, was making quite an impression. And not only were the people around him afraid; even the demons, evil inhabitants of the spirit world, knew his authority and trembled at it.[‡] But we might say, "I can see how having miraculous powers helped Jesus to be a man of impact, but what good does that do *me*? I have no power over nature and no authority in the spiritual realm. How can I impress people with powers that I am not able to tap? Time to move on to the next point...." To the Christians reading this I say, think again! **"The prayer of a righteous man is powerful and effective.** Elijah was *a man just like us.* He prayed earnestly that it would not rain, and it did not rain on the land for three and a half years. Again he prayed, and the heavens gave rain, and the earth produced its crops."[§] **What expectations do you have of your prayer life?** Paul prayed that we might come to know the incomparably great power available to those who believe in Christ. He stressed that the same power that physically raised Jesus from the dead, and also exalted him "far above all rule and authority, power and dominion, and every title that can be given, not only in the present age but also in the one to come"[¶] is available to us today. **But do we believe this?** What fearsome power has ever been unleashed through your prayer life?

There is one particular instance in my life that quickly comes to mind when I think about how the Lord can work powerfully in someone's heart in response to specific prayers. A few years ago we were studying the Bible with a good friend of mine whose wife had recently become a Christian. Three men of God that I highly respected had joined Jim (not his real name) and me as we studied the Bible and tried to help Jim see his need

[†]Mark 4:41
[‡]verses 7 and 10
[§]James 5:16-18
[¶]Ephesians 1:18-21

for God. Jim had heard plenty, and he wasn't denying any of what he had heard. But he wasn't budging. Jim had excelled in many areas of his life, and consequently, was extremely self-reliant and sure of himself. He recognized the truth, but his pride was preventing him from responding to it. I remember thinking, "He's so comfortable, he doesn't see his need. How will he ever begin to accept his desperate state before God? He's so proud! And 'God opposes the proud.'†" I began to pray earnestly for God to humble Jim. I prayed that God would do whatever it took to humble him and take away his casual attitude. A few days later, Jim's wife called me to tell me that he had come down with a serious illness.

Jim was in considerable pain for days and was unable to sleep because of severe and relentless itching all over his body. His face and body were puffed up beyond recognition. Jim called me after the worst had past to tell me that he had never in his life been so afraid. He had realized for the first time just how fragile his life really was. Before I could say a word, Jim told me that he was convinced the Lord had struck him in order to get him serious about becoming a Christian. He decided then and there to make good use of his recovery time by studying the Bible until he was convinced he wanted to give his life to Christ. I remember that while he was speaking to me, **I felt like leaping for joy and falling down in fear at the same time.** I refrained from telling Jim about the role I had played in his getting sick until later. I wasn't sure how he might react! Now we are both convinced that the power of God is no joke. **The people of God need to pray for God's power to be clearly demonstrated, to give this world something it desperately needs—the fear of the Lord.**

---

†James 4:6

Fearlessness

Not only did Jesus strike fear into the hearts of those who saw his power; he himself was fearless of earthly terrors. The storm on the lake mentioned in the previous passage of Mark's Gospel must have been quite intense. These men who were afraid for their lives were fishermen. They had probably been through many life-threatening predicaments on these waters before. When Jesus kept on dozing in the stern of the boat, they must have reasoned that this ex-carpenter simply didn't know enough about "the sea" to be afraid. But when he faced the waves, they realized that he was not in the least afraid. And when Jesus stood his ground as the raging and naked wild man ran at them from the tombs, they must have been impressed at his fearlessness. They probably *took a few steps back* themselves *as Legion went for Jesus.*

A decision to not give in to fear is an essential ingredient for the man or woman who wants to have an impact. Consider how many cowards are respected or held in high regard. **Let us therefore decide to *overcome* our fears.** In my life, I have overcome two major fears to a great extent: the fear of public speaking and the fear of failure. My fear of public speaking was of the most severe kind. "Crowds" of five or six people would intimidate me into silence. I never asked even the simplest question or made any comments "in front of the class" in all my years of university. I started going to Bible discussion groups in my second year of graduate studies. The groups were quite small and everybody said something—well, almost everybody! *It took me weeks to make my first comment.* I soon realized that I would have to overcome my fear if I was going to have *any* positive impact for God. I got a lot of encouragement from my friends along the way. But bottom line, to overcome my fear took a personal resolve to not back down from any opportunity to speak. Today, I am relatively comfortable speaking in front of crowds of up to one or two hundred people. This enables me to effectively contribute to or even lead the groups to which I belong. And I'm sure I could push my panic point further if necessary.

Don't allow your fears to limit your impact. For those of us living with a healthy fear of the Lord this is especially important. We need not fear anything or anyone else.

> Do not be afraid of those who kill the body but cannot kill the soul. Rather, be afraid of the One who can destroy both soul and body in hell. Are not two sparrows sold for a penny? Yet not one of them will fall to the ground apart from the will of your Father. And even the very hairs of your head are all numbered. So don't be afraid; you are worth more than many sparrows. (Matthew 10:28-31)

> For you did not receive a spirit that makes you a slave again to fear, but you received the Spirit of sonship. (Romans 8:15)

> There is no fear in love. But perfect love drives out fear, because fear has to do with punishment. The one who fears is not made perfect in love. (1 John 4:18)

Spectacular Deeds

When Jesus sent the legion of demons into the herd of pigs he must have known that this would cause quite a stir. Imagine two thousand pigs stampeding over a cliff—especially if they were your property! Because the Jews considered pigs "unclean," these must have been the property of a rich gentile. So here we have an itinerant Jewish preacher causing the destruction of a large amount of a gentile's property. Such an event would unquestionably have made front page news in most towns. The "Gerasene Gazette," had there been one, would have put out a "special edition exclusive." I'm no swine expert, no pig professor, no hog handler, no porcine purveyor, but I would guess that two thousand pigs would be worth around a million dollars today. As a renewable resource, unless they fell over a cliff or contracted an epidemic disease, they could provide ongoing income for more than a few people. It would be an understatement to say that the owner suffered a great financial loss. The situation is more akin to a small business closing down in a community. Apparently, Jesus reasoned that freeing this one man from his torment and anguish was more valuable than another man's property and the temporary income reduction of a few other people. One man's freedom was worth creating a public spectacle. Jesus was willing to do something outrageous and controversial for the sake of one needy person.

Very few of us are willing to do something openly controversial in our workplace or our community in order to help someone. **We want to quietly fit in; we don't want to stick out.** Many people are unwilling to stop and talk to "street people" because of how it might appear to the other passersby. As men and women of impact we must not hesitate to cause a stir for the right reasons. **Influential people require visibility, be it complimentary or critical.** The true value of our actions and motives will eventually come to light.

Reinvestment of Dividends

Mark 5:18-20 As Jesus was getting into the boat, the man who had been demon-possessed begged to go with him. Jesus did not let him, but said, "Go home to your family and tell them how much the Lord has done for you, and how he has had mercy on you." So the man went away and began to tell in the Decapolis how much Jesus had done for him. And all the people were amazed.

Jesus didn't surround himself with people who owed him a great debt of gratitude. He didn't need their continuing thanks and he didn't need an ego boost. Essentially, Jesus' message to the man who had been demon-possessed was, "If you're grateful, tell your friends, not only me." He wanted the testimony of God's mercy and grace to be proclaimed firsthand to as many as possible. The impact of a changed life is most profound on those who knew the person before the change occurred. **Jesus wanted the gratitude of people he had helped to be channeled into doing the same work that he was doing.** In this way his influence could spread all the more as those he helped joined in spreading his message. He was, in effect, *reinvesting his profits.* Likewise, we need to view the gratitude others have towards us as a resource which is not for our exclusive enjoyment, but which can also benefit others. We should help people channel their gratitude into positive and purposeful action.

This Gerasene man was deeply moved by what Jesus had done for him. When directed to tell his family how much the Lord had done for him, he did that—and much more. He went throughout the whole metropolitan area proclaiming the power and mercy of God. So we see that Jesus had an excellent return on his investment. Unfortunately, few people are grateful to the Lord, even when he works powerfully on their behalf,† and fewer still are willing to accept their obligation to proclaim God's mercy to others.

Tenderness

Mark 5:21-34 When Jesus had again crossed over by boat to the other side of the lake, a large crowd gathered around him while he was by the lake. Then one of the synagogue rulers, named Jairus, came there. Seeing Jesus, he fell at his feet and pleaded earnestly with him, "My little daughter is dying. Please come and put your hands on her so that she will be healed and live." So Jesus went with him. A large crowd followed and pressed around him. And a woman was there who had been subject to bleeding for twelve years. She had suffered a great deal under the care of many doctors and had spent all she had, yet instead of getting better she

†Luke 17:12-18

grew worse. When she heard about Jesus, she came up behind him in the crowd and touched his cloak, because she thought, "If I just touch his clothes, I will be healed." Immediately her bleeding stopped and she felt in her body that she was freed from her suffering. At once Jesus realized that power had gone out from him. He turned around in the crowd and asked, "Who touched my clothes?" "You see the people crowding against you," his disciples answered, "and yet you can ask, 'Who touched me?'" But Jesus kept looking around to see who had done it. Then the woman, knowing what had happened to her, came and fell at his feet and, trembling with fear, told him the whole truth. He said to her, "Daughter, your faith has healed you. Go in peace and be freed from your suffering."

Jesus wasn't like today's T.V. evangelists, because he insisted on personally interacting with each person he healed. He wanted to see this faithful woman face to face. It wasn't good enough for him to just know that someone somewhere had benefitted from him. Jesus' love for the individual is, for me, his most attractive characteristic. His love for all types of people—from children to the aged, from Pharisees to prostitutes—draws me to him. In this instance he shows exceptional tenderness and compassion to a fragile yet faithful woman. Reread the passage and try to picture the scene. One aspect of this account has puzzled me in the past. This woman was more than a bit afraid of revealing herself to Jesus—she was "trembling with fear." Why was she so afraid? Was she simply very shy? Was she ashamed to speak of her malady? No, she had obviously discussed it frequently with many doctors. I'm convinced that this woman was afraid that she had done an *evil* thing in touching Jesus' clothing. She was, after all, ceremonially *unclean* due to the nature of her affliction.[†] What's more, anyone or anything she touched would also be rendered unclean and would require atonement before the Lord.[‡] How could she, one who was unclean, dare to touch a man so clearly full of the Spirit of God? Yet, at the same time, she was convinced that

[†]Leviticus 15:25
[‡]Leviticus 15:19-30

God would heal her through him. That's why she only dared to touch the Lord's robe, not his person. When Jesus stopped, demanding to know who had touched him, great fear seized her.

To fully appreciate the depth of Jesus' tenderness and compassion, we need to think about the extent of this woman's suffering. She had not only suffered physically from her condition, but she had also suffered from the ineffective treatments that the doctors had given her. Yet far greater than her *physical suffering* was the *emotional pain* she must have endured in a society which had *shunned* her—and everything she touched—*for twelve years*. Her *spiritual anguish* was equally great. She felt like she was *under a curse*. Why had God not allowed her to be healed? She had to struggle every day with feelings of hopelessness and despair.

After hearing the woman's story, Jesus utters some of the most powerful words in all of the gospels. She must have clearly remembered each and every word he spoke to her that day. **His first word to her was "daughter," a term of endearment that served to express his love for her, to protect her and to pull her into the shelter of his presence.** To a woman who was probably completely alone, shunned by her family and friends for twelve years, acceptance and love from this man of God must have flooded her with joy. Then he commended her for her faith: "your faith has healed you." The Greek word for "healed" used here actually means "saved." Jesus is confirming that not only was she now physically whole, but she had also been forgiven and justified by God. He then comforted her and encouraged her as he sent her off with the words, "Go in peace and be freed from your suffering." In addition to her cleansing, he affirmed that she could now begin a new life filled with peace between her and others and between her and God. Consequently, her intense suffering was over. Jesus' message is the same today for all of us who have faithfully accepted that he is the way out from our unclean lives.

We who aspire to powerfully move people have a lot to learn from Jesus' sensitivity and compassion. We will do well to imitate his use of his tongue to build people up, to give them a new hope and a new life. While this woman was healed because of her personal faith in God, she also received healing from the few words that Jesus spoke to her that day. He didn't babble on and on as we often do, hitting and missing with his words. Instead, he said just what she needed to hear.

The book of Proverbs has a great deal to say about how we speak. With the benefit of Jesus' example, implementation of these principles for effective speech is easier to envision, and more possible to attain.

> Reckless words pierce like a sword, but the tongue of the wise brings healing. (Proverbs 12:18)

> The tongue that brings healing is a tree of life, but a deceitful tongue crushes the spirit. (Proverbs 15:4)

> A wise man's heart guides his mouth, and his lips promote instruction. Pleasant words are a honeycomb, sweet to the soul and healing to the bones. (Proverbs 16:23-24)

Assertiveness

Mark 5:35-43 While Jesus was still speaking, some men came from the house of Jairus, the synagogue ruler. "Your daughter is dead," they said. "Why bother the teacher any more?" Ignoring what they said, Jesus told the synagogue ruler, "Don't be afraid; just believe." He did not let anyone follow him except Peter, James and John the brother of James. When they came to the home of the synagogue ruler, Jesus saw a commotion, with people crying and wailing loudly. He went in and said to them, "Why all this commotion and wailing? The child is not dead but asleep." But they laughed at him. After he put them all out, he took the child's father and mother and the disciples who were with him, and went in where the child was. He took her by the hand and said to her, "Talitha koum!" (which means, "Little girl, I say to you, get up!"). Immediately the girl stood up and walked around (she was

> twelve years old). At this they were completely astonished. He
> gave strict orders not to let anyone know about this, and told them
> to give her something to eat.

Jesus was not leading a travelling miracle-working sideshow. Showing consideration for the parents of the dead girl, he did not allow anyone but his closest disciples to accompany him. The bereaved parents didn't need any hang-arounders or faithless, spectacle-seeking observers. It is somewhat surprising that Jesus also turned back nine of the twelve. Maybe he just didn't want to burst into Jairus' home and surround the little girl with the faces of thirteen men that she didn't know. Whatever the case, he took charge of the situation. He told the mocking mourners to take a hike. He "put them out," perhaps in the way that we would put out the dog. Jesus was an assertive man who took charge of his surroundings.

Assertive people are exciting to be around. They tailor their world in order to achieve their purposes. They might not always be right, but they do get things done. And there is absolutely no reason why anyone reading this book could not become more assertive. What hinders us is fear in all its various forms: fear of doing the wrong thing; fear of hurting someone's feelings; fear of being opposed; fear of what people might think of us; fear of rejection. If you are not convinced of this, think about what it is that would have stopped you from handling this situation as Jesus did.

Sensitivity

We also need to note that on this occasion, Jesus didn't say a word to those who doubted. He simply ignored them. His words were reserved for the people that he was helping. He knew that the news of his daughter's death would shake Jairus, and he would not allow the synagogue ruler to fall prey to the discouraging words of faithless men. Jesus again shows that he was a sensitive man. He could sense the deep pangs of fear that stabbed into Jairus' heart as he considered his little girl's death. **Assertiveness without sensitivity can be offensive and counterproductive.** On the contrary, Jesus demonstrates that **the combination of assertiveness and sensitivity produces impact.**

A Simple Charge

Jesus gave Jairus a very simple focus: "Don't be afraid, just believe." He probably looked Jairus in the eye as he encouraged him with this single sentence. He didn't burden him with lots of words, he didn't give a lot of explanations, he didn't confuse him with ideology. Because of the intensity of this situation and because of all the negative influences pulling at him, Jairus needed a clear bearing for his thoughts. "Don't be afraid, just believe."

I know that I, for one, am often guilty of over-teaching and over-explaining. Unfortunately, an excessive amount of teaching may cloud the main issue and produce a "paralysis of analysis." When many related points are discussed, the listener is not likely to completely understand all of them. Consequently he may walk away trying to understand rather than trying to change or trying to do the right thing. I know I've been over-teaching when after my detailed and thorough instruction, someone replies, "Yes, I think I understand what you're saying, but what should I do about it?"

Privileging

Jesus gave exclusive privileges to his three closest disciples—Peter, James and John. We've already discussed why he may not have allowed his other followers and the crowd to see him raise this little girl from the dead. Yet it is equally interesting to speculate why he should have insisted on having his closest three with him. It appears that Jesus took these three men with him almost everywhere: on the mountain where Jesus was "transfigured,"[†] to the Mount of Olives (along with Peter's brother Andrew) to discuss the future destruction of the temple,[‡] and to the Garden of Gethsemane on the night that he was captured.[§] Not surprisingly, Peter and John would become two of the "pillars"[¶] of the new church formed after Jesus' death. (James the brother of John was executed by King Herod soon after the birth of the church, probably because he was perceived to be the leader of the movement; the James referred to by Paul as the third pillar was actually James, the brother of Jesus).

Sometimes we may feel guilty when we center out certain people for special attention and privileges. However, leaders who attempt to lead more than a few people at once will find that they must narrow their focus at times, as Jesus did, or the most capable and reliable of their followers (or players or students or workers) will not reach their full potential. In any training situation, the trainer will better invest his or her time in some exceptional people than in the rest of the trainees. It is not unfair to the group to focus on those who will be the future leaders of the group. In fact, **to make only limited use of the hearts and talents of those few who are exceptionally gifted would be an injustice not only to the few, but also to the rest of the group.**

I must admit that I have been somewhat envious at times when I found myself standing among "the other nine." I have seen the chosen few— on the job, on the team, and especially, in the

[†]Matthew 17:1-9
[‡]Mark 13:3
[§]Mark 14:32-35
[¶]Galatians 2:9

church—being given special attention. I have also seen them quickly rising to the challenge, handling very important and visible responsibilities much better than I could imagine myself handling them. On rare occasions their hidden shortcomings have outweighed my unrecognized strengths. But usually, these young men ("young" being a term relative to the speaker, that is, less than thirty years of age) who are put on the "fast track" in the church turn out to be my heroes in the faith. Though I may have helped Andrew, Mark and Ron to understand before they were even "wet behind the ears" (ie. before they were baptized into Christ), I now honestly hold them in the highest regard[†] for they are truly leading the way. It is much easier to accept the usefulness of the fast track after having personally benefitted from it!

There have also been a few times in my life when I felt sure that I was one of "the Three." I mentioned earlier how Ken Guidroz believed in me and called me out of the crowd into a position of leadership in the church. In so doing, Ken helped turn my life for the better. But that was only the beginning of his impact on my life. When he and Joyce invited my wife and me over to spend Christmas day with them that year, we expected that some of their many other friends would also be coming. When we found out that we were their special guests, we were even more excited about the invitation. Joyce cooked a phenomenal meal. We laughed, we talked, we played games, and we ended up spending the whole day and evening with them. We left feeling that we held a special place in their life and ministry. Soon after, they took us with them to spend some time with the couple who were leading our church. Several times over the next couple of months they repeated to us and to others that they considered us to be among their best and most trustworthy friends. Unfortunately, their time to leave the city

[†]I Thessalonians 5:12-13

we lived in came shortly thereafter. We felt an emptiness when they left. Yet along with the emptiness was a good feeling. In six short months they had, in effect, turned our lives around. By focussing their love and attention on us, they had forged in us the confidence to lead the way and to do great things for God.

Consideration

In addition to being empowered to raise the dead, Jesus was also exceptionally considerate. While everyone else was standing around with their eyes agape and their mouths dropped to the ground in wonderment, Jesus was thinking about how to meet this little girl's needs by getting her some food. When Peter, James and John told others (like Mark the author of our text) about how Jesus had raised this little girl from the dead, they did not fail to mention this detail which showed his kindness. **A little consideration goes a long way.** We may not be able to raise the dead, but we can send our secretaries home when they look a bit under the weather; we can buy our colleagues lunch, and we can remember people's birthdays. We can be alert to meeting other people's needs.

Amazing Speech

Mark 6:1-6 Jesus left there and went to his hometown, accompanied by his disciples. When the Sabbath came, he began to teach in the synagogue, and many who heard him were amazed. "Where did this man get these things?" they asked. "What's this wisdom that has been given him, that he even does miracles! Isn't this the carpenter? Isn't this Mary's son and the brother of James, Joseph, Judas and Simon? Aren't his sisters here with us?" And they took offense at him. Jesus said to them, "Only in his hometown, among his relatives and in his own house is a prophet without honor." He could not do any miracles there, except lay his hands on a few sick people and heal them. And he was amazed at their lack of faith. Then Jesus went around teaching from village to village.

People were amazed when they heard Jesus' teaching. Later, it was his turn to be amazed at their lack of faith. Have you ever been "amazed" at someone's teaching? Although I have completed ten years of post-secondary education, I don't believe that I have ever been "amazed" in the classroom. The first time I can remember being amazed by someone's teaching was at a Sunday church service in Boston after having attended a "campus retreat." The retreat had knocked down a great many of my defenses. Most, but not all, of my suspicions and fears about this particular church had evaporated because of the tremendous love and openness that I had seen at the retreat. But then again, it was only a retreat, and not the real world. Almost everyone at the retreat was young and idealistic. (At that time "young" for me was around twenty, for I was almost twenty-three myself.) I would be able to see what the rest of the congregation was like at the Sunday service. I would also be able to hear this man who people referred to as "Kip." Many of the people at the retreat had spoken about him with great respect and admiration. It sounded like I was in for an exciting time. But what kind of minister would be called "Kip" anyway?

I will never forget my amazement that Sunday morning. The church was full of people of all ages and races. Despite their diversity, they exuded the same confidence and exuberance as the college crowd at the retreat. My first impression of Kip was that he was an intense but otherwise ordinary guy. He wasn't wild, weird or overly formal (hence the nickname), instead he seemed gut-level honest and relatable. But let me tell you, there are very few men like Kip; his message, his frankness, his wisdom and passion "knocked my socks off" (my vernacular for "amazed me"). I remember sitting in the back row thinking, "how does this man know about me?" No one had ever spoke so directly and so correctly about my life (misguided as it was), my attitudes, my motivations and my purpose (or lack thereof). No friend had ever said these things to me in private, and here was a man preaching them to twelve hundred people! **I simultaneously felt like running down the aisle to shake his hand, and running out the back door as fast as I could.** His message was practical: it told me what to do and how to do it. And his message was so very positive that I was inspired to live for God. I appreciated what Kip had done for me. Four days later, I was baptized into Christ.

We need to strive to speak and to teach in such a way that it will amaze our listeners. It is my strong conviction that God's Holy Spirit was working on my heart that Sunday morning, and that He was using Kip to do it. However, there are practical elements of amazing speech that can be examined and imitated. Looking again to Jesus' example, I've compiled the following seven tips:

1. Deep Convictions. The amazing speaker will have deep convictions about his message. Undoubtedly, on a scale of one to ten measuring strength of convictions, we would have to give Jesus a ten. Jesus believed that how individuals responded to his words would determine their eternal destiny and lead them to either condemnation or eternal life.[†] He was convinced that those listeners who put his words into practice were wise, and that those who did not were fools.[‡] One of the best pieces of advice I ever received was from a good friend a day before one of my first experiences of public speaking. I was petrified, and felt sure I would never get my message across because of my nervousness. When Joyce found this out, she asked me one question: "How convinced are you about what you'll be saying?" She told me not to try to say things that sounded good. If I had deep convictions about what I was saying, I

[†]John 12:47-50
[‡]Matthew 7:24-27

wouldn't have to worry about how well I said it. My heart would show through. In fact, if I was thinking about *what* to say, I wouldn't have time to be nervous about *how* I'd come across. That night I edited my message, throwing out whatever I thought I "should say," and adding what I really felt "needed to be said." The next evening when I spoke I found out that I could indeed muster enough conviction to overcome my fears. I amazed myself that night.

2. Passion. The speaker who has no passion for his message and his listeners should stay home. If the speaker isn't moved by his own message, how can he expect to move anybody else? Jesus preached with great passion. To be convinced of this, one need merely read through the Sermon on the Mount out loud.† Just try to say, "You have heard that it was said... But I tell you... " six times in a row without passion, and you'll know how Jesus must have really said it. Try to imagine Jesus saying, "If your right eye causes you to sin, gouge it out and throw it away. It is better for you to lose one part of your body than for your whole body to be thrown into hell. And if your right hand causes you to sin, cut it off and throw it away. It is better for you to lose one part of your body than for your whole body to go into hell."‡ Passionate speech makes for powerful communication.

3. Integrity. The speaker must have integrity both in regard to the subject he is speaking about and in regard to the way he lives his life. Everyone loathes hypocrisy. Although we may not always be able to sniff out the two-faced speaker, we can usually discern the speaker who has integrity. One sure sign of integrity in a speaker is his or her openness about personal shortcomings. If a speaker is trying to take a sliver out of your eye, so to speak, yet does not acknowledge that he has a

†Matthew 5:3-7:27
‡Matthew 5:29-30

railroad tie that needs to be taken out of his own eye, he will
fail to amaze his audience. Jesus was not able to lead the way
for us in this one area alone, that of how to publicly reveal
mistakes and shortcomings. He had no sin and no shortcomings
to expose. In fact, he boldly and publicly challenged his
opponents to prove him guilty of sin.[†] He was able to
completely open up his heart and his life for inspection. Jesus
was a clean, fresh scent in a city stinking with hypocrisy. That's
why the people flocked to listen to him.

4. Person To Person. The speaker must speak to her
audience "at their level," while yet helping them to take
several strides ahead. Speaking "at the level" of your audience
means to not "talk down" to them and to not "talk up" to
them. The person who apologizes without reason, belittles
herself, and thinks she has no right to speak to a particular
assembly is talking up to the audience. Jesus did not "talk up"
to the Pharisees, the Teachers of the Law, or to Pontius Pilate.
Even though they were educated and powerful he was not
intimidated by them because of the moral authority he had from
God. On the other hand, although Jesus is the Son of God, and
although he was usually teaching with great authority and often
rebuking the faithless spiritual leaders of the day, he didn't
come across as having an air of superiority. Although he was a
patron, protecting his followers from those that opposed them,[‡]
the gospels don't portray him as patronizing. He often professed
his deity, yet he wasn't condescending. He is above us, but he
came down to our level to talk to us. "You are from below; I
am from above. You are of this world; I am not of this world."[§]
The speaker should not think of herself as being greater than the
people in her audience. Rather she should see herself as being
alongside and somewhat ahead of the individuals in her

[†]John 8:46
[‡]John 17:12
[§]John 8:23

audience, leading them and urging them onward.

5. Inspirational. The speaker must aim to inspire his audience. If he is conservative and low-key he will have no impact. If he doesn't try to inspire people, he for sure will not. But if he tries to inspire them, he probably will. In our discussion of Mark 4:26-32, we have already seen how Jesus inspired his disciples by using examples of amazing and unexplainable growth to describe the kingdom he was building. He knew that people long to be and need to be inspired. We all want our lives to count for something.

6. Practical. The speaker must bring the message down to earth. She must make it practical and applicable. Otherwise there will be no changed lives. The most exciting events in life are soon forgotten. Yet a changed life continues to speak out, loud and clear. Jesus did not wander from place to place debating philosophies or formulating impressive arguments about the existence of God. He wasn't esoteric or academic in his discussions. Jesus went around telling people how they had to change their lives. His message hit people right where they lived. He specifically addressed the sins in their lives. He gave them direction, and at times told them exactly what to do. If we do likewise, we will have an impact.

7. Meet The Need. The speaker must adapt his message to the needs of the group. To the proud, to the hypocrites and to the comfortable, Jesus issued stern rebukes and challenges. To the blind, to the lepers, and to the broken hearted, Jesus gave words of hope and comfort. A speaker who is out of touch with the situation and needs of his audience may actually make a bad situation worse.

Patience

Someone in the crowd exclaimed, "Isn't this the carpenter?"
This onlooker stood bewildered at the phenomenal impact an
ordinary and unremarkable carpenter was having. Perhaps Jesus
had worked for a summer building a stable for his brother-
in-law. Or maybe Jesus had helped carve the benches in the
Nazareth synagogue. Isn't it wonderful to consider that our
prototypical man of impact, who was himself the Son of God,
spent between ten and fifteen years doing manual labor! He was
known in his hometown as "the carpenter." You don't earn a
label like that with a six-month career. The Bible tells us that
Jesus started his ministry at around age thirty, and that he
finished three short years later. **So for most of his life he was
just a carpenter, waiting for his time to come.** This should be
a tremendous encouragement to someone who is stuck in what
seems to be a nowhere job, or who looks back on her years as a
Christian and realizes that she has not yet had much of an
impact on her world. Let us not "throw in the towel," or resign
ourselves in our hearts to be "do-nothings" and "also-rans."
**Some flowers bloom with the first warm rays of sun in the
spring, while others bloom in late summer.** Let us patiently
await our "day in the sun." **And when that day arrives, we
must not squander it; we must live it and each following day
as if it were our last. "Carpe diem"—seize the day!**

Challenger

Unfortunately, Jesus' neighbors and friends could not accept
that he had become a man of impact, and "they took offense at
him." Jesus was disappointed at their response and he told them
so to their faces. He spoke out against the dishonorable
treatment that he had received from them. How many of us

would do the same? Jesus wasn't looking for praise from men,† yet he was concerned that these "children of God" didn't treat him with honor and respect even though God was so clearly working through him. **Most of us take disrespect and undue criticism too personally. We fail to understand that such treatment usually comes from disrespectful and critical people.** Such people need to be alerted to the condition of their hearts. Disrespect comes from a disrespectful heart; criticalness comes from a critical heart. This past year thousands of people from my home city loudly booed and heckled their national leader before an international audience. The event was the annual All-Star baseball game held at the Toronto Skydome. The audience saw fit to humiliate the Prime Minister en masse in front of literally millions of people around the globe. Perhaps individuals in the crowd thought that they would show the people from the United States and elsewhere how much they disapproved of this man and his policies. They may have achieved this goal to some extent. However, they communicated something else much more clearly: that they were disrespectful, inconsiderate and shameless. By the polls it is evident that most Canadians agree that this man didn't make the best decisions for the country. I personally concur with some of the dissatisfaction. Yet disapproval does not justify disrespect. I was embarrassed for our country because of this shameless display of disrespect for our Prime Minister. Human nature being what it is, it is likely that most of us would have acquiesced to the crowd's irreverent behavior had we been there. But Jesus was the type of man who would recognize such behavior as being wrong and would then boldly address it.

We may think it inappropriate to challenge disrespectful people, especially when they are being disrespectful of us. After all, won't they think that we are only trying to look good? Jesus was not afraid of what people might think of him. He was very

†John 5:41

concerned, however, with their attitudes towards God and the people of God, and he didn't hesitate to speak out. One clear application of this principle for women is when they are discriminated against in their workplace. A woman who in such situations is able to set aside her hurt feelings and express alarm and disappointment at the disrespectful attitudes of her male colleagues is to be admired. By exposing their disrespect, she may even help some of them to turn away from these destructive attitudes. Another application for Christians is when other Christians or interested friends are late or don't show up at all to an appointment to study the Bible. We should not say, "Oh, no problem. It's O.K.. I know you're busy." Would these same people be late to pick up an award check for a million dollars? Their attitude shows a lack of respect towards God's word and towards us as their teachers. It may not hurt us in the least, yet we should be concerned about their hearts. **If we do nothing more than shrug our shoulders in disappointment, they will not change. And we will have had no impact on them.**

The Sending

Mark 6:7-13 Calling the Twelve to him, he sent them out two by two and gave them authority over evil spirits. These were his instructions: "Take nothing for the journey except a staff—no bread, no bag, no money in your belts. Wear sandals but not an extra tunic. Whenever you enter a house, stay there until you leave that town. And if any place will not welcome you or listen to you, shake the dust off your feet when you leave, as a testimony against them." They went out and preached that people should repent. They drove out many demons and anointed many sick people with oil and healed them.

The day finally arrived. It was time for some of Jesus' followers to take their first steps away from the overseeing hand of their master. It was time for them to get some practical experience on their own. Now they would do themselves what Jesus had been doing. But Jesus didn't send them out all alone; instead, he allowed them to go out **two by two.** Not only would this more than double their courage, but it would also teach them how much they needed each other for encouragement, accountability and support. On top of providing each of them with a partner, he personally prepared them for this endeavor by giving them authority to do what he had been doing, and by giving them **specific instructions** to guide them on their way. Matthew, one of the Twelve, records for us in greater detail the specific instructions that Jesus gave that day.[†] In his account, we see that Jesus told them what to say, who to say it to, who not to say it to, what to do, what not to do, how to do it, what to take, what not to take, where they should stay, when they should move on, what attitude to maintain, how to respond to those who are favorable, and how to respond to those who are not favorable.

It is the responsibility of the sender to ensure that those sent on a mission be adequately prepared for it. On occasion, out of sheer laziness, I have sent out novices without first giving them clear and thorough instructions. Two things always occurred when I did this: first of all, my expectations were not met; and secondly, and more importantly, my "sendees" did not have a victorious first experience. I have made this mistake with young Christians who were eager to share their new-found faith, but didn't know what to say or how to say it. They needed to be informed in advance about how to talk to people, what to say, and how to respond to those who rejected their message and denounced what they were trying to do. It can be quite devastating to find out the hard way that not everyone is interested in God! The blatant complacency of the majority in matters dealing with God can be especially exasperating when you don't realize that it is right to be upset about such an

[†]Matthew 10:5-16

attitude. And the pious self-righteousness of religious people who are not shaken by the cross or do not tremble at God's Word is even more infuriating. It can shake the faith and dampen the zeal of new converts. They need to be instructed to "shake the dust off their feet as they leave."

I have made a similar mistake with new research assistants in my laboratory. I have come to realize that if I find myself to be too busy to thoroughly introduce them to the work they will be doing, I am simply too busy. It is easy for them to be overwhelmed by a new assignment, when so much is new and nothing comes naturally. **A failure at the outset of a project can easily shake a new worker's confidence.** Even if nothing does go wrong, her frustration can still be intense if she is floundering because of inadequate preparation by her "too-busy-right-this-second" boss. It can take months of extra effort and encouragement to right this wrong.

In contrast, at other times, I have given more experienced workers too many specific instructions. This is much less likely to happen than sending people out ill-prepared, but it can happen. Excessive instructions can turn out to be unnecessarily constraining, and can cause those sent out to become legalistic and lose sight of their true goal. I have learned that those who have demonstrated their proficiency should not be treated the same as those who are inexperienced.

Forcefulness

A forceful leader gives specific directions and then fully expects his followers to carry them out. Jesus didn't make vague suggestions that his disciples should go about preaching repentance. He didn't wait until they decided themselves that it was time to go out. When they came back, there would be no question as to whether or not they had done as they were told.

Jesus could ask very simple and specific questions to determine this. Jesus was an unabashedly forceful man. At one point in his ministry he told the crowds, ''From the days of John the Baptist until now, the kingdom of heaven has been forcefully advancing, and forceful men lay hold of it.''[†]**Jesus did not apologize for strong leadership; he promoted it.**

In a similar way, Paul was in no way ashamed of his own forceful leadership. He called others to follow him as he followed Christ:[‡]

> We demolish arguments and every pretension that sets itself up against the knowledge of God, and we take captive every thought to make it obedient to Christ. And we will be ready to punish every act of disobedience, once your obedience is complete. For even if I boast somewhat freely about the authority the Lord gave us for building you up rather than pulling you down, I will not be ashamed of it. (II Corinthians 10:5-6,8)

Strong leadership is offensive to many these days. Although it is practised in almost every sector of society—business, government, the military, athletics, education—some people believe that it infringes on their personal liberties. Perhaps these people, because of their pride, simply do not want anyone else to tell them what to do. People seem particularly offended by strong leadership in religious groups. Even some who like to call themselves Christians, and who would claim to follow Jesus, disapprove of strong church leadership. Either they are ignorant of the leadership style of Jesus and his first century followers, or they have been inundated with twentieth century philosophy and are unwilling to exchange these more ''sophisticated'' and ''appropriate'' ideas for those of Omniscient God. Sounds pretty foolish to me! Perhaps those who promote tolerant and passive leadership in churches are responsible for the present day reputation of Christianity. This reputation—laid-

[†]Matthew 11:12
[‡]I Corinthians 11:1

back, unobtrusive and boring—is a far cry from that of the first century church. Of them it was said:

"What are we going to do with these men?" (Acts 4:16)

"We gave you strict orders not to teach in this name... Yet you have filled Jerusalem with your teaching and are *determined to make us guilty of this man's blood.*" (Acts 5:28)

"These men who have *caused trouble all over the world* have now come here... " (Acts 17:6)

"We have found this man to be a *troublemaker*, stirring up riots among the Jews all over the world. He is a *ringleader* of the Nazarene *sect* [cult]." (Acts 24:5)

"But we want to hear what your views are, for we know that people everywhere are talking against this *sect*." (Acts 28:22)

"Christianity" has become much more palatable and socially acceptable in our age. The world hasn't changed, but people's perception of "Christianity" has.

Those of us who desire to make a difference in this world must decide to be forceful leaders. We cannot back down when faced with the condemnation of the those who are too proud to willingly obey anyone else's direction.

Fame

Mark 6:14-29 King Herod heard about this, for Jesus' name had become well known. Some were saying, "John the Baptist has been raised from the dead, and that is why miraculous powers are at work in him." Others said, "He is Elijah." And still others claimed, "He is a prophet, like one of the prophets of long ago." But when Herod heard this, he said, "John, the man I beheaded, has been raised from the dead!" For Herod himself had given orders to have John arrested, and he had him bound and put in prison. He did this because of Herodias, his brother Philip's wife, whom he had married. For John had been saying to Herod, "It is not lawful for you to have your brother's wife." So Herodias nursed a grudge against John and wanted to kill him. But she was not able to, because Herod feared John and protected him, knowing him to be a righteous and holy man. When Herod heard John, he was greatly puzzled; yet he liked to listen to him. Finally the opportune time came. On his birthday Herod gave a banquet for his high officials and military commanders and the leading men of Galilee. When the daughter of Herodias came in and danced, she pleased Herod and his dinner guests. The king said to the girl, "Ask me for anything you want, and I'll give it to you." And he promised her with an oath, "Whatever you ask I will give you, up to half my kingdom." She went out and said to her mother, "What shall I ask for?" "The head of John the Baptist," she answered. At once the girl hurried in to the king with the request: "I want you to give me right now the head of John the Baptist on a platter." The king was greatly distressed, but because of his oaths and his dinner guests, he did not want to refuse her. So he immediately sent an executioner with orders to bring John's head. The man went, beheaded John in the prison, and brought back his head on a platter. He presented it to the girl, and she gave it to her mother. On hearing of this, John's disciples came and took his body and laid it in a tomb.

Jesus became well known because he was making an impact. Reciprocally, because his name had become well known, he was able to have a greater impact. **Fame facilitates influence.** This principle is easily seen in the advertising field. Famous people such as Michael Jordan (basketball), Michael Jackson (music), M.C. Hammer (music), Paula Abdul (music), Tommy LaSorda (baseball), and Bo Jackson (baseball and football) have been paid many millions of dollars by various companies who wanted to use their names to promote products. Famous people are the first choices when representatives are selected for telethons, chairpersons for charitable organizations, and spokespersons for various social causes. **Influence begets additional opportunities to influence.**

The same principle holds true on a smaller scale. The researcher who has earned prominence in her field because of groundbreaking research will be asked to write key editorials and to speak at international conferences. Disciples of Jesus who have demonstrated an ability to win others to Christ will be given opportunities to lead small groups having the same goal.

Those of us who are eager to impact others but not interested in being in the public spotlight have a small problem. We must decide to accept being more widely known as a necessary cost of our impact. This cost may manifest itself in many different ways. Perhaps it will include speaking to groups of tens, hundreds, or thousands of people. Maybe it will come out in an unfavorable newspaper article written about us. Or it could involve struggling to resist the temptation of thinking too highly of ourselves as numerous people express to us their appreciation for what we have done. I personally have a strong preference to work behind the scenes. In fact, I originally intended to write this book under a pen name in order to avoid both the applause and the criticisms it might bring! I soon realized that such a move would mean ignoring my own advice. May that never be! I have a problem with those who don't live what they preach.

Reputation

It is interesting that some people thought Jesus was John the Baptist raised from the dead. Others thought he was Elijah or one of the prophets of long ago. John the Baptist had been a radical and outrageous prophet who wore strange clothes and ate strange foods. He condemned the life-style of Herod and eventually lost his head for it. Elijah stood up alone to a murderous king and queen, and nine hundred and fifty false prophets. He called down fire from heaven. Clearly the people perceived Jesus to be quite unlike most people they knew. He had developed a reputation for intensity, non-conformity and zeal. They saw him as a powerful man.

What type of reputation do you have? For years I fought against my reputation. People said that I was a quiet, laid-back analytical sort. I used to cringe every time I heard the words "laid-back." I also didn't like to hear that others perceived me as an anxious and somewhat unhappy person. I defended myself in my own mind: "That's not the real me; reputations aren't necessarily truth. I'm not lacking joy; I just don't like to smile. I'm really very zealous for God. Sure, I get anxious at times, but I'm not an anxious person. Who cares what people think anyway?" Eventually, however, I began to realize that **although my reputation didn't *define* who I was, it did reveal how I was perceived by others.** Not that I now live for the perceptions of others, but I have come to see my reputation as a form of partially objective criticism. I do believe that we need to listen to our critics; there is usually some truth in what they say. For example, consider what other people said about Jesus: "Here is a glutton and a drunkard, a friend of tax collectors and 'sinners.'"[†] The grain of truth in the first criticism was that Jesus did indeed enjoy eating and drinking. But he could laugh at the accusation because he had never been drunk and he wasn't a "habitually voracious eater." I haven't known many gluttons to go on a forty-day fast! The second criticism was absolutely true. Although it was intended as a slur, he would consider it a compliment to be seen as a friend of the riffraff who were ignored or shunned by most religious people.

Evaluating yourself on the basis of what other people say about you is somewhat like looking at yourself in a carnival mirror. It can be a bit distorted, but it still shows your reflection. Many things can distort how we appear to others. For example, **first impressions are lasting impressions** and it takes considerable time to erase them, even after we have made tremendous and obvious changes in our lives. Consequently, our reputation "mirror" may reflect who we *were* more than who we now *are*. If we cannot point to radical changes in our lives, though, this "mirror" probably shows who we are right now, like it or not.

[†]Matthew 11:19, Luke 7:34

Shepherding

Mark 6:30-44 The apostles gathered around Jesus and reported to him all they had done and taught. Then, because so many people were coming and going that they did not even have a chance to eat, he said to them, "Come with me by yourselves to a quiet place and get some rest." So they went away by themselves in a boat to a solitary place. But many who saw them leaving recognized them and ran on foot from all the towns and got there ahead of them. When Jesus landed and saw a large crowd, he had compassion on them, because they were like sheep without a shepherd. So he began teaching them many things. By this time it was late in the day, so his disciples came to him. "This is a remote place," they said, "and it's already very late. Send the people away so they can go to the surrounding countryside and villages and buy themselves something to eat." But he answered, "You give them something to eat." They said to him, "That would take eight months of a man's wages! Are we to go and spend that much on bread and give it to them to eat?" "How many loaves do you have?" he asked. "Go and see." When they found out, they said, "Five—and two fish." Then Jesus directed them to have all the people sit down in groups on the green grass. So they sat down in groups of hundreds and fifties. Taking the five loaves and the two fish and looking up to heaven, he gave thanks and broke the loaves. Then he gave them to his disciples to set before the people. He also divided the two fish among them all. They all ate and were satisfied, and the disciples picked up twelve basketfuls of broken pieces of bread and fish. The number of the men who had eaten was five thousand.

Jesus cared for his disciples and the crowds who followed him. In this passage he shows them the care and protectiveness of a shepherd for his sheep. He didn't drive them into the ground or try to break their spirits. Instead, he looked to refresh them when they were exhausted. The person who has had a hard driving boss knows from personal experience the correctness of Jesus' actions here. Upon successful completion of a project, employees need to be encouraged to catch up on their rest and to celebrate. "Do not muzzle the ox while it is treading out the grain."†"The hardworking farmer should be the first to receive a share of the crops."‡ If employees have no reason to look forward to completing a project, they are more likely to plod along. They will make sure to pace themselves and take the breaks they deserve along the way. Enforcing deadlines becomes much more difficult if the spoils belong exclusively to the boss. Jesus' disciples were secure in his love for them. They knew that even as he called them to his schedule and his priorities, he would not neglect their personal needs. He would keep watch over them.

If we fail to pause to experience the thrill of victory, if we minimize our own accomplishments, if we have no time to rest and recreate, we will squeeze the joy right out of our lives. If we live this way, we will not allow ourselves to feel contentment. We will never be happy and our lives will be unattractive to others. If we drive our employees or our co-workers in the gospel in the same way, they too will be miserable people who are not able to find joy in their work. Long ago, Solomon understood that although it was impossible to find complete fulfillment in life through your work, to find satisfaction in your work is a blessing from God.§

I learned this **principle of rest and celebration** from Noel, a man who cared for me as Jesus did for his disciples. Prior to learning this important lesson I would feel pangs of guilt if I didn't push myself—and those who were with me—continually forward. I would always remind myself that my rest was not here but in heaven. How very noble! I consistently burned out about every four months. Not so noble. These days, my wife and I always make sure to rest and celebrate upon the event of any hard-earned achievement. For example, we celebrate when my research is accepted for publication, when either of us gets a raise, and when someone we have intensely studied the Bible

---

†I Timothy 5:18, I Corinthians 9:9, Deuteronomy 25:4
‡II Timothy 2:6
§Ecclesiastes 2:22-25

with is baptized. When we are exhausted our performance in all areas of our lives suffers. Therefore **we try to push ourselves only until we reach the point of diminishing returns.** We get away when we need to; yet sometimes we still overdo it.

Work Ethic

In addition to being well aware of the needs of his followers, Jesus fully expected them to work hard. He made no apologies for the demanding schedule they kept, and he didn't pamper them. **Important causes are worthy of extreme levels of effort.** On this occasion, a large and desperate crowd of people arrived unexpectedly while they were trying to get away for some much needed rest. Without hesitation Jesus denied himself and began meeting the needs of the crowds. The disciples, however, were perturbed by what was happening and asked Jesus to disperse the crowd. Instead of sending the people away, Jesus instructed his disciples to meet the needs of the crowd themselves. Not surprisingly, his disciples were a bit miffed at this response, and they protested. But Jesus stood his ground. Consequently, his disciples were trained to "go the second mile"† for others.

Crowd Appeal

When they saw Jesus leaving, a large number of people ran ahead on foot to meet him. I am reminded of a time when a young man just barely missed the street-car that I was on. It was the end of a work day and everybody was heading home. When the doors of the car closed in his face he sprinted along-side us toward the next stop which was two blocks away. Unfortunately

†Matthew 5:41

for him, no one was waiting for the street-car at this stop and, without stopping, we went on to the next stop, two more long city blocks away. I was thinking that he would probably give up and wait for the next street-car when, just as we were pulling away from this third stop, he suddenly appeared again, slapping the door of the car to get the driver's attention. He succeeded in getting the attention of everyone in the car except the driver, who seemed oblivious to his distress. About a kilometer down the street he appeared again. This time a sympathetic passenger rang the bell to get the driver's attention, but to no avail. At last, after twenty minutes of chasing the streetcar, he put on an amazing burst of speed, reached the streetcar while it was at a light, and climbed on board. He tried to say something to the driver, but because he was out of breath, nothing came out. As he walked down the center of the car all eyes were upon him. He didn't seem to care; he really, and I mean really, wanted to be on this particular streetcar. He was the personification of urgent determination.

Jesus was able to create that same level of urgency and determination in the people who listened to him. People did not want to miss out on anything he might say or do. Imagine a whole crowd of people running along the shore of a lake to catch up with Jesus. Perhaps this was the first annual Sea of Galilee 10k race, or at least it appeared that way to the people in the area. Few people have ever had so much charisma and such crowd appeal.

Participation

Jesus taught his disciples to have faith by having them participate in his acts of faith. His disciples had to seat approximately ten thousand people on the grass, all the while knowing that there was virtually nothing to give them to eat. Jesus fostered faith in his men by getting them to stick their necks out. They personally handed out the food and witnessed first hand (pun intended) the miracle of the loaves and the fish. They were the ones who gathered up twelve basketfuls of leftovers.

Visible Sincerity

Jesus didn't just meet the crowd's need for spiritual food and then leave them to fend for themselves to meet their physical needs. **He was concerned about them in a complete way, and met the needs of the whole person.** He didn't feel that his duty was simply to preach and heal. He didn't draw the line anywhere. He was a "people person" who continually met other people's needs asking for nothing in return. Compare Jesus' selfless ministry with the work of some effective communicators today who are able to teach people how to live more productive lives. There are many similarities and many differences. The two most obvious differences are first of all, that Jesus was ultimately concerned with how people fared after this life and not just in this life, and secondly, that he gained nothing materially from his work, unlike most of his modern-day "self-help" counterparts, who may get quite wealthy from their books, tapes and seminars. A worker is worth his wages,[†] but one has to wonder about the motivation of someone who derives more than a modest income from "helping others." Seems to me that the person who benefits the most from some of these self-help programs is the person doing the teaching. **In whatever we do, if we want to have a true and lasting impact, we should give to people without expecting anything in return.** If we are more concerned with what we will get ourselves we probably won't have much of an impact.

[†]1 Timothy 5:18

Toughness

Mark 6:45-46 Immediately Jesus made his disciples get into the boat and go on ahead of him to Bethsaida, while he dismissed the crowd. After leaving them, he went up on a mountainside to pray.

Jesus worked harder and longer than anyone else. Trying to get some rest for his disciples, he sends them on ahead. He stays behind to dismiss the crowd. Then, as if the day hadn't been long enough already, he goes up a mountain to pour out his heart in prayer. Jesus expected more from himself than from his disciples. He was tough on himself. Such is **the cost of leadership; the one who is leading the way must pay the greatest price.** This principle is true for entrepreneurs, in rock-climbing, cycling and many other areas.

Unwavering Excellence

Mark 6:47-56 When evening came, the boat was in the middle of the lake, and he was alone on land. He saw the disciples straining at the oars, because the wind was against them. About the fourth watch of the night he went out to them, walking on the lake. He was about to pass by them, but when they saw him walking on the lake, they thought he was a ghost. They cried out, because they all saw him and were terrified. Immediately he spoke to them and said, "Take courage! It is I. Don't be afraid." Then he climbed into the boat with them, and the wind died down. They were completely amazed, for they had not understood about the loaves; their hearts were hardened. When they had crossed over, they landed at Gennesaret and anchored there. As soon as they got out of the boat, people recognized Jesus. They ran throughout that whole region and carried the sick on mats to wherever they heard he was. And wherever he went—into villages, towns or countryside—they placed the sick in the marketplaces. They begged him to let them touch even the edge of his cloak, and all who touched him were healed.

At this time in Jesus' ministry, he was extremely well recognized and consequently swamped with needy people, "wherever he went." The hearts of so many people in this region were like fertile soil to his message. We can rest assured that many of these people, having been personally touched by Jesus, would go on to become a part of the church when it began on the day of Pentecost. Many of them may have been among the three thousand who were baptized on that day. They would also be a large contingent of the Jerusalem church of some ten thousand men and women described in the book of Acts.[†] **Jesus' personal, one-on-one impact was nothing less than phenomenal.** Sometimes we fail to recognize that most members of the early church, which exploded at a greater rate initially than it ever has since, were not the "fruit" of Peter, John or any of the other apostles. These men merely harvested what another had sown[‡]—what Jesus had sown. Such is God's way; one sows and another reaps so that the two can rejoice together. Jesus didn't feel the need to do all the work himself so he could put a new notch on his belt with each person he converted to God. He did the hard work of planting seeds into people's hearts. He broke through the hard soil of their hearts and got something started. He woke them up to the love of God. He started them down the road that would eventually lead to eternal life. But he personally "harvested" (ie. brought into the kingdom of God) only a few.

It doesn't seem like Jesus could have escaped the pressure of the crowds even if he had wanted to. Yet he didn't get overwhelmed by all their needs. He just kept on healing and teaching. He never stopped and he never complained. I'm sure he got some rest, but not a lot. Although he directed the efforts of many followers, he didn't become an administrator. He didn't hide away in his office, orchestrating his Movement. He was always out among the people. He must have had an

[†]Acts 4:4
[‡]John 4:36-38

unbelievable schedule, with frequent interruptions, time conflicts, and people clamoring for his attention. After all, people are people. Yet Jesus handled everything so well that not one of the gospel writers even mentions any problems. Jesus simply kept on meeting the needs of the people around him. I feel confident to say that none of us are now, or will ever be, as able as Jesus was to fully handle all of the responsibilities and needs that confront us. Yet we have him to imitate, the one who has set the ultimate example. Yes, he even walked on water!

Sounding the Alarm

Mark 7:1-13 The Pharisees and some of the teachers of the law who had come from Jerusalem gathered around Jesus and saw some of his disciples eating food with hands that were "unclean," that is, unwashed. (The Pharisees and all the Jews do not eat unless they give their hands a ceremonial washing, holding to the tradition of the elders. When they come from the marketplace they do not eat unless they wash. And they observe many other traditions, such as the washing of cups, pitchers and kettles.) So the Pharisees and teachers of the law asked Jesus, "Why don't your disciples live according to the tradition of the elders instead of eating their food with 'unclean' hands?" He replied, "Isaiah was right when he prophesied about you hypocrites; as it is written: '"These people honor me with their lips, but their hearts are far from me. They worship me in vain; their teachings are but rules taught by men.' You have let go of the commands of God and are holding on to the traditions of men." And he said to them: "You have a fine way of setting aside the commands of God in order to observe your own traditions! For Moses said, 'Honor your father and your mother,' and, 'Anyone who curses his father or mother must be put to death.' But you say that if a man says to his father or mother: 'Whatever help you might otherwise have received from me is Corban' (that is, a gift devoted to God), then you no longer let him do anything for his father or mother. Thus you nullify the word of God by your tradition that you have handed down. And you do many things like that."

Jesus publicly bashed tradition. He told those who lived by tradition that their religion was in vain, a waste of time. He described those who followed tradition as people going through the motions, their hearts far from God. These are tough and revolutionary words. People who live by traditions handed down by people they respect find security in them. To declare them worthless is to tear apart the foundations of some people's lives.

Jesus was not afraid to rebuke people, to "lay it out" when necessary. He called the religious leaders of his day, and by inference all subsequent tradition-following religious leaders, hypocrites with hearts far from God. No wonder they wanted to kill him! Sometimes we can't understand why anyone would want to kill "sweet Jesus." I don't think these religious folks found Jesus all that sweet. **Jesus had an intense distaste for the religious and societal systems that kept people's hearts numb to God's Word.** When he stirred things up, as he did here, some people would wake up to discover a true relationship with God, while others would wake up furious that he had interrupted a dream which they had wanted to continue.

People who have a true impact with their lives wake up the masses. They insist that people think more carefully about the ways they have always done things. They do not hesitate to raise their voices in order to shake people out of their slumber. They are not afraid of how people will react when they are disturbed from their sleep. **It is right to speak the truth in love even if this means disturbing people. It is wrong to be silent and leave people comfortable in their false sense of security.**

Protectiveness

It was actually not Jesus but his disciples who were caught

disobeying the traditions of the elders. But as we have noticed earlier, Jesus took responsibility for his disciples' actions and omissions. You've got to love a leader that stands up for his followers. Jesus didn't say, "They are the ones who didn't wash their hands, talk to them." but rather, "If you've got a problem with them, you'll have to talk to me." **When a leader stands up for and protects his followers, a strong loyalty is forged.**

A Passion for Truth

Mark 7:14-23 Again Jesus called the crowd to him and said, "Listen to me, everyone, and understand this. Nothing outside a man can make him 'unclean' by going into him. Rather, it is what comes out of a man that makes him 'unclean.'" After he had left the crowd and entered the house, his disciples asked him about this parable. "Are you so dull?" he asked. "Don't you see that nothing that enters a man from the outside can make him 'unclean'? For it doesn't go into his heart but into his stomach, and then out of his body." (In saying this, Jesus declared all foods "clean.") He went on: "What comes out of a man is what makes him 'unclean.' For from within, out of men's hearts, come evil thoughts, sexual immorality, theft, murder, adultery, greed, malice, deceit, lewdness, envy, slander, arrogance and folly. All these evils come from inside and make a man 'unclean.'"

After rebuking the religious leaders, Jesus immediately set the crowd right regarding the false doctrine of their leaders. Apparently due to his passion for accuracy and truth, he had no stomach for the misdirection spread by the Pharisees and Teachers of the Law. He would not allow them to continue to lead the people astray. Later, his disciples asked him to further explain his explanation to them. Big mistake! They obviously weren't thinking for themselves, and now they had asked one too many stupid questions.

High Expectations

Jesus expected more from his Twelve than he did from the crowds. But they were still spiritually dull, even after all that they had been through with their teacher. And now Jesus "let 'em have it." He let them know that they were spiritually stupid. How many of us are willing to rebuke when asked a stupid question by people who should know better? **Jesus was determined that these men would rise above the spiritual rank and file. Instead of giving up on his dreams for them when they didn't meet his expectations, he got upset and urged them to change.** When obstacles are encountered, ineffective people lower their expectations. An effective leader will not give up and easily accept a compromise. **This is the difference between one who wishes things could be different and one who dreams they could: the dreamer, or visionary, never gives up the dream; the well-wisher too quickly accepts that the wish was not granted.**

Blame

Jesus states that a person's behavior is a natural outgrowth of the condition of his heart—that is, his inner self, his desires, his character—and is not merely a conditioned response to his environment. In other words, **the responsibility for our actions resides with us, the decision makers, and not with our environment.** We are empowered to choose our response to the stimuli of life. Jesus claims—a few centuries before anyone else—that each of us is, by nature, *proactive*. We are not simply the product of our environment and experiences. Rather, our environment is to some extent determined by the choices we make. For example, we choose who will be a part of our peer group, and we choose whether or not we will be a part of the church. Such choices affect our environment, which most certainly influence our destiny. Therefore we are the product, for the most part, of our own decisions. If we find that our behavior is fundamentally comprised of conditioned responses to external stimuli, then we have decided, either consciously or by failing to make a decision, to subject ourselves to those external conditions. We have chosen to be *reactive* by relinquishing our ability to choose our response. This is not to say that factors beyond our control have no role to play in developing our character. The sins of the father do affect the son. However, these stimuli play a lesser role, leaving the responsibility for what we do and who we become on our own shoulders. We cannot rightly blame others or fate or our circumstances for our inappropriate behavior. We should not shake our fist at Heaven and blame God for what we have done. Instead, **we must take responsibility for the consequences of our decisions.** In my own life, because I continually gave in to my desire to lust after women and to yearn for things that I could not have, I became like a slave to my desire. I could not find lasting contentment, and my relentless desire drove me ever farther from what I knew to be right and pure. Because I was self-focussed, critical and mistrustful, I became extremely sarcastic and insecure around people. Consequently, I had no deep friendships.

One corollary to this truth stated by Jesus is that changes in people occur from the inside out. **It is only when we accept responsibility for who we are and what we have or have not done that we can make significant changes in our lives.** If a leader accepts this truth it will dramatically affect how he interacts with others. The negative and hurtful behaviors in people's lives arise out of the evil in their hearts. Admittedly, classical "behavior modification," which does not deal directly with the "inner man" but only with external behaviors, can work. A conscious behavioral change can also change what lies deeper; that is to say, we can "act ourselves into a new way of feeling." However, what I would refer to as "Christian behavior modification" involves helping people to acknowledge what they are really like deep down and then to deal with their inner self. With continued help from other people, an internal cleansing always produces an amazing external transformation. A leader who accepts Jesus' teaching here can have great confidence that people are able to change if they are willing to deal with their hearts.

"But if evil in my own heart causes me to do evil, how can I change my heart in order to do good? And if the ultimate impact that I can have on others is to help them change their hearts, how can I do this?" The answer, according to Jesus, is you cannot; on your own, you cannot change your own, or anyone else's heart. Jesus claimed that only he, as the Son of God, could set people free from their bondage to evil. Only God is greater than our hearts:

> Jesus replied, "I tell you the truth, everyone who sins is a slave to sin. Now a slave has no permanent place in the family, but a son belongs to it forever. So if the Son sets you free, you will be free indeed. (John 8:34-36)

> For God is greater than our hearts, and he knows everything. (I John 3:20)

> I will give you a new heart and put a new spirit in you; I will remove from you your heart of stone and give you a heart of flesh. And I will put my Spirit in you and move you to follow my decrees and be careful to keep my laws. (Ezekiel 36:26-28)

If we accept that there is evil present in our hearts (ie. moral imperfections that we are not able to overcome on our own), and if we believe that only God can change our hearts, then we are very close to a happy eternity. For it is precisely at this point of understanding that we realize how desperately we need God's intervention in our lives. On the other hand, if we are blind to or feel comfortable with the evil in our hearts, or if we are confident that we can change our inner self on our own, we will not be able to fully respond to the grace of God, regardless of how faithful we are to our religious traditions.

All true Christians have had to humbly face their own imperative need to change, at the heart level, in order to even enter the kingdom of God. **The Bible exposes, in an unbiased way, the true quality of our hearts.** It reveals that we all alike have chosen a path diverging from God's moral perfection. Subsequently, the change demanded by the Bible strikes at the very root of our being: an immediate and complete reversal in the direction of our lives, regardless of whether or not we have grown up in a "Christian family." It follows then that true converts to Christ, more than any other people, should be ready and able to make ongoing radical and lasting changes in their lives. I have found this to be consistently and indisputably true. Unfortunately, deceitful or hypocritical people who say they are Christians make this comparison rather difficult for the person who knows little Bible teaching. If you are unfamiliar with the radical "transformation" of true Christians, or if you perceive the United States to be a "Christian" nation, or if you think a person is a "Christian" if they do their best to be a good person, or if you can admit that you honestly don't know what a true follower of Christ would look like in our day, then please leave the jury out on this one. Don't accept or reject this teaching until you get to know someone who has radically changed their inner self because of Christ. As for me, **the deep and permanent character changes that I observe in my own life, as well as in the lives of other disciples, fuels my faith.** Every leader in the church of Christ should fervently believe that his or her people can change, totally and dramatically!

Firmness and Flexibility

Mark 7:24-30 Jesus left that place and went to the vicinity of Tyre. He entered a house and did not want anyone to know it; yet he could not keep his presence secret. In fact, as soon as she heard about

> him, a woman whose little daughter was possessed by an evil
> spirit came and fell at his feet. The woman was a Greek, born in
> Syrian Phoenicia. She begged Jesus to drive the demon out of her
> daughter. "First let the children eat all they want," he told her,
> "for it is not right to take the children's bread and toss it to their
> dogs." "Yes, Lord," she replied, "but even the dogs under the
> table eat the children's crumbs." Then he told her, "For such a
> reply, you may go; the demon has left your daughter." She went
> home and found her child lying on the bed, and the demon gone.

Are you able to say "no" to people? Jesus was. His main
objective was not to be a "nice guy." Here he initially denies
the request of this woman because she was not an Israelite, and
his personal ministry was directed exclusively to the "people of
the covenant." He wasn't going to back down just because this
woman might not be able to understand the big picture. He even
refers to her people as the "dogs" of the children of God. That
was a pretty strong "no!" Yet because of her determination, her
humility and her faith, he is won over. He makes an exception
because of her exceptional qualities. **Some of us are unable to
deny anybody anything.** We want people to agree with our
decisions and we want them to like us. We are too ready to
compromise for no good reason. **Others of us are too
inflexible. We are unwilling to make any exceptions.** Jesus
had both the strength of character to deny someone a reasonable
request and the flexibility to make an exception to his own rule.
He was not afraid of people talking against him for "discrimi-
nating against an immigrant." He also was not afraid to change
his mind.

The world does not need any more "yes men" or "yes
women." Nice and easily swayed people don't become movers
and shakers. Not that we don't need to follow the advice of
those more experienced or more successful than ourselves. We
need wise counsel! **But we must also think for ourselves and
not succumb to the whims and fancies of everyone around
us.**

If we want to make a difference, we must be willing to

disappoint some people. Unfortunately, not everyone will be able to understand our other obligations, our agendas and our schedules. We need to take charge of our lives and hold to our convictions, yet not in a way that is inflexible.

Communicator

Mark 7:31-37 Then Jesus left the vicinity of Tyre and went through Sidon, down to the Sea of Galilee and into the region of the Decapolis. There some people brought to him a man who was deaf and could hardly talk, and they begged him to place his hand on the man. After he took him aside, away from the crowd, Jesus put his fingers into the man's ears. Then he spit and touched the man's tongue. He looked up to heaven and with a deep sigh said to him, "Ephphatha!" (which means, "Be opened!"). At this, the man's ears were opened, his tongue was loosened and he began to speak plainly. Jesus commanded them not to tell anyone. But the more he did so, the more they kept talking about it. People were overwhelmed with amazement. "He has done everything well," they said. "He even makes the deaf hear and the mute speak."

Jesus knew that people would be amazed at the miracle he was about to perform on this deaf and mute man. Not needing the applause of the crowds, he takes this man away from the crowd before he heals him. We have already mentioned how Jesus was seeking impact, not fame.

After taking the man aside but prior to actually healing him, Jesus does something that we haven't seen him do before. He puts his fingers in the deaf man's ears and he spits and touches his tongue. Through these touches and gestures, I believe Jesus was *telling* the deaf man in a visible, non-verbal way that he had the power to heal him. In so doing, he encouraged the man to have faith so that he could be healed. As any good communicator does, Jesus took upon himself the responsibility of communication. He didn't use phrases or words or jargon that his audience could not understand. He wasn't trying to impress anyone. Instead he was creative and resourceful. In a situation where verbal communication was impossible, he found a way to influence this man. He did whatever was required to get through to the individual he was "speaking" with.

It is a fact of life that some people are more difficult for us to communicate with than others. It is especially difficult for us to persuade someone who comes from a vastly different socioeconomic background. Sometimes it is quite hard to win the trust of someone who is physically challenged, or the respect of someone who is older than us. On the other hand it may be quite difficult to win the respect of a teen when we are unfamiliar with the current lingo and fads. **Jesus found a way to win the hearts of all types of people. His** *secret* **was an overwhelming love for all people. His** *method* **was communication that fit the individual.**

A Standard of Excellence

Jesus not only opened this man's ears to hear, he also gave him the ability to speak. The people responded by declaring that Jesus did everything well. **Jesus never did a shoddy job. He never quit halfway.** We remember that when Jesus turned water into wine at a wedding banquet in Cana, he produced the best wine the master of the banquet had tasted.† Jesus had a standard of excellence in everything he did—and, as is always the case, his audience eventually took notice. More than noticed; they were overwhelmed with amazement! They could not stop talking about what he had done. **We may not be able to do miracles, but with a passion for excellence, we too will eventually amaze those around us.**

†John 2:10

Caterer

Mark 8:1-10 During those days another large crowd gathered. Since they had nothing to eat, Jesus called his disciples to him and said, "I have compassion for these people; they have already been with me three days and have nothing to eat. If I send them home hungry, they will collapse on the way, because some of them have come a long distance." His disciples answered, "But where in this remote place can anyone get enough bread to feed them?" "How many loaves do you have?" Jesus asked. "Seven," they replied. He told the crowd to sit down on the ground. When he had taken the seven loaves and given thanks, he broke them and gave them to his disciples to set before the people, and they did so. They had a few small fish as well; he gave thanks for them also and told the disciples to distribute them. The people ate and were satisfied. Afterward the disciples picked up seven basketfuls of broken pieces that were left over. About four thousand men were present. And having sent them away, he got into the boat with his disciples and went to the region of Dalmanutha.

When another "sell-out" crowd gathered to hear him speak, Jesus began an impromptu three-day seminar on God and righteous living. He had no warm-up band, no laser light show, not even a sound system! Yet large crowds were the norm for Jesus' ministry. He didn't sneak around stating his case behind closed doors. He was good with crowds because he was always ready to speak. He was dynamic and charismatic. He was not afraid of the crowds.

On this occasion, Jesus again shows his compassion for the crowds, his sensitivity to their needs. He was concerned that they get home safely after coming a long distance to hear him. The crowds were not there for his benefit; he was there for the benefit of the crowd. He wasn't performing, he was serving. A *caterer* is a person who supplies food for an event, or less specifically, **a person who supplies what is required or desired.** Jesus was a comprehensive caterer: as well as being concerned with the task of sowing the seed of God's Word in their hearts, he was also alert to their condition, and concerned about their physical needs. Shortly before being crucified, Jesus sensed his disciples grief and said to them, "I have much more to say to you, more than you can now bear."[†] If only today's speakers could be as sensitive to the condition and receptivity of their listeners! What a marvelous example Jesus is to those of us who interact with "crowds." Jesus shows us how to be effective in leaving a lasting impression on a crowd.

Delegator

Once again, Jesus lets his disciples do a lot of the footwork in his ministry. The art of delegation is essential in order to free a leader's time to do more important tasks. In addition, and equally valid, it is an effective training method to give a leader's trainees a thorough understanding of the details that are involved in executive decision-making. It prepares subordinates to be able to take over the tasks of leadership. Delegation also tests the abilities of subordinates to successfully handle responsibility. It exposes how attentive they are to details, and how solution-oriented they can be when an unexpected problem arises.

Effective delegation—like many other aspects of the nature and proper use of authority—is a subject unto itself. Delegating does not mean "dumping" unwanted chores on subordinates; delegation is different than abdication. It is important to realize that one can inadvertently "over-delegate," and in so doing, lose control of the outcome of the project. The delegator (who is ultimately responsible for the final outcome) puts herself in a vulnerable position when she over-delegates. She becomes excessively dependent on the exceptional performance of people who do not have as much incentive as she does to successfully

†John 16:12

complete the task. In such a situation, her work load is probably too low, and her stress level too high. **Effective delegation implies careful selection of appropriate tasks to delegate, clear communication of expectations, thoughtful assessment of the delegatee's performance, and constructive criticism.** Through his example here and elsewhere, Jesus helps us to begin to understand the rudiments of effective delegation.

Prudence

Mark 8:11-13 The Pharisees came and began to question Jesus. To test him, they asked him for a sign from heaven. He sighed deeply and said, "Why does this generation ask for a miraculous sign? I tell you the truth, no sign will be given to it." Then he left them, got back into the boat and crossed to the other side.

Sometimes Jesus simply didn't bother to deal with his adversaries—he just up and left. He could see that these Pharisees weren't at all open to his message; instead, they just wanted to pick a fight with him. So Jesus didn't waste any time. He just sighed in frustration, laid the truth out before them and left them standing there. **Sometimes we need to be able to determine when the best thing to do is to walk away.** In some situations involving, shall we say, difficult people, there is simply nothing to be gained in continuing a fruitless argument. At such times we need to lay the truth out to them and leave. Too often we waste our time arguing with people who are not in the least open to seeing things any other way than they already do. Why do we waste our time? Are we naive enough to think that everybody can be won over to our way of thinking? It is more likely that we enjoy a good argument. Either that or we enjoy beating our heads against a wall. We should "shake the dust off our feet" and move on to find people who show some interest in our message. It is much more likely that those who have some interest will eventually respond favorably.

Moving On

Jesus kept moving. One reason he kept moving was so that he wouldn't get pinned down by his adversaries. If he stayed in any one place for too long they would come to him en masse and stifle his efforts among those who were open to his message. Another reason Jesus kept moving was to help a larger number of people to reach spiritual maturity. He was like a farmer working the soil. A good farmer doesn't simply scatter seeds around his farmhouse; he plants seed across all of his fields. If he desires a good crop, he won't exclusively water and weed one small patch and leave the rest of his fields unattended. He must cover a large area in order to produce an abundant crop.

To lose sight of the fields for the sake of one plant would be foolish. Yet that is what many of us do. We focus all of our attention on one problem, one goal, or one person's need, and we neglect the rest of our "fields." Because of a problem at work, we may be pensive at home, and give only shallow, one-word responses to our family. Or a problem in one relationship may somehow sour all of our other relationships. Or we may spend months, even years, to achieve one particular goal, alienating our family and completely neglecting other responsibilities along the way. It is too easy to get bogged down if one "patch" of our "fields" is not growing as we had planned. We may find it hard to accept failure, and let everything else fall to pieces while attempting to restore a perfect state. We should rather attempt to see the whole "field"—the big picture—and not allow ourselves to get stuck in one corner. We should do our best with our plans and with what arises unexpectedly. Yet we must always move on. As a consequence of the first man's decision to disobey God, our life is not an easy, painless roller-coaster ride. After Adam had broken God's commandment, God said to him: "Cursed is the

ground because of you; through painful toil you will eat of it all the days of your life. It will produce thorns and thistles for you.... By the sweat of your brow you will eat your food... "†
No painful toil, no gain or spoil. We have been banished from the garden of Eden; therefore we must always move on. **To not move on is to stagnate. And stagnation leads to apathy, hopelessness, numbness and death.**

Jesus also kept moving in order to keep his life and work fresh, vibrant and spontaneous. He kept moving in order to keep things moving. *Momentum* **is an invisible yet critical element in any type of movement.** To understand what momentum is and how it works, visualize the weighted wheel of an exercise bicycle. Much more energy is required to start up the wheel than to keep it going once it is up to speed; that is, it takes less energy to *keep up* the momentum than to *build up* the momentum. Because we cannot readily see momentum, it can quietly slip away if energy is not consistently being put into the system. This happens on an exercise bicycle when our foot slips off the pedal. When we start up again after a few seconds we sense that a little of the momentum has been lost. Fortunately, we can get up to speed again very quickly. If we stop pedalling for a much longer period of time, however, much more energy will be required in order to get back up to speed. **Neglect necessitates extra energy. So keep moving.**

Scout

Mark 8:14-21 The disciples had forgotten to bring bread, except for one loaf they had with them in the boat. "Be careful," Jesus warned them. "Watch out for the yeast of the Pharisees and that of Herod." They discussed this with one another and said, "It is because we have no bread." Aware of their discussion, Jesus asked them: "Why are you talking about having no bread? Do

†Genesis 3:17-19

> you still not see or understand? Are your hearts hardened? Do you have eyes but fail to see, and ears but fail to hear? And don't you remember? When I broke the five loaves for the five thousand, how many basketfuls of pieces did you pick up?" "Twelve," they replied. "And when I broke the seven loaves for the four thousand, how many basketfuls of pieces did you pick up?" They answered, "Seven." He said to them, "Do you still not understand?"

Jesus warned his disciples to be alert to the maneuvers of those who opposed their movement. He wanted to make them aware of those who were against them. That Herod, an amoral political opportunist, would be in opposition to them came as no surprise at all. However, it probably came as somewhat of a surprise when they realized that the religious leaders of Jesus' day opposed him much more than did anyone else. It was not the Romans who fought his work; it was not those living blatantly sinful lives; it was not people from a different religious background. In the same way it may surprise followers of Jesus today to find that the leaders of "Christian" denominations may offer the greatest opposition to a radical adherence to the teachings of Christ.

A good coach warns his players of the strengths and possible strategies of the opponent. This is preceded by what is called "scouting out the opponent"—or, if the rivalry between the two teams is intense, "scouting out the enemy." The basic principles of assessing the opponent and informing one's teammates holds true in any competitive arena, be it sports, warfare, or business. Each side designates one or more people to assess the abilities and determine the tactics of the other side. The "scout" is typically very knowledgeable and experienced in the nature of the confrontation that is about to occur. He is able to quickly size up the competitive ability of the opponent in a way that will *inform* but not *intimidate* his own teammates. He protects his own people and helps them prepare for victory by warning them about the strengths of their opponent and the types of activity to expect.

I can remember the first time I was on a team where our coach helped us to prepare in this way to face our opponent. It was my second year in "squirt" league ice hockey. I was fortunate to be placed on a team of relatively talented boys, ages nine and ten. Consequently, we routed many of the other teams in our league and routinely won outside tournaments on the weekends. Nearing the end of our regular season, we were undefeated and feeling invincible. Although many years have passed since then, I can still remember our coach's warning before we faced the number two team in our league for the first time. He told us about their record, and how they had intimidated some of the other teams. They weren't pretty, but they were tough and effective. He told us to keep on top of their number seven, a small guy with thick glasses who was faster than any ten-year old on skates ought to be. He liked to hang out between the other team's defensemen and their goal-keeper looking for stray pucks so he could race down and shoot with no one but the goalie to stop him. It was up to us defensemen to make sure he didn't get between us and our goalie. Sure enough, we were able to take away their primary offensive threat. Even though we lost the game when they scored a fluke goal in the last few seconds, we eventually beat the team in the league championship game. They were every bit as good as we were; in reflection, I think we won because we knew them better than they knew us.

If we want to be effective leaders, then we cannot afford to neglect scouting out the opposition and warning our subordinates about who they are up against. This is a crucial leadership responsibility. There will always be opposition, and our people need to be aware of the weapons and tactics of our adversaries in order to be able to resist and overcome them.

Rebuke

We also see from this passage that Jesus was aware of the
private discussions of his disciples. He made it his business to
know what they were thinking and what they were discussing
among themselves. **Uninhibited discussions can be very
revealing.** As leaders we should always try to be aware of what
our followers are saying to each other. Our people may say
things to each other that they would never discuss with a
supervisor.

Jesus recognized, on this occasion, that his disciples had no clue
what he was trying to teach them. Apparently they were looking
at things from a very unspiritual perspective. This made Jesus
very angry, and he proceeded to hit them with a barrage of
questions—some of which were very cutting. He wasn't trying
to be "Mr. Nice Guy." They had been listening but not
hearing. Even though they had been a part of his miracles, they
had not paid attention. They were seemingly stuck in unspiritual
thinking. Yet Jesus didn't just throw up his hands in frustration.
He asked them embarrassingly simple questions to both remind
them of what had happened and to help them to see how stupid
they had been to so soon forget.

Try to imagine how Jesus' disciples must have felt after this
conversation. He had intended to humble and convict them. I
wouldn't be surprised if you could have heard a first-century
pin drop when Jesus finished speaking. Perhaps Judas felt
picked on. Possibly the rest were more eager to change. As we
today survey this somewhat uncomfortable interaction, ask
yourself an important question: Can you see yourself being so
firm and convicting with your friends? Would you be willing to
humble and convict them for a senseless action, when they
should have known better? If your answer is "no," you
shouldn't expect to be a man or a woman of impact. As
important as a genuine concern for others, a willingness to

be strong and forthright is a required characteristic of one who would have lasting influence.

I find that in regard to the willingness to confront others, there are two types of people. For the first type, it is an extremely difficult thing to do; for the second, it comes all too easily. Six years ago it was quite natural for me to criticize and put down the people around me. I was continually making myself feel like dirt for the mistakes in my own life, so I found it quite easy to be just as tough on other people. Since then, due to the influence of my wife and a number of other friends, I've learned to love other people and express myself in a much different way. Paradoxically, I now find it very difficult to humble and confront my friends. I have to push myself to say hard things to people. Then after I've said what I had to say, I feel just as uncomfortable as they do. But **I am convinced that people can grow in significant ways when a friend rebukes them.** Proud people who are not convicted of their need to change will not change. But humble people who are willing to change can be molded into the very image of God. I ask you to chew on this next proverb, and ask yourself the question, "am I a friend or an enemy to ____?" (Fill in the blank with the name of your wife, husband, neighbor, employees, etc..)

> Proverbs 27:5,6 Better is open rebuke than hidden love. Wounds from a friend can be trusted, but an enemy multiplies kisses.

Second Effort

> Mark 8:22-26 They came to Bethsaida, and some people brought a blind man and begged Jesus to touch him. He took the blind man by the hand and led him outside the village. When he had spit on the man's eyes and put his hands on him, Jesus asked, "Do you see anything?" He looked up and said, "I see people; they look like trees walking around." Once more Jesus put his hands on the man's eyes. Then his eyes were opened, his sight was restored, and he saw everything clearly. Jesus sent him home, saying,

"Don't go into the village."

Jesus again went to extremes in order to do his miracles of healing in secret. It seems that there were a great number of "miracle hounds" in the cities of Galilee. Unfortunately these people, although they did have enough faith to be healed of various deficiencies and diseases, did not have enough faith to be willing to turn away (the biblical word is "repent") from the sins in their lives. They had witnessed many miracles, but these miracles had not produced a humility in their hearts towards God. They still refused to "tremble at his word."[†] This was not the case for all of the Galileans. In fact, all of his disciples, except perhaps Judas Iscariot, were from the region of Galilee. Yet the masses of people in these regions would not repent. Consequently, Jesus pronounced the judgement of God on the unrepentant people of these cities. He claimed that they would be worse off than the gentile cities of Tyre and Sidon which were proud, historic centers of Canaanite paganism:

> "Woe to you, Korazin! Woe to you, Bethsaida! For if the miracles that were performed in you had been performed in Tyre and Sidon, they would have repented long ago, sitting in sackcloth and ashes. But it will be more bearable for Tyre and Sidon at the judgment than for you." (Luke 10:13,14)

Mark tells us that Jesus led the blind man out of the city by the hand. He didn't take him by the arm. The difference is significant. To hold someone's hand, in any culture, is more intimate and more affectionate than to take them by the arm. **Jesus was not afraid to show affection to people in public.**

Imagine walking hand-in-hand down the street with God. It is encouraging to know that Jesus is the kind of friend who would take us by the hand. This blind man had the privilege of walking with God. But my guess is that he didn't know it, and he wasn't even convinced that Jesus was sent by God. This man was quite different from blind Bartimaeus who we will read about later. Bartimaeus could not be dissuaded from trying to

[†]Isaiah 66:2

get Jesus' attention. This man from Bethsaida was brought to Jesus by his friends. They begged Jesus to heal him. I'm sure Jesus and the blind man had a good talk as they walked out of the village together. **Yet it still took *two attempts by Jesus* to give the man his sight.** This is about the closest thing we can find to a failure in Jesus' life in all of the gospel record. And we see that **Jesus didn't allow an unsuccessful first try to discourage him from trying again.** He didn't doubt himself or his abilities. He was convinced that the problem must lie in the blind man's lack of faith. (For this same reason, Jesus had been unable to do much healing in Nazareth.†) Jesus' power had not mysteriously faded; this man was weak in his faith. Therefore Jesus worked with him, and sought to increase his faith. He didn't give up on him, or rebuke him for doubting. Instead he gave him more of his time and personal attention. Jesus demonstrated in this instance what it means to be *solution-oriented:* **He recognized the problem, did what was in his power to do, and persevered until his goal was achieved.**

Time Management

Mark 8:27-30 Jesus and his disciples went on to the villages around Caesarea Philippi. On the way he asked them, "Who do people say I am?" They replied, "Some say John the Baptist; others say Elijah; and still others, one of the prophets." "But what about you?" he asked. "Who do you say I am?" Peter answered, "You are the Christ." Jesus warned them not to tell anyone about him.

It is my personal conviction that the pace of urban life has never been faster than it is today. Consequently, time management is critically important for every person who hopes to live a life of impact. Fortunately for those of us who look to imitate his example, **Jesus lived a very busy life.** The demands

†Mark 6:1-6

on his time were unceasing. He took upon himself an unenviable amount of responsibilities, he met every need within earshot, and he faced interruptions every step of the way. Accordingly, Jesus made good use of his time, often accomplishing several things at once. For the most part, Jesus taught his disciples by having them accompany him wherever he went. A great many of his conversations with them occurred as they were travelling from one place to another. **He could walk, talk, obtain information and influence people's lives all at the same time.** Some of us have convinced ourselves that we can't walk and chew gum at the same time. We have to finish this before we can begin that. Others of us feel guilty if we are not constantly doing at least two things at the same time. Jesus knew that his time was limited and his task great; therefore he strove to get double-duty from his time.

From reading each of the gospel records, it is clear that most of Jesus' days were long, his rest was intermittent, and his schedule was full. Yet he never seemed harried or "stressed out." He never complained about not having enough time, or about being too busy. **Since none of us can claim the same success, we could most likely benefit from imitating his attitudes toward time management. His most fundamental attitude seemed to be to simply *make the most of each day*, and to *not worry about tomorrow*.† Yet he did *plan for tomorrow*; he had *long and short term goals*.‡ He frequently spoke out *against running after the urgent and having no time left for the important*.§**

Reputation

Jesus had at least a passing interest in his public image. He

---

†Matthew 6:34
‡Luke 13:31-33, Luke 19:10
§Matthew 6:33, Luke 10:38-42, Luke 12:16-21

certainly wasn't consumed with it as would be a present-day politician. As we have mentioned before, the way others perceived him did not control his behavior. Yet he kept informed of what the public was thinking by staying on top of what they said about him.

In the same way, Jesus was curious about what his disciples thought about him. He wanted to know if he was getting through to them. He was openly disappointed when they remained so long in the dark regarding his identity. It would probably hurt very much to be the Son of God and to have the men in whom you were investing your life fail to really understand you. Yet Jesus risked making the inquiry.

We also need to find out how others perceive us. We shouldn't fear their disapproval. If we are truly laying down our lives for them and they fail to appreciate the fact, we shouldn't take it personally. Their ignorance tells us something about the present state of their hearts. If they fail to appreciate that we are more experienced, knowledgeable and capable than they are, we shouldn't feel insecure. If they don't think they have much to learn from us, it is their loss, for they will not grow. On the other hand, we may discover that they fully appreciate who we are or what we are doing for them. Such was the case on this occasion; Peter made Jesus' day!

Timing

Mark 8:31-33 He then began to teach them that the Son of Man must suffer many things and be rejected by the elders, chief priests and teachers of the law, and that he must be killed and after three days rise again. He spoke plainly about this, and Peter took him aside and began to rebuke him. But when Jesus turned and looked at his disciples, he rebuked Peter. "Get behind me, Satan!" he said. "You do not have in mind the things of God, but the things of men."

Only after Peter's proclamation that Jesus was the Savior did he
begin to tell them plainly about the suffering ahead of him, and
the death that he would die. Jesus knew the importance of
timing. Consequently, he did not reveal things prematurely; he
did not give in to the anxieties which always accompany
undisclosed information. In so doing, he adhered to the advice
of King Solomon: **"For there is a proper time and procedure
for every matter, though a man's misery weighs heavily
upon him."**[†] There can be no doubt but that the suffering and
humiliation awaiting Jesus at the cross were ever on his heart.
Yet until this moment in his ministry, even his closest friends
were not at a point to bear this difficult truth. If he had told
them earlier, he would have burdened them with more than they
could handle. Only after they had developed a strong faith that
he was the Messiah, could they honestly begin to wrestle with
the fact that he would lay down his life. The implications for
their own lives were all too clear: if their leader was going to be
persecuted and killed, what might happen to them?

Approachability

This new revelation obviously did not go down too well for
Peter. He drew Jesus aside and rebuked him. "Never, Lord!"
he said. "This shall never happen to you!"[‡] Imagine rebuking
God face to face! Another gleaming quality of Jesus that we
may miss at first glance is revealed here: he was exceptionally
approachable. Sure, Peter was still feeling good about the
golden answer that he had so recently been commended for, and
no doubt he often suffered from "foot-in-mouth disease." But
in addition to this, **Peter and all the other disciples knew that
they could say anything to Jesus and he would continue to
accept them.** They were convinced that nothing they could say

[†]Ecclesiastes 8:6
[‡]Matthew 16:22

would cause him to distance himself from them.

A leader must be approachable. If people don't feel comfortable with their leader, they will simply not discuss with him or her what is really on their hearts. **No communication means no conflict resolution, no transfer of courage, no constructive criticism given and no lives changed.** Jesus shows us that being approachable does not mean being a "push-over." Approachability is not the product of timidity, or of an unwillingness to challenge people, or of a lack of conviction. In fact these qualities may reduce a person's approachability because **people won't open up to someone they perceive as being weak and unable to help them.** Rather, approachability is derived from emotional stability, kindness and patience. It reflects inner strength and confidence, and belongs to the people who are not preocupied by their image, by how people are perceiving them. Approachability is the fruit of those who have the ability to listen completely before responding, those who have self-control. Approachable people can be stern, but they are never harsh. They can be uncompromising with regard to a moral standard, but never argumentative or self-righteous. They may demand openness, but they must also practice a high standard of confidentiality. They can get angry, but they are also warm and full of praise. Unapproachable leaders are frequently out of touch with how people are feeling about their organization's policies and goals. Unless they change, they will ultimately fail.

With regard to confidentiality, Jesus held to this principle: public offenses demand public discipline. Mark tells us that when Jesus turned and saw that all of the disciples were aware that Peter was rebuking him, he rebuked Peter in front of them. *What goes around comes around!* If a person is not careful to discuss disagreements privately he had best be prepared for a public rebuke. If someone is publicly critical of a leader, he has committed two offenses: he has shown disrespect, and he has maligned the leader, whether he intended to or not. He deserves to be publicly reprimanded. His offense was committed for all the world to see; why should he be allowed the dignity of private retribution? I'm sure that Peter learned to bring up his grievances and disagreements with Jesus in private. The disciples also learned not to imitate Peter's bad example. Publicly rebuking Peter was for his own good, and for the good of the group.

Hardline

Mark 8:34-9:1 Then he called the crowd to him along with his disciples and said: "If anyone would come after me, he must deny himself and take up his cross and follow me. For whoever wants to save his life will lose it, but whoever loses his life for me and for the gospel will save it. What good is it for a man to gain the whole world, yet forfeit his soul? Or what can a man give in exchange for his soul? If anyone is ashamed of me and my words in this adulterous and sinful generation, the Son of Man will be ashamed of him when he comes in his Father's glory with the holy angels." And he said to them, "I tell you the truth, some who are standing here will not taste death before they see the kingdom of God come with power."

With Peter cringing at the news of his leader's imminent and bloody departure, Jesus knew that he had to address the crowd. Jesus understood what I call **"the whistling teapot principle."** When the teapot whistles, it is not because of some isolated steam; the pot is full of boiling water. In the same way, if one of the players on your team is expressing ill-will, there is probably a "teamful" of attitudes to be dealt with. If one of your top executives is disgruntled, you probably have a whole department of discontented people. Such **attitudes generally don't float in isolation, they filter up and down and across the ranks.** If a leader under your direct supervision handles difficult news poorly, why should you expect a better response from those who will hear it from them second hand? How would the crowds react when they heard through the grapevine what Jesus had predicted about his death? Peter wasn't about to leave Jesus at this moment, but might other followers walk away thinking Jesus had lost his mind?

Jesus clearly needed to put things in perspective for his followers. If Peter was shocked at the predicted final outcome of Jesus' committment to God, and if the Twelve reacted by clinging to life as they knew it, then they all needed to get a glimpse from God's perspective. They were unaware of the true plight of mankind, of the inevitable doom they themselves faced apart from divine intervention. They failed to grasp the severity of their situation. They clung to life in a world which was tragically opposed to its Maker. Jesus wasn't choosing to lay down his life on a whim; he was fully aware of the prophesy of Scripture regarding his death. He was convinced that his death would be excruciatingly painful (Psalm 22); he knew that his body would be so torn and battered that when it was all over, he wouldn't even be recognizable:

> See, my servant will act wisely; he will be raised and lifted up and highly exalted. Just as there were many who were appalled at him—his appearance was *so disfigured beyond that of any man and his form marred beyond human likeness*—so will he sprinkle many nations, and kings will shut their mouths because of him. For what they were not told, they will see, and what they have not heard, they will understand. (Isaiah 52:13-15)

At this moment, only Jesus was fully convinced of the judgement that was to come upon the world. No one else could yet understand why he should have to die such a horrible death. They had not yet grasped the holiness of God, or realized that God could not be close to them because of the evil in their hearts. They had not yet fathomed their own unworthiness; they placed too much focus on their present life and not enough on the life to come. It was time for them to hear one "barn-burner" of a message!

Jesus chose this time to speak some of the hardest and most challenging words ever spoken by any leader to his

followers. Jesus was not speaking to his opponents. This would not be an appropriate message for those who were not already eager to please their God. This was the ''bottom line,'' reserved for those who intimately knew the one who was speaking to them. Let us examine what Jesus said in more detail:

''If anyone... ''—this means ''Listen up, all of you!'';

''... would come after me,''—the crowd knew that Jesus' purpose was to lead them to the kingdom of God;

''... he must... ''—a difficult word for most of us to hear: there are no alternatives, no other ways;

''... deny himself... ''—simple to understand—to do the will of another instead of your own will[†]—but rather difficult to do;

''... take up his cross... ''—people did not wear crosses for jewelry in the first century; a cross was symbolic of a humiliating public execution;

''... whoever wants to save his life will lose it, but whoever loses his life for me and for the gospel will save it... ''—the ultimate cost of following Jesus;

''What good is it for a man to gain the whole world, yet forfeit his soul? Or what can a man give in exchange for his soul?''—Jesus reasons with the people, pleads with them to contrast the value of their soul with the value of what can be attained in the world, and calls them to change their value systems;

''If anyone is ashamed of me and my words in this adulterous and sinful generation, the Son of Man will be ashamed of him when he comes in his Father's glory... ''—he acknowledges how many members of the crowd must have been feeling about what he had said, and implies that they were ashamed because they valued the approval of men more than the approval of God.

[†]''In order to obey God, we must first disobey ourselves; and it is in this disobeying of ourselves wherein the difficulty of obeying God consists.'' —Hermann Melville, *Moby Dick*

Jesus wasn't trying to scare these people off; on the contrary, he was trying to win them over. But he knew that he had to talk to them about topics they found uncomfortable. Jesus was aware that people in general are afraid to talk about such things as self denial, receiving scorn from close friends, losing their life, and changing their value system. Yet Jesus considered no topic too sacred or too personal to talk about or to challenge people on. His primary concern was for their immortal souls. No wonder he had such an impact!

Peer Group

Mark 9:2-13 After six days Jesus took Peter, James and John with him and led them up a high mountain, where they were all alone. There he was transfigured before them. His clothes became dazzling white, whiter than anyone in the world could bleach them. And there appeared before them Elijah and Moses, who were talking with Jesus. Peter said to Jesus, "Rabbi, it is good for us to be here. Let us put up three shelters—one for you, one for Moses and one for Elijah." (He did not know what to say, they were so frightened.) Then a cloud appeared and enveloped them, and a voice came from the cloud: "This is my Son, whom I love. Listen to him!" Suddenly, when they looked around, they no longer saw anyone with them except Jesus. As they were coming down the mountain, Jesus gave them orders not to tell anyone what they had seen until the Son of Man had risen from the dead. They kept the matter to themselves, discussing what "rising from the dead" meant. And they asked him, "Why do the teachers of the law say that Elijah must come first?" Jesus replied, "To be sure, Elijah does come first, and restores all things. Why then is it written that the Son of Man must suffer much and be rejected? But I tell you, Elijah has come, and they have done to him everything they wished, just as it is written about him."

Jesus made a point of spending time alone with his top guys. They were often surrounded by crowds, but he never failed to allow for special, meaningful times together. They didn't merely "veg out" down in the valley; they accompanied him up a high mountain, a place worthy of the exhilarating experience they were about to share. Jesus brought his best men of God to hang out with two of the greatest men of God who had ever lived. **They got to rub shoulders with leaders they had admired from childhood.** This encounter had a tremendous impact on them; it left them speechless. **Jesus knew that providing an opportunity for his three most committed disciples to associate with these "superstars" and to see him interacting with them as** *peers* **would inspire them powerfully.**

Affirmation

But there was a more important reason for this extraordinary meeting. Jesus' prediction about his own death had been extremely difficult for his disciples to accept. Even these three had responded poorly. Although they had often failed to understand in the past what Jesus was doing and why he was doing it, this time was different; for the very first time they had actually opposed him. Perhaps they had even begun to question his sanity. Therefore Jesus decided to confirm in their minds that he was indeed fulfilling the expectations of his Father in Heaven. His previous actions had been pleasing to God and so was his plan for the future, however grim it might appear to his followers.

The Three were completely overwhelmed when they heard the voice of Jesus' father, affirming his love for Jesus and calling them to accept Jesus' words as truth. How privileged they were that God would personally encourage them to remain faithful to his son! Apparently, God intended for these three to play significant roles in his plan to win the world back to himself through the death of his son. Undoubtedly, they never forgot this experience. Though they would stumble and fall in the days ahead—being just like us—they would indeed go on to play substantial roles in turning the world upside-down for Jesus.

Just a few moments with their leader's leader (and his peers) made an impact on them for the rest of their lives.

Once again, we would do well to imitate Jesus' example. In the critically important times with our key people, we must not hesitate to pull in the "big guns," ie. our superiors and our peers. **The people we lead will be encouraged when they realize that we are indeed in line with the expectations of our superiors. They will also be inspired when they understand that their support for us is essential for the overall success of the organization.**

Jesus, knowing why they had asked the question about Elijah, addressed the real issue behind their question. They were still wrestling with the thought of Jesus' death. They were looking for a way around the cross. The disciples knew that Elijah was supposed to "restore all things" before the day of the Lord. The prophet Malachi wrote: "See, I will send you the prophet Elijah before that great and dreadful day of the LORD comes. He will turn the hearts of the fathers to their children, and the hearts of the children to their fathers... "[†] The disciples hoped this might mean that after this "Elijah" came, the nation of Israel would turn to Jesus—including the religious leaders who were plotting to kill him. But Jesus countered by asking them why it was also written that the Christ must suffer and be rejected. It was good that they were trying to understand the Scriptures, but unfortunate that they were avoiding a clear and often repeated prophesy about the Christ. That is why Jesus reminded them of an important principle: don't just take a part of God's word, take it all. He was telling them, "Hey guys, it can't be avoided." After responding to their unspoken question, he went on to answer the question they had actually asked: John the Baptist had been the "Elijah that was to come." And King Herod had beheaded him.

[†]Malachi 4:5-6

Magnetism

Mark 9:14-29 When they came to the other disciples, they saw a large crowd around them and the teachers of the law arguing with them. As soon as all the people saw Jesus, they were overwhelmed with wonder and ran to greet him. "What are you arguing with them about?" he asked. A man in the crowd answered, "Teacher, I brought you my son, who is possessed by a spirit that has robbed him of speech. Whenever it seizes him, it throws him to the ground. He foams at the mouth, gnashes his teeth and becomes rigid. I asked your disciples to drive out the spirit, but they could not." "O unbelieving generation," Jesus replied, "how long shall I stay with you? How long shall I put up with you? Bring the boy to me." So they brought him. When the spirit saw Jesus, it immediately threw the boy into a convulsion. He fell to the ground and rolled around, foaming at the mouth. Jesus asked the boy's father, "How long has he been like this?" "From childhood," he answered. "It has often thrown him into fire or water to kill him. But if you can do anything, take pity on us and help us." "'If you can'?" said Jesus. "Everything is possible for him who believes." Immediately the boy's father exclaimed, "I do believe; help me overcome my unbelief!" When Jesus saw that a crowd was running to the scene, he rebuked the evil spirit. "You deaf and mute spirit," he said, "I command you, come out of him and never enter him again." The spirit shrieked, convulsed him violently and came out. The boy looked so much like a corpse that many said, "He's dead." But Jesus took him by the hand and lifted him to his feet, and he stood up. After Jesus had gone indoors, his disciples asked him privately, "Why couldn't we drive it out?" He replied, "This kind can come out only by prayer."

What clearer description could be written to describe the popular response to one who has a magnetic personality?—"All the people... were overwhelmed with wonder and ran to greet him." There are very few people who possess true magnetism. I am fortunate to know a couple. One man in particular, Henry Kreite, has had me running to greet him on several occasions. In my estimation he is one of a kind, one of the most radical and dynamic men you could ever want to know. I met Henry one evening on the campus of MIT in Cambridge, Massachusetts. He was the MIT "campus minister" for the Boston Church of Christ, totally unconventional and, as I soon discovered, possessing one of the most sensational senses of humor to be found anywhere. He was overflowing with zeal, yet mature beyond his years. He oozed conviction and still managed to maintain an aura of love and respect for others. He seemed to genuinely care about everyone, great and small, with whom he came in contact. Henry's eyes are his most striking physical feature. When you look in his eyes, you can see great hope mixed with great sorrow. Most everyone on campus who knew Henry loved to hear him speak. Even some of those who refused to give up anything in order to follow Jesus could not resist the charisma of this gregarious bear of a man. In recent years the hard living conditions and diseases of the underdeveloped countries in which he has lived have taken their toll on his body. Despite this challenge, he is even more energetic, even more determined, ever more inspiring, and just as funny. I rarely see Henry these days. Yet whenever I think of him, it feels as if someone's hand has reached into my chest and squeezed my heart. I followed Henry to Toronto, and I will continue to pray for him and lend support to him as long as we both are alive. This illustrates **magnetism: an attracting force on the level of the soul which produces deep bonding and enduring loyalty.** When coupled with morality and a good character, this kind of personal magnetism can produce a very positive impact on this world. When used towards selfish or manipulative ends, it can produce devastating results. I believe personal magnetism is a gift from God. Henry has it. Jesus had it even more. He said, "But I, when I am lifted up from the earth, will draw all men to myself."† Jesus used his magnetism to draw people back to God.

†John 12:32

Frustration

Jesus frequently expressed frustration regarding the continuing unbelief of the people around him. He was frustrated that even his closest disciples always needed him around to bolster their faith. He was upset because they still doubted that God was willing and able to work in their lives. The disciples doubted that God could do anything through them, and the people they were with naturally had the same doubts. As long as he was on earth, Jesus had to put up with unbelief. He was frustrated because their unbelief blocked the power of God. It is noteworthy that Jesus didn't lock his frustration up inside where it would eat away at him; rather, he expressed it to the people. Consequently, the people were challenged, as they needed to be, and Jesus was able to move on unburdened by pent up frustration. Yet on the other hand, Jesus didn't just dump his frustration on the people and then go away mad. He didn't abuse them with harsh, demeaning and demoralizing words. He expressed how he felt and then said, "Bring the boy to me."

How do you deal with frustration? Are you a "stuffer," a "slammer" or (to coin a new label) an "expressive resolver?" Stuffers push emotions deep inside; "out of sight, out of mind" is their motto. They fail to deal with either their emotion or the event which spawned the emotion. Slammers, on the other hand, indiscriminately push their emotions out at others; they "fly off the handle," dump on others, blameshift. **It is important to recognize the ways in which we may be stuffers or slammers, and even more important to realize that neither is any good. Both are improper ways of dealing with emotions.** Stuffers may eventually stuff too much inside and, like a balloon, explode (or implode) and hurt themselves or people close to them. Slammers very often scare off everyone who may dare to be close to them. We need to imitate Jesus and deal with our emotions in a productive way.

Perceptiveness

Jesus was alert to what this desperate man's words revealed. The words "if you can do anything" probably sounded quite innocent to anyone else in the crowd, but to Jesus these words rang out faithlessness.

People don't realize how much their own words can betray them. This provides a good listener with a tremendous advantage. Great insight into a person's thoughts and attitudes can often be gained by simply reflecting on why they said what they said. Most of us already know this, but very few of us practice it routinely. We are usually busy thinking about what we are going to say next, or how well we are coming across. Immigration officials, customs officers, counsellors and the like are trained to read between the lines when they listen to people talking. We too must learn to gather more information from what a person says.

Motivation

Again Mark emphasizes that Jesus did not do his good works for others to see. When he saw a crowd running to the scene, he quickly healed the boy. He did not want the praise of men. He wanted to help people and please his father in heaven.

Retreats

Mark 9:30-32 They left that place and passed through Galilee. Jesus did not want anyone to know where they were, because he was teaching his disciples. He said to them, "The Son of Man is going to be betrayed into the hands of men. They will kill him, and after three days he will rise." But they did not understand what he meant and were afraid to ask him about it.

Sometimes the only way that we can truly give ourselves to the few is by making ourselves unavailable to the many. Perhaps you have "made yourself scarce" by taking the phone off the hook or by not acknowledging that you were home. Alternatively, leaving town can enable us to escape the pressures of our responsibilities and focus on a few of our priority relationships. Jesus believed in having "retreats" to provide for some uninterrupted teaching time with his closest disciples. He apparently placed a high priority in his personal ministry on teaching and "raising up" the next line of leadership. At times he put aside all the other demands on his time and focussed solely on preparing his disciples for what was ahead of them.

I have found "getting away" to be indispensible at times in my life. **A change from routine, a new venue, and the time to thoroughly ponder my perspective on life are just a few of the ways in which retreats have helped me in my personal growth.** In fact, I would go so far as to say that retreats have contributed significantly to determining who I am and how I live my life today. At most of the retreats that I attended, I went as one of the "disciples"; not to teach, but to receive life-changing instruction. Just recently, however, I became aware that I too could use this valuable resource in order to help those I was leading. A camping trip that I took "my group" on one spring did more to teach them the concepts of family and a personal walk with God than did many Wednesday night messages. (At the time my church "family group" numbered about 25 and regularly met together for "family time" on Wednesday nights.) It will always be difficult to carve the time out of our busy schedules for a retreat and even the simplest excursions can be relatively expensive. But I have found that the long term benefits of retreats more than justify the costs.

The corporate world is familiar with the benefit of retreats. However, a conference where all the participants run off and do their own thing in their free time does little for forging unity. Similarly, a resort with a long list of facilities and recreational activities is not conducive for those who want to take a meditative, uninterrupted look at life or the business or both. One's character is not moulded at Club Med. Such places are designed to satiate many different appetites all at once. A true retreat leaves behind the busy world, its lusts and its problems. A starry sky, a campfire and some quiet conversation can help to bring the day's messages into proper perspective.

Openness

Jesus was very open with his disciples about the difficult challenges and troubles that lay ahead for him—even though they would not be able to fully understand what he was talking about. Later[†] we will see Jesus exposing his weaknesses and his struggles to these same disciples. Through his openness, Jesus led the way for his disciples to be open and vulnerable with each other. His example fostered closeness and unity in the group. Consequently, the disciples would be able to stay bonded together throughout the tumultuous years ahead. They would cling to each other in the "upper room" during the first few weeks after Jesus was taken from them.[‡] And they in turn would effectively teach new believers to have close, open relationships. Secrecy and hiding behind facades produce shallow relationships and weak bonding. A lack of openness among the members of any group will eventually lead to the dissolution of the group. Every one of us needs the emotional support of others; we need people who will listen and try to understand. Yet few of us are willing to open up about our troubles to someone who has never been open with us.

[†]Mark 14:34
[‡]Acts 1:13,14

Openness breeds openness. Vulnerability precipitates closeness and bonding. Jesus, through his own openness, set the stage for his followers to be tightly knit to each other.

Ambition

Mark 9:33-35 They came to Capernaum. When he was in the house, he asked them, "What were you arguing about on the road?" But they kept quiet because on the way they had argued about who was the greatest. Sitting down, Jesus called the Twelve and said, "If anyone wants to be first, he must be the very last, and the servant of all."

Jesus watched and listened to his disciples when they were on their own. He knew that they probably acted differently when he wasn't around. They were less guarded and more willing to speak their minds when he wasn't in the middle of the conversation. This time they had argued amongst themselves. Let us try to listen in on their discussion....

As they walked along the road, Jesus was in front, leading the way. The disciples trailed behind watching his back and speaking in hushed tones. Being with Jesus all this time had boosted their confidence. They knew they were now men of consequence. Most of the disciples agreed that the greatest among them must be one of the Three—Peter, James or John. However, Simon the Zealot thought that because he was the boldest of the lot evangelistically, he might be more important than the rest. And Matthew found it hard to accept that one of these fishermen could be more highly esteemed than him. He had more education than all of them put together. Not only was he good with numbers and calculations, but he could also read and write in Greek, Hebrew and Aramaic. Those in John's camp said that he seemed to have a special closeness to Jesus. While they said these things John looked down at the ground trying hard to keep from smiling and nodding his head. Peter, on the other hand, wasted no time reminding everyone that he was the one who had walked on the water, and who had correctly confessed that Jesus was the Son of God. Some of the others may have cut him off almost at once and reminded him that he was also the recipient of some of Jesus' most stern rebukes. The ones who were campaigning for James for "Most Valuable Disciple" pointed out that he was a natural leader, strong and level headed. They would rather follow James than the emotional John or the impetuous Peter. As they argued, their discussions grew occasionally louder as one or another of them tried to make his point. The others would shush the overexcited disciple, nodding furtively towards Jesus. Someone would mutter, "He probably heard that!" One by one they dropped out of the discussion until all at once it ended and they walked silently down the dusty path.

Jesus waited until he had them all together and gave them some time to cool down from their argument before choosing to address the matter. They would be less defensive after having some time to think about what they had said. In the heat of the argument, most of us arguers just want to be right; we only care about winning the argument. A fine-sounding argument is more valuable to us at such times than is truth or fairness. Later on, however, cooler heads can prevail. Jesus didn't get involved in a discussion of who said what to whom; instead, he cut to the heart of the issue.

It is important to note that Jesus in no way corrected these men for wanting to be great. **He did not quench the fires of ambition; he refocussed them.** Selfish ambition is a sin, according to the Bible,† but to be ambitious for God and for others is highly esteemed.‡ It has been my experience that people who are high achievers in life tend to want to be great for God after they become followers of Christ. Yet many who have not climbed the mountain of success in life also become

---

†Romans 2:8, Galatians 5:19-21, Philippians 1:15-17, 2:3-4, James 3:14-16
‡Matthew 11:12, Romans 2:7, 15:20, I Thessalonians 4:11-12, I Timothy 3:1

high achievers in the kingdom of God. The former must learn to fight the ongoing battle against selfish ambition; the latter must discover the many difficulties associated with striving for greatness. These inexperienced achievers often trip over every hurdle that they encounter, sometimes falling flat on their faces, wondering why people reacted to them as they did, or why they failed in a particular endeavor. Regardless of which type of person we may be, seeking to be great for God is a noble ambition. God works powerfully in order to bring individuals into a relationship with him; the proper response to this is to turn around and do something extraordinary for God. Was Jesus' message to the ambitious—"whoever wants to be first must be the very last and the servant of all"—a one hundred and eighty degree turn from conventional wisdom and practice? Yes and no. We would concur that a good CEO would likely be the hardest working person in his organization. He would use all his energy, time and resources, and make a radical commitment to the company to the extent of depriving his family, for the good of the company. Yet the attitudes of most CEOs are a far cry from Jesus' appeal to the ambitious to become a slave of all. Jesus didn't merely preach this message; he lived it:

> Your attitude should be the same as that of Christ Jesus: Who, being in very nature God, did not consider equality with God something to be grasped, but made himself nothing, taking the very nature of a servant, being made in human likeness. And being found in appearance as a man, he humbled himself and became obedient to death—even death on a cross! Therefore God exalted him to the highest place and gave him the name that is above every name, that at the name of Jesus every knee should bow, in heaven and on earth and under the earth, and every tongue confess that Jesus Christ is Lord, to the glory of God the Father. (Phil 2:5-11)

Consider what Jesus gave up to "take the position" of the Savior of the world. He was in heaven with God, the God of love,[†] from all eternity. He was with God and he was God.[‡] He

[†]1 John 4:16
[‡]John 1:1

was free from every temptation and in complete power over every kind of evil. To be more specific about what Jesus must have given up to be abused by the world would be difficult. In fact, the Bible teaches that we can hardly imagine what will be in store for those who make it to this place called "heaven": "As it is written: 'No eye has seen, no ear has heard, no mind has conceived what God has prepared for those who love him.'"[†] In giving up heaven, equality with God, and eventually his life for us, Jesus clearly had the right to call ambitious people to become the servants of all. **People who aspire to be served by others are not remembered for long. But people who are eager to use their lives to benefit others are remembered and admired for generations** (Martin Luther King, Jr., Gandhi, John F. Kennedy, Abraham Lincoln, and Winston Churchill to name but a few). If we want to maximize our impact we must adopt this attitude: to serve, not to be served.

Win/Lose/Win

In Stephen Covey's book The Seven Habits of Highly Effective People, the author discusses the merits of a "Win/Win" philosophy regarding interpersonal interactions. Win/Win is the continual pursuit of mutually beneficial solutions. It is a way of thinking which challenges the premise that one person's or one group's success can only be attained at the expense of others. Covey states that the tendency of most people to think in terms of dichotomies (ie. mutually exclusive groups such as creator and creation, male and female, winner and loser, leader and follower) is "fundamentally flawed" because this kind of thinking is based on "power and position rather than on principle." He claims that people who are highly effective adopt the habit of Win/Win in their interactions. However, it

[†] I Corinthians 2:9

appears from what Jesus said in Mark 9 that he condoned a "Lose/Win" philosophy for those who want to be the best for God. In other words, it seems that Jesus advocates: I lose that you may win. Many other passages would also seem to support this:

> But he was pierced for our transgressions, he was crushed for our iniquities; the punishment that brought us peace was upon him, and by his wounds we are healed. (Isaiah 53:5)

> Instead, whoever wants to become great among you must be your servant, and whoever wants to be first must be your slave— (Matthew 20:26-27)

> God made him who had no sin to be sin for us, so that in him we might become the righteousness of God. (II Corinthians 5:21)

> I am not commanding you, but I want to test the sincerity of your love by comparing it with the earnestness of others. For you know the grace of our Lord Jesus Christ, that though he was rich, yet for your sakes he became poor, so that you through his poverty might become rich. (II Corinthians 8:8-9)

If the Win/Win interaction paradigm is universally valid, one might question whether or not Jesus really had to die in order for us to live. Couldn't we win—be reconciled to God—without Jesus having to "lose?" Could the gospel message be fundamentally flawed?

I do not consider dichotomous thinking to be flawed or erroneous. While it is true that nearly every apparent dichotomy can be viewed as two extremes along a continuum, or two of three or more alternatives, **dichotomous thinking serves to give us direction in life.** We would be quite lost, literally, without dichotomous thinking. To better understand how frequently we use dichotomies to interpret our universe and to navigate through it, consider how integral the following dichotomies are to our everyday thinking: north and south, night and day, urban and rural, predator and prey, wet and dry, right and left, front and back, top and bottom, etc., etc.. I propose that the continuums of our universe are often best interpreted dichotomistically. **The reason many of us dislike dichotomous thinking is because we fear or hate or refuse to accept failure or exclusion.** We don't want lines to be drawn. **However, when we try to eliminate the agony of defeat, we also take away the joy of victory.** When we eliminate the consequences of doing poorly, we also take away some of the benefits of excelling and we lessen the incentive to achieve.

Dichotomous thinking is a necessary part of our reality, as are power and position. **To think that principle alone can form the basis of our thinking is unrealistic. To think that we can accurately assess our own effort and abilities without comparing ourselves to others is also unrealistic.** In addition, the God who inspired the Bible is clearly a dichotomist and a God of principle at the same time. Light and darkness, heaven and hell, good and evil are just a few of the many biblical concepts of mutually exclusive groups. This biblical paradigm does not change from Old to New Testament, or from book to book. To discard dichotomous thinking is to discard the God of the Bible.

Stephen Covey states, and most of us would agree, that Lose/Win is typically a weak position which is based on personal insecurities. But does Jesus actually advocate Lose/Win thinking? Consider the following passages:

> Blessed are the meek, for they will inherit the earth... Blessed are those who are persecuted because of righteousness, for theirs is the kingdom of heaven. Blessed are you when people insult you, persecute you and falsely say all kinds of evil against you because of me. Rejoice and be glad, because great is your reward in heaven, for in the same way they persecuted the prophets who were before you. (Matthew 5:3,10-12)

> "I tell you the truth," Jesus replied, "no one who has left home or brothers or sisters or mother or father or children or fields for me and the gospel will fail to receive a hundred times as much in this present age (homes, brothers, sisters, mothers, children and fields—and with them, persecutions) and in the age to come, eternal life. But many who are first will be last, and the last first." (Mark 10:29-31)

> I tell you the truth, unless a kernel of wheat falls to the ground and dies,

it remains only a single seed. But if it dies, it produces many seeds. The man who loves his life will lose it, while the man who hates his life in this world will keep it for eternal life. Whoever serves me must follow me; and where I am, my servant also will be. My Father will honor the one who serves me. (John 12:24-26)

From these passages we can better understand the full message of Jesus. Yes, Jesus was tortured and killed so that we might have an opportunity to come back to God, but that is not the end of the story. He was raised from the dead! In each of the passages above he promises a reward for interactions in which we apparently lose. God's blessings, true happiness and eternal life await the person who adopts Jesus' approach to life's interactions. Jesus, therefore, is not advocating Lose/Win. His philosophy could perhaps best be described as **"Win/Lose/ Win": I win by losing so that you may also win. The loser becomes the ultimate winner!**

It must be pointed out that **while many of Jesus' teachings on leadership and personal effectiveness agree with conventional wisdom, this one most certainly goes against the grain.** What reasonable person would try to promote the philosophy of winning by losing so that others can win? Many people find distasteful this "martyr complex" at the very center of Christianity: that the Creator willingly became part of the creation to be killed by the creation in order to bring it back into a relationship with the Creator. In fact, this philosophy can be accepted only by faith in God. And that is exactly the way God wanted it:

For the message of the cross is foolishness to those who are perishing, but to us who are being saved it is the power of God. For it is written: "I will destroy the wisdom of the wise; the intelligence of the intelligent I will frustrate." Where is the wise man? Where is the scholar? Where is the philosopher of this age? Has not God made foolish the wisdom of the world? For since in the wisdom of God the world through its wisdom did not know him, God was pleased through the foolishness of what was preached to save those who believe. (I Corinthians 1:18-21)

I wholeheartedly believe Win/Lose/Win to be the preferred

paradigm of human interaction. Although it is a philosophy that faithless scholars cannot accept, I am sure that it is true. Perhaps this belief qualifies me to be a fool. I don't know; one can only hope.

Warmth

Mark 9:36-37 He took a little child and had him stand among them. Taking him in his arms, he said to them, "Whoever welcomes one of these little children in my name welcomes me; and whoever welcomes me does not welcome me but the one who sent me."

Often children are terrified of bold, assertive adults. They don't come into the arms of such people; instead they run away crying. While Jesus was a man's man, he also was gentle and overflowing with warmth. **He was rugged without being rough. He was tough, yet not lacking tenderness. He was forceful and fun at the same time. He was serious, yet a joy to be around.**

The reaction of children to any particular adult can be a very good barometer of how that adult may appear to people in general. Children are not fooled by formalities; they have eyes that see clearly what adults often overlook. But do we have the humility to learn from their insights into our own characters? *Think about how children behave around you.* Are they out of control and manipulative? If so, they probably perceive you to be unsure of yourself and without strength of character. Are children fearful around you? It is probably because they perceive you to be an ogre, and they may not be the only people uncomfortable around you.

Friend Or Foe?

Mark 9:38-41 ''Teacher,'' said John, ''we saw a man driving out demons
in your name and we told him to stop, because he was not one of
us.'' ''Do not stop him,'' Jesus said. ''No one who does a miracle
in my name can in the next moment say anything bad about me,
for whoever is not against us is for us. I tell you the truth, anyone
who gives you a cup of water in my name because you belong to
Christ will certainly not lose his reward.

This man was apparently a convert to Jesus but he was not
converted by Jesus or one of his disciples. Jesus' disciples
opposed him because he was not a result of their personal
ministry. They felt in competition with him. Jesus taught his
disciples not to oppose someone who is doing the work of God
in Jesus' name. Although this man was an outsider, he was a
friend, not a foe. At another time Jesus had some choice words
for others seemingly doing the work of God in his name:

Not everyone who says to me, 'Lord, Lord,' will enter the kingdom of
heaven, but only he who does the will of my Father who is in heaven.
Many will say to me on that day, 'Lord, Lord, did we not prophesy in
your name, and in your name drive out demons and perform many
miracles?' Then I will tell them plainly, 'I never knew you. Away from
me, you evildoers!' (Matthew 7:21-23)

So this friendly outsider may or may not have been in a right
relationship with God. He may have been self deceived, not
known by God and not fully obeying the will of God.
Regardless of his situation, Jesus instructed his disciples not to
interfere with such a person. If he was actively on their side of
the struggle, they needn't worry about him hindering their
cause. In fact, he would be rewarded by God for even a small
act of kindness directed toward Jesus' followers.

In any struggle, it is important to know who is for you and who
is against you. **To wrongly oppose an ally is wasteful, and to
aid an adversary out of ignorance is embarrassing.** Either
situation can easily happen if we are not careful. Fans booing

their own players and an employee slandering his boss are examples of wrongly opposing an ally. On the other hand, the Swiss aided their adversary when they failed to protect their invention of the digital timepiece. This mistake led to a considerable loss of market share to the Japanese who took their idea and ran away with it.

Jesus was so focussed on his purpose—advancing the kingdom of God—that he categorized everyone according to whether they were aiding or opposing his purpose. Not that Jesus was paranoid or overly sensitive, but as would any good leader, he wanted to know which side people were on. He needed to know who was for him and who would betray him.

It is interesting that Jesus did not recognize anyone as being "neutral" about him. He considered everyone to be either "for" him or "against" him. Then again, it would be very difficult to remain undecided or neutral for long about a man who was radical, controversial and convicting. People sometimes "sit on the fence," trying to make a decision about Jesus. Fence-sitting can be quite painful! Once a person is adequately informed, neutrality is doomed.

Hell-Fire Speech

Mark 9:42-50 "And if anyone causes one of these little ones who believe in me to sin, it would be better for him to be thrown into the sea with a large millstone tied around his neck. If your hand causes you to sin, cut it off. It is better for you to enter life maimed than with two hands to go into hell, where the fire never goes out. And if your foot causes you to sin, cut it off. It is better for you to enter life crippled than to have two feet and be thrown into hell. And if your eye causes you to sin, pluck it out. It is better for you to enter the kingdom of God with one eye than to have two eyes and be thrown into hell, where "'their worm does not die, and the fire is not quenched.' Everyone will be salted with fire. "Salt is good, but if it loses its saltiness, how can you make it salty again?

> Have salt in yourselves, and be at peace with each other.''

Jesus could say very hard and striking things to get his point across. He often spoke about fire, and his messages themselves were quite fiery. He talked about plucking out one's eye, being eaten by worms and being burned in everlasting fire. That is awfully scary stuff, probably not very palatable to those who would prefer to view a nice little world with a nice little God from their nice little church as they live out a nice little life with no harsh realities. Jesus seriously offended these types of people. He still does today. **A man of impact does not hold back explicit details regarding uncomfortable realities. The truth hurts sometimes.** When a person steps into sea water, he becomes acutely aware of open wounds on his feet; the salt in the water produces a burning sensation. Similarly, "Salty" speech is good for producing impact. Perhaps no public figure in recent times better exemplified this principle than Malcolm X. His proclamation of the harsh treatment of African-Americans by American whites was often quite explicit and disturbing to many people. Unsurprisingly, his impact on this world carries on long since his violent death. **As we strive to grab people's attention, we must not allow our words to become bland, boring or impotent.**

Teacher

Mark 10:1 Jesus then left that place and went into the region of Judea and across the Jordan. Again crowds of people came to him, and as was his custom, he taught them.

One of Jesus' titles was "Rabbi" or "Teacher," and he certainly earned it: teaching was second nature to him. He was always teaching. As anyone who has tried teaching would admit, it can be quite exhausting to continually remain in "teacher mode," ever explaining, illustrating, correcting, questioning, testing, and evaluating. Some teachers eventually wear thin and grow impatient. They stop taking the trouble to explain and instead begin to make demands. But Jesus remained committed to the spiritual enlightenment of those around him, whatever the personal cost. We must similarly accept the responsibility of being good teachers if we want to have his impact.

Taking the Offensive

Mark 10:2-12 Some Pharisees came and tested him by asking, "Is it lawful for a man to divorce his wife?" "What did Moses command you?" he replied. They said, "Moses permitted a man to write a certificate of divorce and send her away." "It was because your hearts were hard that Moses wrote you this law," Jesus replied. "But at the beginning of creation God 'made them male and female.' 'For this reason a man will leave his father and mother and be united to his wife, and the two will become one flesh.' So they are no longer two, but one. Therefore what God has joined together, let man not separate." When they were in the house again, the disciples asked Jesus about this. He answered, "Anyone who divorces his wife and marries another woman commits adultery against her. And if she divorces her husband and marries another man, she commits adultery."

When Jesus was tested by this hostile audience, he took the offensive. Instead of backing down or becoming apologetic, he answered their question with a question. After turning the question back upon his adversaries, he saw more clearly just how they were trying to catch him. Perhaps that is why he began the second part of his answer with some inflamatory words: "It was because your hearts were hard.... " They initiated this discussion and he was going to finish it. He backed up everything he said with Scripture, knowing that they also believed it to be the Word of God. He began with the principles and then followed up with specific practicals. His answer was clear and definitive. He didn't use a lot of words to say nothing as politicians of today have been known to do. He didn't avoid their question, and he didn't care if his answer offended some people. He simply let them have it.

Judgement

Jesus held that the ultimate authority in matters of judgement is God. The "Divine Court" will be the final place of judgement, not the Supreme Courts of this world. The courts and legislatures of this world may legalize some forms of murder (eg. abortion), tax evasion and theft. They may look the other way in the face of corruption and abuse. But according to Jesus, God's requirements have been clearly laid out from the beginning, and God's judgement will be final. Not only are they written in the Bible, but they are also written on our hearts and on our consciences so that none of us is beyond accountability:

> "God 'will give to each person according to what he has done.' To those who by persistence in doing good seek glory, honor and immortality, he will give eternal life. But for those who are self-seeking and who reject the truth and follow evil, there will be wrath and anger. There will be trouble and distress for every human being who does evil: first for the Jew, then for the Gentile; but glory, honor and peace for everyone who does good: first for the Jew, then for the Gentile. For God does not show favoritism. All who sin apart from the law [meaning the law of Moses handed down by God on Mount Sinai, including the Ten Commandments†] will also perish apart from the law, and all who sin under the law will be judged by the law. For it is not those who hear the law who are righteous in God's sight, but it is those who obey the law who will be declared righteous. (Indeed, when Gentiles, who do not have the law, do by nature things required by the law, they are a law for themselves, even though they do not have the law, since they show that the requirements of the law are written on their hearts, their consciences also bearing witness, and their thoughts now accusing, now even defending them.)" (Romans 2:6-15)

Jesus accepted that a person may hold fastidiously to the letter of the law (or regulation or guideline), but explained that God

---

†Exodus chapters 20-31, Deuteronomy chapters 5-26

was ultimately more concerned that this person hold to the spirit of the law. The Bible teaches that God is concerned above all with the condition of our hearts. "For the LORD searches every heart and understands every motive behind the thoughts."[†] Laws serve to expose our sinful hearts by making clear—even to us—that we have done something wrong: "For before the law was given, sin was in the world. But sin is not taken into account when there is no law."[‡] Unfortunately, exposing the evil in our hearts is not always a pleasant experience. Sometimes we may even want to edit the laws governing our lives so that we can do what we would like to do without feeling guilty. But one of Jesus' points here is this: to avoid or eliminate the consequences of disobeying the law will not enable us to escape God's judgement. Again Jesus shows a fundamental concern for character: what people do or say is of secondary importance to the condition of their hearts. Sometimes actions expose a person's true character, but sometimes a person's character remains hidden behind a facade: insincere actions and correct sounding replies can cloak the truth about the goodness of a person's heart. **Jesus maintained a *character ethic* in his teaching, calling people to live lives founded on solid principles and morals, and not on what they could get away with.** The same can be said for anyone who seeks to imitate Jesus' impact. **What we may say or do is not as important as *who we are*.** "Man looks at the outward appearance, but the LORD looks at the heart."[§]

People Oriented

Mark 10:13-16 People were bringing little children to Jesus to have him touch them, but the disciples rebuked them. When Jesus saw this, he was indignant. He said to them, "Let the little children come

[†]I Chronicles 28:9
[‡]Romans 5:13
[§]I Samuel 16:7

to me, and do not hinder them, for the kingdom of God belongs to such as these. I tell you the truth, anyone who will not receive the kingdom of God like a little child will never enter it." And he took the children in his arms, put his hands on them and blessed them.

Jesus was neither too important nor too busy to spend time with little children. He became indignant with his disciples for turning away the people who were bringing their children to see him. The disciples may have felt that these children were simply a nuisance, distracting their group from more urgent matters with adults. Jesus, however, respected and praised the humility and purity of children. He did not primarily perceive children as immature people, but rather as innocent people who had not yet fallen from God. The kingdom of God belonged to them and to adults who were like them. Jesus chastised those who did not show respect for these little people. **He valued people for themselves, and not merely for what could be gained through them or from them.**

For which reason do you value people? Could you rationalize your way out of taking care of a friend's children for a day because you "couldn't afford the time?" Would you honestly love to spend time with your grandmother, but unfortunately you have something to get done this evening? Perhaps you would love to spend more time with your family, and get to know your neighbors, but the demands of your career right now are just too intense. Maybe later you can fit them in to your schedule. If this describes you, the problem you face is not a matter of time, but of value. Performance and achievement are more important to you than are people. It is highly unlikely that this attitude will spontaneously change as your circumstances change. "Maybe later" is equivalent to "not now." It's your choice. **People of true impact value people and make them a priority.** Being "people oriented" needn't hinder one's effectiveness; most likely it will greatly enhance it.

Tough Love

Mark 10:17-31 As Jesus started on his way, a man ran up to him and fell on his knees before him. ''Good teacher,'' he asked, ''what must I do to inherit eternal life?'' ''Why do you call me good?'' Jesus answered. ''No one is good—except God alone. You know the commandments: 'Do not murder, do not commit adultery, do not steal, do not give false testimony, do not defraud, honor your father and mother.''' ''Teacher,'' he declared, ''all these I have kept since I was a boy.'' Jesus looked at him and loved him. ''One thing you lack,'' he said. ''Go, sell everything you have and give to the poor, and you will have treasure in heaven. Then come, follow me.'' At this the man's face fell. He went away sad, because he had great wealth. Jesus looked around and said to his disciples, ''How hard it is for the rich to enter the kingdom of God!'' The disciples were amazed at his words. But Jesus said again, ''Children, how hard it is to enter the kingdom of God! It is easier for a camel to go through the eye of a needle than for a rich man to enter the kingdom of God.'' The disciples were even more amazed, and said to each other, ''Who then can be saved?'' Jesus looked at them and said, ''With man this is impossible, but not with God; all things are possible with God.'' Peter said to him, ''We have left everything to follow you!'' ''I tell you the truth,'' Jesus replied, ''no one who has left home or brothers or sisters or mother or father or children or fields for me and the gospel will fail to receive a hundred times as much in this present age (homes, brothers, sisters, mothers, children and fields—and with them, persecutions) and in the age to come, eternal life. But many who are first will be last, and the last first.''

This rich young man was looking for reassurance from Jesus. Although he was confident that his personal righteousness compared well with just about everyone else he knew, a nagging feeling deep down inside told him that he might not have it all together after all. Initially, Jesus gave the man the answer that he expected. The man was quick to point out that he had been obedient to all the commandments since he was a boy. Frankly, if he was telling the truth, that would be a pretty good reason for him to feel good about himself. Probably none of us could begin to say the same thing, and nobody else in the crowd with Jesus that day made a similar claim. Such a complete obedience must have come from a reverent and believing heart. This man must have revered and loved God's Word. Yet everyone, however good he may look, is lacking something: all people are in need of God's mercy.[†] As usual, Jesus hit the nail on the head. This young man was secure in his own material goods. He lacked a willingness to let go of his riches and depend completely on God.

One thing that impresses me in this passage is that Jesus was able to love this self-righteous, religious, "goody-goody" person. Jesus openly loved him and invited him to become a disciple and accompany him on the road. I myself often find it easier to love the self-deprecating pagan who is up to his eyeballs in self-centered sensuality than I do the super-religious sort. Thankfully, Jesus demonstrated perfect love. He had the capacity to deeply love all types of people.

This man went away sad because he was unwilling to let go of the security of his wealth to follow God—but Jesus made no attempt to run after him. He did not try to change the man's mind, even though he cared about him. Jesus was hurt by the man's decision; he may have even felt pangs of rejection. But this young man had made his own decision, in full awareness of the consequences. He knew what he was leaving behind. Jesus, in his disappointment, exclaimed to those present, "how hard it is for the rich to enter the kingdom of God!" But in the end he let him go. There would be no use in chasing after him; he could never be a true disciple until he was able to gladly give up everything for a relationship with God.[‡] In light of Jesus' course of action here, there are some questions we need to ask ourselves. **First of all, are we willing to lay such tough, "make-or-break" challenges before people, even when it means putting our relationship with them on the line? And**

[†]Romans 11:32
[‡]Luke 14:33

secondly, are we willing to let people walk away? Do we allow people the responsibility to make their own decisions? Or do we lower our standards to make it easier for people to stay a part of our group? This young man, walking away dejected, was morally upstanding and talented and could have contributed an awful lot to Jesus' cause. Wouldn't we have been tempted to compromise our standard for such a "special" situation? I mean, let's be reasonable here. Wasn't Jesus being a bit too tough on this guy? Didn't he deserve some kind of special status? Hardly! On the contrary, no one deserves an easier path into the kingdom than anyone else. Each person must put his hope fully in God. Besides this, if basic selection criteria can be waived, then has not the integrity of the group been forsaken? And **without integrity, can a group avoid drowning in a sea of politics? If we compromise our standards, our standards become meaningless. Jesus absolutely refused to compromise his standards however much it might hurt him personally.**

Reassurance

After this impressive man walked away from him, Jesus was clearly disappointed. In contrast, his disciples were outright discouraged, insecure about whether or not they themselves would make the grade. If this apparently righteous man couldn't make it, what hope would they have? Sensing their feelings, Jesus immediately set aside his own disappointment and called them to faith: "all things are possible with God!" Peter began to see the light before the others. Although he had lived a sinful life, he had gladly left behind his career, his friends, even his family when given the opportunity to follow Jesus. Remembering this, he exclaimed, "We have left everything to follow you!" Jesus thoroughly encouraged Peter and the rest of his disciples with his response at this critical moment. He inspired them by reminding them of the rewards awaiting them and all

others who sacrifice for God. He spoke of the rewards they
would have both in this life and, more importantly, in the life to
come.

**A leader needs to first overcome her own negative thoughts
and feelings in order to help her followers avoid becoming
discouraged.** If a leader mopes around, her followers are
already defeated. On the other hand, if she quickly turns herself
around and immediately begins to call those around her to faith
and fills them with hope, the group will quite possibly become
more effective than before and achieve more in spite of any
setback.

———————————————

Jesus' followers now needed his encouragement more than ever,
because public opinion regarding him was beginning to shift.
There was a new feeling in the air, one of hostility and danger.
Time was running short for this preacher from Galilee. He
would soon begin the last lap of his race, and they could all
sense it.

3

FULFILLING
HIS DESTINY

Leading the Way

Mark 10:32-34 They were on their way up to Jerusalem, with Jesus
leading the way, and the disciples were astonished, while those
who followed were afraid. Again he took the Twelve aside and
told them what was going to happen to him. "We are going up to
Jerusalem," he said, "and the Son of Man will be betrayed to the
chief priests and teachers of the law. They will condemn him to
death and will hand him over to the Gentiles, who will mock him
and spit on him, flog him and kill him. Three days later he will
rise."

It would be completely unheard of today for a military leader to
physically lead the troops into battle. Generals, admirals and
commanders-in-chief tend to stay back behind the front lines in
well-fortified bunkers. Jesus, however, was more courageous; he
led the way up to Jerusalem where he knew what lay in store
for him. This is a passage that needs to be visualized in order to
be appreciated, one of my favorites in all of the Bible. As I
picture the scene, it is a cloudy and windy day. A small crowd
of people with fear etched on their faces quietly follows a little

knot of men down a dusty road. The afternoon shadows lengthen as the group begins to ascend a gradual incline. The man leading the procession is strong and fit, but not handsome. His stare is fixed not on the road ahead but on the city in the distance. His eyes, narrowed against the wind, accentuate the pained determination on his face. His strides are long and deliberate. The men immediately behind him shuffle to keep up; they are ten or so in number. They are all strong young men, and on each of their faces is an expression of awe mixed with bewilderment. They are tense, and their gait betrays their anxiety. Yet they are not fearful as the crowd is; rather, there is an air of stressful excitement, like that of men going off to war. They frequently glance around them, but the scene doesn't change. When they pause to look at their leader there is admiration on their faces; then they lean forward into the wind, gather their cloaks around them, and press on.

Mark tells us that "those who followed were afraid." And well they should be! Although they were all confused about what Jesus meant when he spoke of dying and rising again, they all knew that there was a price on Jesus' head. They had all seen for themselves the jealousy of the religious leaders; they had perhaps personally felt the fire of their anger.[†] They were afraid for Jesus, and they were afraid for themselves. Although they could slip away into the crowd if they had to, many of them probably had enemies who would be more than happy to point out their association with "the Jesus cult." Their thinking may have followed these lines: "Don't I have anything better to do than to go up to Jerusalem to be harrassed? Would I be able to stand up to the anger of the Pharisees if it were to turn my way? Then again, Jesus has been able to handle everything that the Pharisees have dished out so far; why should this be any different? After all, he must be from God; how else could all the powerful things he's been doing be explained? *But why does*

[†]John 7:47-52, 9:28,34, 12:10-11

it sound like he's predicting his own defeat? Can't the one who has the power to heal the sick and even raise the dead protect himself from these old men? And more to the point, can I be sure that he will protect me? True, I haven't been as visible to the general public as the twelve who are his closest friends, but someone might still point the finger at me!'' Despite such ambivalent thoughts, they still followed Jesus with fascination and fear. They wondered, ''Am I sure that this man is the Messiah?—sure enough to suffer for him?''

The disciples, Mark tells us, were ''astonished.'' Questions flooded their thoughts: ''What in the world is happening? Is Jesus really going to Jerusalem to die, or is this another one of his parables? Everyone knows that his enemies are lying in wait to murder him when he returns to Jerusalem. Yet he seems determined to go back there. Doesn't he have any sense of caution at all? And if he does get killed, what will become of this movement? What could we possibly do without Jesus leading us? Perhaps he is merely testing our faith. But then again, if Jesus says that they are going to do all these terrible things to him, it must be so; he has never been wrong before. But if he knows this is so, then why isn't he avoiding Jerusalem? Maybe he has gone mad!''

It is important to ''see'' Jesus leading this crowd into ''the city that stones the prophets.'' With an understanding of the circumstances we can better appreciate why the disciples were astonished. Not only was Jesus physically leading the way to Jerusalem, but he was also leading the way in courage, determination and fearlessness. What I also find fascinating is this: **after spending day and night with his disciples for three years, Jesus had never stopped astonishing them.** Consider how hard it is to actually astonish people who know you well. Some people astonish us when we first meet them, but after getting to know them, we grow accustomed to their unusual actions or characteristics, and they become predictable to us. However, Jesus' actions continued to surpass the expectations

of his disciples. And now, clearly seeing his bitter end, **he
would allow nothing to stand between him and his destiny.** I
am thoroughly inspired by Jesus' resolve. I want to see myself
develop a similar strength of character; I want to be like him.

The Attitude of a Servant

Mark 10:35-40 Then James and John, the sons of Zebedee, came to him.
"Teacher," they said, "we want you to do for us whatever we
ask." "What do you want me to do for you?" he asked. They
replied, "Let one of us sit at your right and the other at your left
in your glory." "You don't know what you are asking," Jesus
said. "Can you drink the cup I drink or be baptized with the
baptism I am baptized with?" "We can," they answered. Jesus
said to them, "You will drink the cup I drink and be baptized
with the baptism I am baptized with, but to sit at my right or left
is not for me to grant. These places belong to those for whom
they have been prepared."

James and John wanted Jesus to agree to do something for them
even before they told him what it was they wanted. But Jesus
didn't fall for it. He asked them what they wanted before
agreeing to anything! After all, who would agree to doing
something for you before they knew what it was you wanted?
Surely not your boss! Your brother? Maybe. A friend? Perhaps.
One of your parents? Probably. Here we see that James and
John expected to pull this one over on Jesus. **They *expected*
that he would automatically do for them what they wanted,
that he was there for their benefit. It seems clear that Jesus'
servant-like attitude must have made a strong impression on
them.** And Jesus did not seem to get the least bit upset that they
had asked such a question of him. He didn't correct them for
being manipulative or disrespectful. Instead, he was humble and
unassuming. Let's read on to get the rest of the story.

Servant Leadership

Mark 10:41-45 When the ten heard about this, they became indignant with James and John. Jesus called them together and said, ''You know that those who are regarded as rulers of the Gentiles lord it over them, and their high officials exercise authority over them. Not so with you. Instead, whoever wants to become great among you must be your servant, and whoever wants to be first must be slave of all. For even the Son of Man did not come to be served, but to serve, and to give his life as a ransom for many.''

Let's look again at what Jesus says about ''servant leadership'' and see how he contrasts it with ''lording leadership.'' Not only was this a focus of Jesus' teaching, but Mark also seems to be highlighting it in these passages. Have you ever laughed when you heard a government leader referred to as a ''civil servant?'' You laugh because the word ''servant'' seems so out of place when used in reference to contemporary politicians. Staying in power, looking good and not making any costly mistakes seem to be the goals of most government leaders. Campaign promises are less reliable than the weather, and acts of corruption are more common than opportunities to vote offenders out of office. The same could probably have been said to an even greater degree about the political establishment of Jesus' time. Civil liberty and social reform had not yet seen the light of day. Consequently, Roman rulers were oppressive authoritarians. They used their positions of leadership to extract whatever they wanted from the people who were under them.

As we look back through history, it is unfortunate to note that very few great leaders have lived as servants, and none the way Jesus did: laying down his life for both friend and foe. We will continue to observe this unique style of leadership below. Let us simply note at this point that **Jesus taught his leaders-in-training the difference between *lording leadership* and *servant leadership*, and he called them to become servant leaders. Indeed he encouraged them to become great**

leaders. Again we note that Jesus didn't try to discourage his disciples' desire for greatness. Rather, he corrected their understanding about what greatness in leadership entails.

Popularity

Mark 10:46-52 Then they came to Jericho. As Jesus and his disciples, together with a large crowd, were leaving the city, a blind man, Bartimaeus (that is, the Son of Timaeus), was sitting by the roadside begging. When he heard that it was Jesus of Nazareth, he began to shout, "Jesus, Son of David, have mercy on me!" Many rebuked him and told him to be quiet, but he shouted all the more, "Son of David, have mercy on me!" Jesus stopped and said, "Call him." So they called to the blind man, "Cheer up! On your feet! He's calling you." Throwing his cloak aside, he jumped to his feet and came to Jesus. "What do you want me to do for you?" Jesus asked him. The blind man said, "Rabbi, I want to see." "Go," said Jesus, "your faith has healed you." Immediately he received his sight and followed Jesus along the road.

In this and many other passages, we find Jesus drawing a large crowd. This detail alone speaks volumes about what it means to be a man or woman of impact. Jesus was intense, dynamic and charismatic. This made him very exciting to watch. For those of us who feel good about our own laid-back "coolness," this is a challenging example to follow. Being "cool" is the same thing as being a people pleaser; it is safe to conform to the "in" crowd. To be laid-back is to be lazy and selfish. Laid-back people hardly stand out from the crowd. Speaking from personal experience, to change from being reserved to being out-going can be a difficult task. **Being *out of one's self* is a much more vulnerable position, and it takes much more energy.** For the person resolved to make such a change I have but one piece of advice (handed down to me by my previously mentioned friend Scott): **when you feel like you are acting like a lunatic, you are probably just beginning to get out of yourself.**

The Words of a Servant

Mark is trying to show us something here. Jesus repeats the exact same words that he said to James and John earlier. This time he asks a blind beggar: "What do you want me to do for you?" These are the words of a servant, or an employee: "How may I be of service?" Are they also characteristic of a person of impact?

Jesus was "in very nature a servant."† When people spent time with him they had the clear impression that he was there for them, that he was at their bidding. Yet Jesus did not have some of the characteristics we associate with a servant or a slave. **He didn't grovel; he didn't try to appease; he wasn't afraid to speak his mind. He was a servant with great strength.** The King of kings and Lord of lords was also a Servant of servants and the Slave of slaves.

Impressed by Desperation

Desperate people got Jesus' attention. Bartimaeus, when told to shut up by the people who were around him, shouted all the more. He desperately wanted an audience with Jesus, and Jesus granted it to him. Some people don't believe in rewarding desperation; they would rather respond to a display of cool self-control. But **Jesus encouraged intensity of any kind. He hated complacency, he rewarded persistent determination.** Likewise, we should be eager to listen to a person who is really worked up about something. People who always strive to be politically and socially correct are boring "play-it-safers" who will never shake up themselves, much less anyone else. On the other hand, people who are intense about getting a need met

†Philippians 2:7

will likely be exuberant in gratitude when their need is met. Jesus stopped what he was doing to attend to such people; so should we.

Specific Delegation

Mark 11:1-10 As they approached Jerusalem and came to Bethphage and Bethany at the Mount of Olives, Jesus sent two of his disciples, saying to them, "Go to the village ahead of you, and just as you enter it, you will find a colt tied there, which no one has ever ridden. Untie it and bring it here. If anyone asks you, 'Why are you doing this?' tell him, 'The Lord needs it and will send it back here shortly.'" They went and found a colt outside in the street, tied at a doorway. As they untied it, some people standing there asked, "What are you doing, untying that colt?" They answered as Jesus had told them to, and the people let them go. When they brought the colt to Jesus and threw their cloaks over it, he sat on it. Many people spread their cloaks on the road, while others spread branches they had cut in the fields. Those who went ahead and those who followed shouted, "Hosanna!" "Blessed is he who comes in the name of the Lord!" "Blessed is the coming kingdom of our father David!" "Hosanna in the highest!"

It would be rather difficult for us to imitate Jesus' ability to know things which he would have no way of knowing if he did not have a special power from God. Such knowledge thoroughly impressed Mark and the other followers of Jesus. However, there is in this passage a demonstration of leadership skills which we can imitate. Jesus gave his disciples specific instructions which enabled them to be successful in fulfilling the responsibilities he had delegated to them. In this situation, he even tells them exactly what to say if they were questioned about their actions. Borrowing a colt for Jesus to ride into the city wasn't a matter of great significance, but by giving them very specific instructions, he ensured their success. This was probably just one of many tasks that Jesus delegated to his disciples over the course of their three years with him. Other examples include seating and feeding several large crowds,[†] going out to preach and heal,[‡] and making arrangements for the Passover feast.[§] In each of these examples we see that Jesus is not at all vague in what he says; **it was his practice to give very specific instructions.**

Exultation

People who were around Jesus were at times overwhelmed with wonder and praise. They were often so excited by Jesus and by what he was doing that they could not restrain their exclamations of joy. Such a response cannot be sought; it is one of the inevitable outcomes of a life of impact. Another inevitable outcome is persecution, because "you can't please all of the people all of the time!"

Anger

Mark 11:11-19 Jesus entered Jerusalem and went to the temple. He looked around at everything, but since it was already late, he went out to Bethany with the Twelve. The next day as they were leaving Bethany, Jesus was hungry. Seeing in the distance a fig tree in leaf, he went to find out if it had any fruit. When he reached it, he found nothing but leaves, because it was not the season for figs. Then he said to the tree, "May no one ever eat fruit from you again." And his disciples heard him say it. On reaching Jerusalem, Jesus entered the temple area and began driving out those who were buying and selling there. He overturned the tables of the money changers and the benches of those selling doves, and would not allow anyone to carry merchandise through the temple courts. And as he taught them, he said, "Is it not written:

[†]Mark 6:39-44, Luke 9:14-17
[‡]Matthew 10:5-15, Mark 6:7-11, Luke 9:1-6, 10:1-16
[§]Matthew 26:17-19, Mark 14:12-16, Luke 22:7-13

> "'My house will be called a house of prayer for all nations'? But you have made it 'a den of robbers.'" The chief priests and the teachers of the law heard this and began looking for a way to kill him, for they feared him, because the whole crowd was amazed at his teaching. When evening came, they went out of the city.

I've often wondered why Jesus cursed this fig tree. Didn't he know that figs weren't in season? Was he acting like I sometimes do after a crack in the sidewalk jumps up and trips me, or after a wall jumps out and bangs my big toe? I'm not usually proud of how I handle my anger at these moments. So what made Jesus so angry? Although I rarely have one, he must have had a good explanation. But what was it? A second source of confusion exists for me in this passage: Why does Mark connect Jesus' clearing of the temple with the end of his ministry while John describes it as happening at the beginning of his ministry?† Could this be one of those elusive "contradictions" in the Bible that I have heard so much about, yet never found? After considerable meditation on this passage I think I have finally figured it out! The explanation for why Jesus cursed the fig tree is linked to the reason why Mark and John apparently disagree about the timing of the "temple-clearing" event. Jesus was angry, but not just at the tree. He was furious about the fruitlessness of another "tree" which he had been earnestly watering, weeding and fertilizing. Indeed, Jesus did clear the temple at the beginning of his ministry, but he did it again here near the end of his ministry. That is why he was so angry at the fruitlessness of this fig tree. The fig tree was a symbol of the holy city, Jerusalem, which had refused to repent even after all that he had said and done. The money-changers and merchants were right back where they had been before he cleared the temple for the first time. Still no one feared God! So Jesus cursed the city. No longer would it waste the soil, no longer would it be called the City of God. (The same fate awaits us as individuals if we fail to respond to God

†John 2:11-17

by bearing good and lasting fruit.)† **Once again I realized that apparent contradictions in the Bible may actually serve as maps pointing the way to hidden treasures—the treasures of undiscovered truths and fresh insights.**

Restraint

Jesus was very clearly angry with what was going on in Jerusalem, yet he didn't lose control. Mark tells us that when Jesus arrived in Jerusalem, "he looked around at everything." He went to the temple, but because it was late he waited until the next day to deal with the situation. This is another tremendous example for us to imitate. **Jesus knew how to choose the right time and place to do what he had to do.** He demonstrated considerable restraint and self-control; he didn't react on the spot, despite his great disappointment. The intensity of his feelings were revealed in Matthew's account, when he exclaimed: "O Jerusalem, Jerusalem, you who kill the prophets and stone those sent to you, how often I have longed to gather your children together, as a hen gathers her chicks under her wings, but you were not willing. Look, your house is left to you desolate. For I tell you, you will not see me again until you say, 'Blessed is he who comes in the name of the Lord.'"‡

Relentlessness

What made Jesus angry was the stubborn refusal of most of the people of Jerusalem to change. It was as if his passionate appeals had made little difference in how they lived their day-to-day lives. He had not come to entertain them, but to call them to live different lives. Because little had changed in their

†Matthew 3:8-12, Matthew 7:16-20, Luke 13:5-9, John 15:1-8
‡Matthew 23:37-39

lives, there could not have been any significant change in their hearts; they had not truly believed him. Even in this matter of mocking the holiness of God's temple—blatantly wrong even by Jewish and Old Testament law—they weren't willing to change.

A willingness to change is a precious and seemingly rare behavioral characteristic. It is a trait which usually diminishes with age, and which is closely linked with the level of comfortability in one's life. **Ironically, most of us dread changing, but we love changes. We loathe being stuck in a rut, we don't want to stagnate, yet we are often too proud to even admit that we could stand to make some changes.** We get angry with the people in our lives, even those we love the most, when they point out a desperate need for change in some area of our lives. We become exceedingly insecure and defensive when we are awakened to the existence of personal deficiencies. We would rather sink than assume a sense of urgency about abandoning ship. Yet at the same time, we would like things to be fresh, new and exciting.

A sluggishness in making changes seems to be common to all people regardless of culture, race or era. Jesus would be just as upset with us today as he was with the people of Jerusalem in his day. It stands to reason, then, that in order to produce significant changes in the world in which we live, we must—like Jesus—get angry with the obstinancy in our own and other people's lives. We may not have opportunity to make a whip and clear out a temple, but we need to make some noise and shake people out of their mulish stupor.

Jesus certainly knew how to get people's attention! Most of us have probably experienced very similar situations: someone calls for a big change; things are initially different, but quickly revert back to the way they were. I have heard this phenomenon referred to as "backsliding." Backsliding can occur in our marriages, in our jobs, in our personal discipline and in our moral standards. Backsliding can be especially frustrating for the person who had enough conviction to "turn over some tables" in order to initiate the change in the first place. When people turn back, the instigator of change may be tempted to give up, to turn a blind eye to what is happening once again, and to quietly accept defeat. Instead of doing this, Jesus turned up the volume. He would not relent. He got their attention again.

Fearsomeness

Why didn't anyone try to stop Jesus as he was taking over the temple and turning over the tables and benches of the merchants? It seems that nobody was willing to stand up to this radical as he completely disrupted their marketplace. Jesus wasn't a frail shepherd, slow-moving and soft featured. He had been a carpenter all of his life, and had a body toughened by years of hard physical labor. During the days of his ministry he had walked thousands of miles as he traveled from village to village in Palestine. But even the most physically impressive man is only one person. Surely two or three merchants could have overpowered him and thrown him out of the temple area, but no one dared try. This may have been partly because most of the people knew that they were in the wrong. But besides this, Jesus' intensity, fearlessness and strength of character combined to make him a respected and fearsome individual. Mark tells us that even the teachers of the law and the chief priests feared Jesus. He was an imposing threat to their lives and their livelihoods. They couldn't laugh him off or ignore him. But Jesus didn't deliberately try to scare or intimidate people; that was not his goal. We must remember that this is the same Jesus that children loved to be around, the same man that touched lepers and comforted women. But people who knew they were living in opposition to Jesus feared him. The fear which gripped their hearts was simply a natural by-product of the intensity with which Jesus lived his life. They knew that he was more powerful than they; they knew that he was unstoppable.

Some of us couldn't scare a mouse if we tried. **You probably shouldn't go around trying to be scary, but if people around you aren't at least a little bit in awe of you, if you are considered a "nice guy" or a "nice lady" by others, you probably won't have much of an impact.** When you turn up the intensity in your life you will notice that some people will be intimidated, some people will feel uncomfortable around you, some will hate you, some will love you, some will give you their respect and many more will notice you.

An Emphasis on Fundamentals

Mark 11:20-25 In the morning, as they went along, they saw the fig tree withered from the roots. Peter remembered and said to Jesus, "Rabbi, look! The fig tree you cursed has withered!" "Have faith in God," Jesus answered. "I tell you the truth, if anyone says to this mountain, 'Go, throw yourself into the sea,' and does not doubt in his heart but believes that what he says will happen, it will be done for him. Therefore I tell you, whatever you ask for in prayer, believe that you have received it, and it will be yours. And when you stand praying, if you hold anything against anyone, forgive him, so that your Father in heaven may forgive you your sins."

Peter was amazed that the fig tree that Jesus had cursed had withered from the roots in one day. Surely, any one of us would have been equally amazed. But because Peter was the kind of person who didn't usually conceal his thoughts and feelings, he openly expressed his surprise at what had happened to the tree. As if to say, "Of course, what did you expect to happen?", Jesus challenged Peter's faith in God. Jesus was clearly not amazed that the tree had withered; rather, he would have been amazed had it not withered. Therefore Jesus took this opportunity to teach his disciples the mechanics of a conceptually difficult topic: faith. He explained very practically how they could "pray in faith." At this relatively late stage in Jesus' ministry, he was teaching his disciples fundamentals.

It has been my experience that **a person can be effective at almost anything by simply mastering the basics.** Even in the realm of professional sports, winning coaches are almost always well known to be those who stress fundamentals when training their players. For example, in American football it doesn't matter how intricate or spectacular a particular play is, if the players cannot execute it correctly, it is not likely to be very effective.

It is interesting that Jesus was not pleased that Peter was so amazed at the effectiveness of his words. Peter's amazement revealed that he didn't really believe that God could and would do mighty deeds in response to prayer. Answered prayers will only amaze those who are not themselves faithful in prayer. Faithful prayer is not a hit and miss proposition. Upon noticing where Peter was at in his faith, Jesus proceeded to teach him the basics: Faithful Prayer 101. Jesus noticed things that told him what his disciples were thinking, and where they were at spiritually. He responded accordingly by teaching them whatever it was that they lacked. His teaching was flexible; he often produced an impromptu lesson in order to meet the needs of the hour.

Apparently Jesus' disciples already understood that unforgiven sin in their own lives would diminish God's willingness to give them what they prayed for,[†] for Jesus' second instruction regarding successful prayer concerned how to receive forgiveness. He probably went on to explain further, but Mark has not recorded this for us.

[†]Psalm 66:18-20, Isaiah 59:1-2

Never Intimidated

Mark 11:27-33 They arrived again in Jerusalem, and while Jesus was walking in the temple courts, the chief priests, the teachers of the law and the elders came to him. "By what authority are you doing these things?" they asked. "And who gave you authority to do this?" Jesus replied, "I will ask you one question. Answer me, and I will tell you by what authority I am doing these things. John's baptism—was it from heaven, or from men? Tell me!" They discussed it among themselves and said, "If we say, 'From heaven,' he will ask, 'Then why didn't you believe him?' But if we say, 'From men...' '" (They feared the people, for everyone held that John really was a prophet.) So they answered Jesus, "We don't know." Jesus said, "Neither will I tell you by what authority I am doing these things."

Jesus was not intimidated by "leaders of men." As we try to envision this situation we must remember that these were influential, prominent and forceful men. They came to him 'en masse', when he wasn't necessarily expecting them. They challenged his authority in front of his disciples and followers and friends. They were out to get him. Yet Jesus knew that they were mere men, and stood his ground. He decided to turn this pressure situation back on them. First he took control of the situation and said that he would answer their question only if they first answered his. Then he asked them a doozy of a question, and basically outwitted them. By his question he forced them to choose between either exposing their critical, unbelieving hearts toward another prophet of God, or their unrepentant hearts toward the Word of God. When they refused to have their hearts exposed, he refused to answer their question.

How do we handle it when confident and aggressive people challenge our way of life, our doctrine or our work? How would you react if you were publicly put down in front of your friends or co-workers? At times I have felt intimidated and backed down or said nothing in reply to impressive people who have opposed me. Some people try to appease a challenger: they squirm, smile and try to say what the challenger wants to hear. Once I was challenged at work for not allowing the software used in my laboratory to be used elsewhere in the company. The issue came up because I would not allow the secretary of a high-level administrator to duplicate and use some proprietary software which we had been licensed to use in the lab. I explained to her that my policy had always been to not use pirated software, and that by the authority delegated to me, I had decided to not allow it to be present in the lab. In the same way, I would not allow our legal software to be pirated by others. The senior administrator subsequently sent me a note which said that "it is all right to duplicate the lab's software." Unfortunately, he had never bothered to read the licensing agreement which we had accepted in order to use the software, nor did he have any intention of so doing. His secretary returned, confident of victory, and again asked me for the software. I refused. She responded, "but so-and-so said I can take it." I simply told her that so-and-so was not aware of the licensing agreement and that I would not break the law for him or for myself or for anyone else. "But everyone does it!", she said. I stood my ground and she left. I never again heard another word on the subject from her or from the senior administrator. Through this confrontation—and a few others—I earned the respect of my co-workers as one who would stand up eye to eye with the powerful men and women in our company. I certainly can't say that I outwitted them at every turn, or that I was clearly in the right on every issue, but that is not the point. **I made a decision not to buckle when things got hot.** I am not sure that some of my co-workers understood when I explained to them that I had learned to stand my ground from the example of Jesus. But that is the truth.

In the same way, those of us who are disciples need to be ready to contend with those who might challenge our authority to "proselytize" anyone we come into contact with, wherever we go (ie. "make disciples of all nations"†).   We must have an answer ready‡ when challenged by people who claim that we have no right to influence other people for Christ. After all, what could be morally wrong with teaching those who are interested in learning, and calling everyone to make a decision about Jesus? The decision itself—and the consequences of the decision—will remain with them. You can't force someone to love God no matter how hard you try. Yet many will oppose the active disciple of Jesus; many people just want to be left alone, and others simply hate the message of the cross. Following Jesus' example in the above passage, we may have to ask some of our more religious opponents, "Jesus' teaching, was it from heaven or from men?" If they say "from heaven," we will ask them why they don't follow him. If they respond, "from men," we must find out why they say this and either challenge their ignorance with regard to the Scriptures, or challenge their critical, unbelieving hearts which refuse to accept the truth about Jesus. Just before he left for heaven, Jesus said:

> "All authority in heaven and on earth has been given to me. Therefore go and make disciples of all nations, baptizing them in the name of the Father and of the Son and of the Holy Spirit, and teaching them to obey everything I have commanded you. And surely I am with you always, to the very end of the age." (Matthew 28:18-20)

We have the delegated authority of God to live out this great commission. We therefore have the permission of God himself to expose the hearts of those who would challenge our way of life. And even if our opponents are men and women of stature, intimidating leaders who may have authority over us and others, we must remember that they are mere men and women, and that we have the authority of God Almighty.

†Matthew 28:18-20
‡I Peter 3:15-16

Subtlety

Mark 12:1-12 He then began to speak to them in parables: "A man planted a vineyard. He put a wall around it, dug a pit for the winepress and built a watchtower. Then he rented the vineyard to some farmers and went away on a journey. At harvest time he sent a servant to the tenants to collect from them some of the fruit of the vineyard. But they seized him, beat him and sent him away empty-handed. Then he sent another servant to them; they struck this man on the head and treated him shamefully. He sent still another, and that one they killed. He sent many others; some of them they beat, others they killed. He had one left to send, a son, whom he loved. He sent him last of all, saying, 'They will respect my son.' But the tenants said to one another, 'This is the heir. Come, let's kill him, and the inheritance will be ours.' So they took him and killed him, and threw him out of the vineyard. What then will the owner of the vineyard do? He will come and kill those tenants and give the vineyard to others. Haven't you read this scripture: 'The stone the builders rejected has become the capstone; the Lord has done this, and it is marvelous in our eyes'?" Then they looked for a way to arrest him because they knew he had spoken the parable against them. But they were afraid of the crowd; so they left him and went away.

Jesus was very wise. On the offensive here, he uses a simple story to subtly accuse the religious leaders of being murderous and disrespectful towards God. He infers that it would be foolish for anyone of us to think that we deserve heaven (ie. able to take the son's inheritance) when because of our sins the Son of God was crucified. His audience at the time had an undeniable history of killing the prophets God had sent them, yet they smugly felt they were right with God. Jesus teaches them from the Scriptures that the Christ had to be rejected by the Jews just as the other prophets had been rejected. He also teaches by his analogy of the vineyard that God deserves a harvest from our lives, that we have no right to deny him our obedience. Jesus shows that God has first given to us in order that we might be in a position to give back to him. He gives us everything we need and provides us with an opportunity to work for him, yet many of us reject the very idea that we owe him anything. **Whole books could be written on the above issues, but Jesus taught all of this in one simple parable.**

Since Jesus used parables in such a powerful way, we should also learn to communicate truth through the use of parables, stories and analogies. I have recently found these to be extremely useful teaching tools even for describing scientific and computer principles and structures. Besides to instruct, parables can also be used to accuse and to convict.[†] Often, people will be more effectively convinced of their own wrongdoing by seeing themselves in a parable than by direct confrontation. The parable first brings them to realize and to condemn the wrongdoings of characters in the story. When they finally make the connection and realize that they have acted in a similar way, the message comes through loud and clear. Direct statements, on the other hand, are often completely disregarded.

Wisdom

Evidently, a considerable measure of wisdom is required by those of us who wish to imitate Jesus' effectiveness in motivating people. **To be more like Jesus, and to be men or women of impact, we *need* wisdom.** We need to make the right calls at the right times. We need the "apt reply": "A man finds joy in giving an apt reply—and how good is a timely word!"[‡] So often how we act or speak in the pressure times of life dictates the impact that our lives will have. Fortunately, wisdom is a characteristic which we can seek out and acquire. Wisdom and knowledge never come easily. Learning the Bible is an excellent path to understanding:

[†]See II Samuel 12:1-13
[‡]Proverbs 15:23

My son, if you accept my words and store up my commands within you, turning your ear to wisdom and applying your heart to understanding, and if you call out for insight and cry aloud for understanding, and if you look for it as for silver and search for it as for hidden treasure, then you will understand the fear of the LORD and find the knowledge of God. (Proverbs 2:1-5)

The Bible also says that we can directly ask God for wisdom:

If any of you lacks wisdom, he should ask God, who gives generously to all without finding fault, and it will be given to him. (James 1:5)

You may not be convinced that God dishes out wisdom upon request. On the contrary, I have absolutely no doubt that he does. One day several years ago I was encouraged to find out that Henry, the man who initially taught me the Bible, prayed for wisdom every day. Because Henry impressed me as someone with exceptional wisdom, I decided at the time that I too would cash in on God's promise through James. Never before that time but frequently since then, I have been complimented for my wisdom. Even on a work performance review one of the few specific compliments given by my supervisor was that I had excellent judgement and always made wise decisions. I recently found out that my current boss has made a similar comment to his secretary. I don't mind it one bit when people say things like that behind my back! But I do know where this wisdom is from, and I must acknowledge my source. I am often surprised by my own insights and by the advice that comes from my lips when I am providing counsel for friends. I pray for it, God produces it, and I praise him for it.

A Higher Plain

Mark 12:13-17 Later they sent some of the Pharisees and Herodians to Jesus to catch him in his words. They came to him and said, "Teacher, we know you are a man of integrity. You aren't swayed by men, because you pay no attention to who they are;

> but you teach the way of God in accordance with the truth. Is it
> right to pay taxes to Caesar or not? Should we pay or shouldn't
> we?'' But Jesus knew their hypocrisy. ''Why are you trying to
> trap me?'' he asked. ''Bring me a denarius and let me look at it.''
> They brought the coin, and he asked them, ''Whose portrait is
> this? And whose inscription?'' ''Caesar's,'' they replied. Then
> Jesus said to them, ''Give to Caesar what is Caesar's and to God
> what is God's.'' And they were amazed at him.

Jesus wasn't deceived by flattery. He was alert to the
conspiracies and hidden agendas of the people he was dealing
with. When facing a trap, Jesus didn't try to appease everyone;
instead, he spoke openly about their attempt to trap him. Then
he amazed them—not with diplomacy, but with a radical
application of spiritual principles. In this passage he taught
them that a spiritual man won't be as eager to keep what goods
he has away from the governing powers of this world, as he will
be eager to give of what's his to God. **Jesus amazed them with
a spiritual perspective which made simple all the complications and debates they had tried to spring on him.** He
showed that what we give to God is a far more important issue
than what we give to the taxman. In so doing, Jesus not only
escaped from their trap, but he humbled and convicted at least
some of them on their worldly perspectives.

Unity

''They'' say it's not good to talk about religion and politics
because such talk just ends up causing arguments and divisions.
Yet we learn from Jesus that the spiritual man is able to easily
resolve the contentious issues of life. While it is true that
different religions may alienate, the singular truth of God is
intended to completely unify those who accept and submit to it.
Consider, for example, the apostle Paul's pleas for unity in the
following passages:

> As a prisoner for the Lord, then, I urge you to live a life worthy of the

calling you have received. Be completely humble and gentle; be patient, bearing with one another in love. Make every effort to keep the unity of the Spirit through the bond of peace. There is one body and one Spirit—just as you were called to one hope when you were called—one Lord, one faith, one baptism; one God and Father of all, who is over all and through all and in all. (Ephesians 4:1-6)

I appeal to you, brothers, in the name of our Lord Jesus Christ, that all of you agree with one another so that there may be no divisions among you and that you may be perfectly united in mind and thought. (I Corinthians 1:10)

If you have any encouragement from being united with Christ, if any comfort from his love, if any fellowship with the Spirit, if any tenderness and compassion, then make my joy complete by being like-minded, having the same love, being one in spirit and purpose. Do nothing out of selfish ambition or vain conceit, but in humility consider others better than yourselves. Each of you should look not only to your own interests, but also to the interests of others. (Philippians 2:1-4)

Quite clearly, these passages testify that the disciple of Jesus has the secret to complete unity. **Unity *is* achieved as God's people strive together to attain God's thinking on all of life's issues.** Admittedly, it is sometimes difficult to agree on what God would want us to do. But with his Word as a guide, it can be achieved. When people are willing to deny themselves and accept their Creator's thinking above their own opinion they achieve a closeness and a bonding that this world does not know and cannot achieve. It is important to note that the unity that God wants is not built strictly on uniformity. Quite to the contrary, **it is God's plan for diversity and unity to complement each other** as the church of Christ grows and builds itself up in love.[†] **Individuality is wonderful and variety truly is the spice of life.** Sameness is bland and boring, while God's kingdom is one big happy family made up of every nation, every race and every type of people.[‡] If this is true, then why do we see such disunity among all the groups professing to be Christians?   There are, after all, thousands of different

[†]Romans 12:4-8, I Corinthians 12:12-30
[‡]Acts 10:34-36, Revelation 7:9

denominations of Christianity in the United States alone. The answer to this question is actually quite simple and reasonable: a plurality of denominations exists because men and women have not obeyed the above passages (and others) which call followers of God to be perfectly united. Men and women have not done so because it is difficult to deny oneself and accept the truth of God above and beyond one's own understanding. It is much easier for us to align ourselves with others who think as we do, or to grasp teachings which are more flattering to us. Paul long ago correctly predicted that denominationalism would occur:

> "Preach the Word... For the time will come when men will not put up with sound doctrine. Instead, to suit their own desires, they will gather around them a great number of teachers to say what their itching ears want to hear." (II Timothy 4:2-3)

There is considerable evidence to support the theory that a common goal can produce exceptional unity. The marriage that will last and deepen will inevitably be one in which husband and wife not only like each other and love each other but also share the same aspirations, values and truths. The work groups that will be the most productive come rain or shine, good times or tough times, will be those that ascribe to the same dreams and goals, and that stick to their principles. The organizations with the best ideas and greatest talent will not necessarily be the most successful, though they may have their season of greatness. Rather, those with enduring standards, perspectives and ideals will prosper, those that possess a well defined mission statement and those who will not sacrifice integrity for the sake of a quick fix will successfully reach maturity.

Contentedness

Jesus lived in quite modest circumstances and yet he was

content. In this passage we see that he didn't even have a denarius to his name. On another occasion, he had Peter obtain their tax payment from the mouth of a fish.† There was not even a hint of greed in Jesus' life. When his group had money it was kept and dispersed by Judas Iscariot, one of the Twelve. This kind of contentedness with little has a great impact on people. **The teaching, advice, and time of the greedy person always has its price.** People don't trust someone whom they suspect to be greedy or overindulgeant. This distrust may culminate in conflict and alienation. Proverbs 28:25 says that ''a greedy man stirs up dissension.'' Yet someone who is clearly unconcerned about his personal financial status is easy to trust. He will keep no record of what he is owed, be it time, love, or money.

Cockiness

Mark 12:18-27 Then the Sadducees, who say there is no resurrection, came to him with a question. "Teacher," they said, "Moses wrote for us that if a man's brother dies and leaves a wife but no children, the man must marry the widow and have children for his brother. Now there were seven brothers. The first one married and died without leaving any children. The second one married the widow, but he also died, leaving no child. It was the same with the third. In fact, none of the seven left any children. Last of all, the woman died too. At the resurrection whose wife will she be, since the seven were married to her?" Jesus replied, "Are you not in error because you do not know the Scriptures or the power of God? When the dead rise, they will neither marry nor be given in marriage; they will be like the angels in heaven. Now about the dead rising—have you not read in the book of Moses, in the account of the bush, how God said to him, 'I am the God of Abraham, the God of Isaac, and the God of Jacob'? He is not the God of the dead, but of the living. You are badly mistaken!''

Jesus wasn't always a ''nice guy.'' Imagine saying these phrases to someone who is generally respected as an expert on

†Matthew 17:27

the Bible: "Are you not in error?"; "you do not know the
Scriptures or the power of God"; "have you not read... ?";
"you are badly mistaken!." Every one of those phrases cuts
like a knife. Jesus was so confident that he might even be
described as cocky! It was his intention to challenge his critics.
As much as he came to *comfort the disturbed,* he also made it
his goal to *disturb the comfortable!* He wasn't afraid to rock
their boats. Of course, Jesus did not focus exclusively on
challenging and rebuking the religious establishment—but he
did not at all shy away from it, as a "nicer" man might have
done.

And so we see that in order to have a lasting impact it is
necessary for us to be polemic and willing to challenge our
opponents to their faces. **When people are proud and
comfortable, blind to their own ignorance, we need to be the
ones who will say something to disturb them.** We encounter
these types of people everywhere. Some of our bosses may fit
into this category: no one ever dares to say anything to them to
challenge the way they mistreat people and misunderstand and
mishandle situations—at least not to their faces! We live in a
world filled with comfortable religious leaders who have never
come to understand or accept the basic principles of God's
Word. Are we willing, like Jesus, to stand up and speak out
against the ignorance and unbelief of these so-called priests,
ministers and pastors? Even in our personal relationships we
must be willing to "mix it up." Many times a husband or wife
of our acquaintance may be completely confident of their own
innocence in a particular conflict with their spouse. They are
sure that it is their spouse alone who needs correction.
Husbands especially can be quite sure that any "reasonable
human being" would be able to see how their wife's behavior is
the source of the problem. A friend who in any way feeds this
perception will push a reconciliation farther away, while a
friend who exposes and rebukes the pride of the self-righteous
spouse will save the marriage. **"Better is open rebuke than**

hidden love."†

Expertise

Mark 12:28-34 One of the teachers of the law came and heard them
debating. Noticing that Jesus had given them a good answer, he
asked him, "Of all the commandments, which is the most
important?" "The most important one," answered Jesus, "is this:
'Hear, O Israel, the Lord our God, the Lord is one. Love the Lord
your God with all your heart and with all your soul and with all
your mind and with all your strength.' The second is this: 'Love
your neighbor as yourself.' There is no commandment greater
than these." "Well said, teacher," the man replied. "You are
right in saying that God is one and there is no other but him. To
love him with all your heart, with all your understanding and with
all your strength, and to love your neighbor as yourself is more
important than all burnt offerings and sacrifices." When Jesus
saw that he had answered wisely, he said to him, "You are not far
from the kingdom of God." And from then on no one dared ask
him any more questions.

Jesus impressed people with his right answers and his apt
replies. He was prepared to give an answer on any topic that
anyone might choose to challenge him. He was a verifiable
expert. He didn't have shallow Bible knowledge, but could
demonstrate his expertise on a level that impressed and silenced
all of his critics. In the same way, **before we can expect the
people around us to trust us and to believe in us, we must
devote ourselves to developing the necessary expertise in our
chosen field.** We need to do our homework. We must become
authentic experts who cannot easily be embarrassed at our lack
of knowledge on any point. We need to know our stuff, to know
the whys and the wherefores in order to make an impact on the
job. This kind of expertise comes only through study, through
good teaching, and through hard work. Even Jesus, the
Incarnate Word of God, sat at the feet of the Teachers of the

†Proverbs 27:5

Law and the Pharisees when he was a boy.† Jesus knew what he was talking about; consequently, he silenced his critics.

Here is a trustworthy saying: **Good students make the best teachers. Likewise, good listeners are worth listening to.** Unfortunately, some of us want to skip over the student phase and jump right into the teacher phase. We feel that we already know all there is to know about something without having received any instruction. We know how to have a great marriage, we know how to raise our children, we know how to get to heaven—and all of this without ever seeking advice or reading a single book! We must think that we are the Mozarts of life, having an intuitive wisdom and not needing to imitate the example of proven experts or to learn from the mistakes of the experienced. ''The way of a fool seems right to him, but a wise man listens to advice.''‡ Jesus said: ''Therefore consider carefully how you listen. Whoever has will be given more; whoever does not have, even what he thinks he has will be taken from him.''§

A Champion

Mark 12:35-37 While Jesus was teaching in the temple courts, he asked, ''How is it that the teachers of the law say that the Christ is the son of David? David himself, speaking by the Holy Spirit, declared: 'The Lord said to my Lord: ''Sit at my right hand until I put your enemies under your feet.'' 'David himself calls him 'Lord.' How then can he be his son?'' The large crowd listened to him with delight.

Everybody loves a winner. Having quieted all of his opponents, Jesus, in victory, tells the crowd the riddle he had up his sleeve in case the teachers of the law had not quit when they did. The Old Testament teaches—and the Jews all knew—that

†Luke 2:40-51
‡Proverbs 12:15
§Luke 8:18

the Messiah would be a descendent of King David.† However, Jesus reminds the Jews that David himself, not in error but by the Spirit of God, declares the Messiah to be his Lord (ie., his superior or master). The false belief that he was addressing was the one that painted a picture of the Messiah as being less than or at best equal to King David. Jesus shows the people from the Scriptures that while the Messiah would be from the lineage of David, he would be far greater than David. This is quite a bold teaching, especially from one actually claiming to be the Messiah. But at this point, everyone in the crowd was delighted. They had witnessed an apparent underdog win a decisive victory over his many well-robed opponents.

Winning isn't everything, but for the man or woman who desires to make an impact in life, it is extremely important. Winning a contest, a debate, or a battle immediately establishes the victor as someone for others to imitate and follow. People want to win and they want to be on the side of a winner. **Few people rush to associate themselves with a loser.** Of course, a victor's actions on the road to victory are also extremely important. Mud-slinging, cheating and other reproachful actions, while perhaps effective in bringing about a short-term victory, are counterproductive for one seeking to have a long-term influence on others. Therefore, fight fair—and do your best to win. Second-place finishers are all but ignored in the championship celebration.

Reprobation

Mark 12:38-44 As he taught, Jesus said, "Watch out for the teachers of the law. They like to walk around in flowing robes and be greeted in the marketplaces, and have the most important seats in the synagogues and the places of honor at banquets. They devour widows' houses and for a show make lengthy prayers. Such men

†Isaiah 11:1-3, Jeremiah 23:5-6, Ezekiel 34:23-24

will be punished most severely."

After establishing himself as a prophet with wisdom far greater than any of the contemporary religious leaders, Jesus immediately warned the people to watch out for the hypocrisy of these men. He knew that he had gained the upper hand, and that the people were delighted with his superior wisdom. Yet he also knew that popular opinion would turn. He therefore wasted no time in alerting the people to discern those who used religion for show from those who were committed to do the will of God. He made it clear that these hypocritical leaders would be blown away when they faced God. Their smugness would melt away when they were forced to answer to God. Jesus let the people know that these men were damned.

Discernment

Mark 12:41-44 Jesus sat down opposite the place where the offerings were put and watched the crowd putting their money into the temple treasury. Many rich people threw in large amounts. But a poor widow came and put in two very small copper coins, worth only a fraction of a penny. Calling his disciples to him, Jesus said, "I tell you the truth, this poor widow has put more into the treasury than all the others. They all gave out of their wealth; but she, out of her poverty, put in everything—all she had to live on."

Jesus was careful to select worthy people for public honor. Here he applauded sacrifice above generosity. In a similar way, we applaud those who win gold medals in the Olympic Games—yet we have begun to wonder how many of these victories are purchases of a rich country, the performance of its athletes merely the product of the best training facilities, the best drugs, the best masking agents, the best psychologists, and the best biomechanics technology. I get the biggest thrill out of watching the runners from Kenya who do not train in the United States or Europe. These athletes from relatively poor countries seem to simply love to run. They run not for the gold, for their countries, for show, or to get rich from endorsements. They run from the heart, for the sheer excitement of pouring themselves out to win the race. **We need to learn how to discern the *relative* merits of people's deeds. If we do, we will be able to find those people around us of exceptional *character.*** They may not always have had the best opportunities in life, but they will be those who inspire others to live by principle, to hold nothing back as they pursue truth and love and righteousness.

It is interesting to contrast what Jesus said about the poor widow with what he said about the religious leaders. There can be little doubt but that Jesus esteemed good character and thought little of whatever else people gained or achieved in this life. The Bible teaches that "God 'will give to each person according to what he has done.' To those who by persistence in doing good seek glory, honor and immortality, he will give eternal life. But for those who are self-seeking and who reject the truth and follow evil, there will be wrath and anger."† Likewise, we need to be sensitive to demonstrations of good character. **We judge too many books by their covers. We applaud glitzy winners, and we often fail to notice the hidden glory of those who deny themselves.**

Snoopiness

Some bystanders might have asked Jesus what business he had watching to see how much money people were putting into the temple treasury. Was he not invading their privacy? Apparently Jesus made it his business to know the details about other people's relationships with God. He wanted to know the extent of other people's love for God. Therefore, **he carefully watched people; he assessed their level of commitment by**

†Romans 2:6-8

observing their actions. It is important to note that Jesus was not interested in getting something to hold against people. He never gossipped; he slandered no one. Rather, he was genuinely concerned about the condition of people's hearts before God. This genuine concern gave him license to find out the details.

It is a mistake to think that we can effectively help people when we don't know the details of what is going on in their lives. Likewise, we will miss the extraordinarily good actions of others if we are not making it our business to know what they are doing. Society today seems to uphold a seldom stated but widely accepted agreement: "You mind your own business and I'll mind my business and we will all be better off." This practice is intended to ward off gossip, but it also eliminates constructive interaction. Unfortunately, because we do live in a world which is consumed with a passion for juicy gossip, people are ever suspicious of other people's interest in their lives. But men and women of impact must not look the other way. We must care enough to see what is really going on in people's lives. And along with our clear vision, **we must** *demonstrate* **a genuine concern for the welfare of others** so that people will have no valid reason for suspicion.

The Warning

Mark 13:1-37 As he was leaving the temple, one of his disciples said to him, "Look, Teacher! What massive stones! What magnificent buildings!" "Do you see all these great buildings?" replied Jesus. "Not one stone here will be left on another; every one will be thrown down." As Jesus was sitting on the Mount of Olives opposite the temple, Peter, James, John and Andrew asked him privately, "Tell us, when will these things happen? And what will be the sign that they are all about to be fulfilled?" Jesus said to them: "Watch out that no one deceives you. Many will come in my name, claiming, 'I am he,' and will deceive many. When you hear of wars and rumors of wars, do not be alarmed. Such things must happen, but the end is still to come. Nation will rise against nation, and kingdom against kingdom. There will be earthquakes in various places, and famines. These are the beginning of birth pains. "You must be on your guard. You will be handed over to the local councils and flogged in the synagogues. On account of me you will stand before governors and kings as witnesses to them. And the gospel must first be preached to all nations. Whenever you are arrested and brought to trial, do not worry beforehand about what to say. Just say whatever is given you at the time, for it is not you speaking, but the Holy Spirit. "Brother will betray brother to death, and a father his child. Children will rebel against their parents and have them put to death. All men will hate you because of me, but he who stands firm to the end will be saved. "When you see 'the abomination that causes desolation' standing where it does not belong—let the reader understand—then let those who are in Judea flee to the mountains. Let no one on the roof of his house go down or enter the house to take anything out. Let no one in the field go back to get his cloak. How dreadful it will be in those days for pregnant women and nursing mothers! Pray that this will not take place in winter, because those will be days of distress unequaled from the beginning, when God created the world, until now—and never to be equaled again. If the Lord had not cut short those days, no one would survive. But for the sake of the elect, whom he has chosen, he has shortened them. At that time if anyone says to you, 'Look, here is the Christ!' or, 'Look, there he is!' do not believe it. For false Christs and false prophets will appear and perform signs and miracles to deceive the elect—if that were possible. So be on your guard; I have told you everything ahead of time. "But in those days, following that distress, "'the sun will be darkened, and the moon will not give its light; the stars will fall from the sky, and the heavenly bodies will be shaken.' "At that time men will see the Son of Man coming in clouds with great power and glory. And he will send his angels and gather his elect from the four winds, from the ends of the earth to the ends of the heavens. "Now learn this lesson from the fig tree: As soon as its twigs get tender and its leaves come out, you know that summer is near. Even so, when you see these things happening, you know that it is near, right at the door. I tell you the truth, this generation will certainly not pass away until all these things have happened. Heaven and earth will pass away, but my words will never pass away. "No one knows about that day or hour, not even the angels in heaven, nor the Son, but only the Father. Be on guard! Be alert! You do not know when that time will come. It's like a man going away: He leaves his house and puts his servants in charge, each with his assigned task, and tells the one at the door to keep watch. "Therefore keep watch because you do not know when the owner of the house will come back—whether in the evening, or at midnight, or when the rooster crows, or at dawn. If he comes suddenly, do not let him find you sleeping. What I say to you, I say to everyone: 'Watch!'"

Jesus prepared his disciples by talking with them and warning them about the future. Moreover, he gave them confidence that they wouldn't be left on their own in any of the struggles they would face, that the Holy Spirit would be with them. He assured them that his day would come, and that it would be the last day. The Lord's faithful would be ultimately victorious. To share in his victory, they needed to pay attention and be on their guard, and they needed to stay faithful to him until the end.

While we may have no ability to predict events of the future, we know that **every venture will be *tested* and every good endeavor will find *opposition*. We must therefore inspire those around us who share a common purpose to be *faithful until the end*.** We need to forewarn them about opposition so that they will be ready to meet it face to face. **Too often people treat life as if it were a fairytale. They hope that the struggles in which they are presently engaged will be their last, and that they will then "live happily ever after."** To warn people that they will have challenges and trials until the very end is not usually what they want to hear. You won't read that kind of thing on a birthday card. **Yet we must, as men and women of impact, deal with life as it really is. Life is a *challenge*, and it is an *adventure*.** If people think that they are building up to some point after which they can relax and coast the rest of the way, they are deceived! On the other hand, if people do accept the struggle but are unable to see the light at the end of the tunnel, they need our help. We must inspire our friends and co-workers to believe that with perseverance our good efforts will produce hoped-for results. We must convince them that good will ultimately triumph over evil, but not without a fight. And we must believe this ourselves.

The Spark

Mark 14:1-2 Now the Passover and the Feast of Unleavened Bread were only two days away, and the chief priests and the teachers of the law were looking for some sly way to arrest Jesus and kill him. "But not during the Feast," they said, "or the people may riot."

The chief priests and the teachers of the law regarded Jesus as a catalyst, able to set off a reaction among the people which they would not be able to control. Jesus was, more precisely, a spark. **His words *ignited* people, both for and against him.** He was a revolutionary, and those who wanted to maintain status quo were afraid of his influence.

Having studied the ways of Jesus, we should not be surprised that he could ignite the masses. We have come to understand how he achieved such a position of influence. Very few of us will ever reach such prominence, because very few of us are willing to be loved and hated that much; few of us could stand to be respected and feared to that degree. But for those who are willing to completely live their lives for a dream, to live for others, to make a difference, Jesus has demonstrated the fullest possible extent of influence. By his words this one man could have started a riot, initiated a revolution, overthrown the rulers and made himself king. But he chose instead to die.

Although most of us will not achieve this level of impact, we must realize that we can be the individuals who turn a crowd. By living a life of impact, we can be those who inspire large groups of people; we too can have the pivotal opinion and sway the vote. This influence needn't come by way of political power, popularity or good looks. Rather it will be achieved by selflessness and by holding to a standard of excellence in all areas of life. Perhaps some people will even be willing to lay down their lives for you—or against you—if you choose to take a stand for what is right.

Romantic

Mark 14:3-11 While he was in Bethany, reclining at the table in the home of a man known as Simon the Leper, a woman came with an alabaster jar of very expensive perfume, made of pure nard. She broke the jar and poured the perfume on his head. Some of those present were saying indignantly to one another, ''Why this waste of perfume? It could have been sold for more than a year's wages and the money given to the poor.'' And they rebuked her harshly. ''Leave her alone,'' said Jesus. ''Why are you bothering her? She has done a beautiful thing to me. The poor you will always have with you, and you can help them any time you want. But you will not always have me. She did what she could. She poured perfume on my body beforehand to prepare for my burial. I tell you the truth, wherever the gospel is preached throughout the world, what she has done will also be told, in memory of her.'' Then Judas Iscariot, one of the Twelve, went to the chief priests to betray Jesus to them. They were delighted to hear this and promised to give him money. So he watched for an opportunity to hand him over.

Jesus exalted passionate action from a person's heart above practicality. He valued passion, and he found beauty in extravagant actions prompted by love. His own ultimate demonstration of extravagant, unrequited love was seen at the cross. He laid down his life because of his passionate love for us.[†] On this occasion, he strongly reprimanded those who were attacking the woman who had shown such extravagant love. (She is elsewhere identified as Mary, the sister of Martha and of Lazarus, whom Jesus had raised from the dead.[‡]) By defending this woman, Jesus provoked bad attitudes in those who disagreed with him. In particular, Judas did not see eye to eye with Jesus on this one.

[†] I John 3:16
[‡] John 12:1-3

Many of us need to "break the alabaster jars" in our own lives. **We have love and passion and gratitude all bottled up and safely stored away.** Prudence is our middle name, and moderation our trusted friend. We are boring to our wives, and we never surprise anybody. But just what are we waiting for anyway? **Spontaneity, extravagance and apparently unreasonable actions are the trademarks of passionate love.** In contrast, the words "routine," "balanced," and "practical" are not descriptors of a passionate relationship. Break that jar today! Express your love and gratitude in a way which will be remembered.

Accepting Praise Graciously

Why do most of us find it very difficult to accept praise graciously? It is probably because we covet it so much and hear it so seldom. And on those rare occasions when we do receive a compliment, we deny, we diminish, we dodge, we discredit or we retaliate. We *deny* the praise by saying: "Oh, it was nothing, really." We *diminish* the compliment by saying: "It wasn't only me, I got a lot of help." We *hide* behind a joke so that our true feelings of gratitude are not exposed. We *discredit* the praise-giver in our hearts by convincing ourselves that he is only flattering us to get something from us. We *retaliate* by praising her back, passing the compliment like a hot potato, and thus taking the focus off of ourselves: "Look who's talking! YOU look gorgeous!" Sometimes the best we can do is to offer back a sheepish "thank you." All of these practices are characteristic of insecurity. **We don't want people to know how much we crave the compliment, so we pretend that it means nothing to us.** Sometimes we even succeed in convincing ourselves that we are not seeking to be appreciated by others. If you are convinced that you don't want or need praise from anyone, then why do you act so funny when you are

complimented? **The way a person responds to a compliment
is a clear indication of the condition of his or her self image.**
I am convinced that we all share a fundamental need to be
appreciated by others. Unfortunately, many of us refuse to
accept that we have this need. We would prefer to think that we
don't need anyone: "I can be quite happy on my own, thank
you." I think this attitude begins at some point in life as a
protective reaction to not being appreciated enough by those we
love.

Jesus acted quite out of the ordinary (here we go again!) with
regard to accepting praise and honor. He found it right and
fitting, yet he didn't get self-absorbed. He even defended the
woman who honored him when she was attacked for being too
extravagant. He held her up for honoring him. Clearly, Jesus
was deeply moved by this beautiful gesture of love and
appreciation. Most of us need to learn to accept praise more
graciously. We often deserve it, and we definitely need it.
Besides, **one person praising or honoring another is
intrinsically beautiful, just as two small children hugging
and kissing each other is beautiful.**

The crucible for silver and the furnace for gold, but man is tested by the
praise he receives. (Proverbs 27:21)

Connections

Mark 14:12-16 On the first day of the Feast of Unleavened Bread, when it
was customary to sacrifice the Passover lamb, Jesus' disciples
asked him, "Where do you want us to go and make preparations
for you to eat the Passover?" So he sent two of his disciples,
telling them, "Go into the city, and a man carrying a jar of water
will meet you. Follow him. Say to the owner of the house he
enters, 'The Teacher asks: Where is my guest room, where I may
eat the Passover with my disciples?' He will show you a large
upper room, furnished and ready. Make preparations for us
there." The disciples left, went into the city and found things just

as Jesus had told them. So they prepared the Passover.

What does it take to get dinner reservations in a busy city... on a holiday weekend... for a large group of people... at the last minute... at a private spot... at a minimal charge? The answer is simple: connections. Jesus had connections; there is no other way to explain it. True, they were miraculous, divine connections, but they were connections none the less. Ask some people what it takes to get a job, especially in the arts, and they will answer but one word: connections. "Sometimes, it's not what you know but who you know." Jesus knew the Sovereign God—the One who either makes it happen, or allows it to happen, or it doesn't happen—and He took care of even the trivial details.

Men and women of impact need connections. **Connections are other people of influence or position who know you and who are willing to help you.** These aquaintances don't have to be the "top dogs" in their organization; if they are respected, or if they themselves have connections with other respected individuals, they can help you. **If you don't have many connections, this is probably either because you are not a very friendly person, or because you are intimidated by influential people.** In either case you can change, and you need to change. I am not at all condoning being friendly towards people for the sake of what you might get from them someday. **Most people can see right through "friends" who only befriend them to get something from them. You cannot hope to have a lasting impact if you use people.** As the Bible teaches, "Love must be sincere."† For those of us trying to live by faith, we need to remember that we already have some great connections. I couldn't begin to count the number of times that a parking spot opened up for me just as soon as I finished reminding God that I was there to do his will, and asking, "Could you please find me a place to put this car?" Usually when I pray that kind of prayer, God responds by providing me with the very best

†Romans 12:9

possible parking spot amidst a crowd of other cars seeking parking spots. The same is true about finding an apartment to rent in a city with a vacancy rate of less than one percent. I tell God that I've got better things to do with my time than to run around for weeks, like everyone else, trying to find a place to live. Apparently, God has always agreed. In the same way, when my wife and I were looking to buy our first house, we made a list of everything we wanted in the house, along with the price range we could afford. The first night we went out looking at houses, we came across *The House*. We found out shortly thereafter that this house had every single thing we wanted, and was within our price range. Just to make sure, we continued to look around. Nothing else came close to matching up one hundred percent with what we were praying about. Fortunately, we wasted no time, and we have had no regrets about our purchase. I could go on and on with personal examples, but the point is clear. Disciples of Jesus have most of the connections that they will need already; they just need to ask. "Ask and it will be given to you; seek and you will find; knock and the door will be opened to you. For everyone who asks receives; he who seeks finds; and to him who knocks, the door will be opened."†

Unconditional Love

Mark 14:17-26 When evening came, Jesus arrived with the Twelve. While they were reclining at the table eating, he said, "I tell you the truth, one of you will betray me—one who is eating with me." They were saddened, and one by one they said to him, "Surely not I?" "It is one of the Twelve," he replied, "one who dips bread into the bowl with me. The Son of Man will go just as it is written about him. But woe to that man who betrays the Son of Man! It would be better for him if he had not been born." While they were eating, Jesus took bread, gave thanks and broke it, and

†Matthew 7:7-8

gave it to his disciples, saying, "Take it; this is my body." Then he took the cup, gave thanks and offered it to them, and they all drank from it. "This is my blood of the covenant, which is poured out for many," he said to them. "I tell you the truth, I will not drink again of the fruit of the vine until that day when I drink it anew in the kingdom of God." When they had sung a hymn, they went out to the Mount of Olives.

Isn't it curious that none of the other disciples knew that Judas was the one who would betray Jesus. Of course Jesus knew; he had known all along. Yet he had never treated Judas any differently than he had the rest of the Twelve. Imagine—he had never given in to telling a single Judas joke. Jesus allowed Judas to be the keeper of the money bag even though he knew that Judas was greedy, often helping himself to what was put into the bag.[†] But beyond being merely equitable and fair toward Judas, Jesus loved him like he did the rest of his closest friends. When he washed the disciples' feet in order to show them the full extent of his love,[‡] he washed Judas' feet along with the others. He loved and gave himself to Judas even though he knew that Judas would eventually betray him for thirty pieces of silver.[§] If Jesus treated Judas this fairly, we can be sure that his love toward everyone else was unconditional as well. He didn't give up on his closest friends when they disappointed him. He never became critical or bitter about any of his relationships. He preached that we should "love our enemies,"[¶] and he lived up to his own preaching.

Conditional love **puts an unbearable strain on relationships.** Eventually, the relationships cannot stand up under the strain, and they disintegrate. *Unconditional love,* **on the other hand, never fails.**[¥] **It allows relationships to become stronger through adversity. It provides the workbench upon which weaknesses can be built into strengths.** It gives security,

[†]John 12:3-6
[‡]John 13:1-17
[§]Zechariah 11:12-13, Matthew 26:15
[¶]Matthew 5:44
[¥]I Corinthians 13:8

wipes away fear, builds confidence, adds hope, teaches perseverance, and erases discouragement and doubt. Marriages built on conditional love will not last. If a wife gives of herself in love to her husband only as long as he satisfies her needs and fulfills all of her expectations, she is at least in part responsible for the inevitable downward spiral their marriage will take. Likewise, if a husband only feels obligated to love his wife when she is pleasing him, then his love is not sufficient for building a great marriage. But if husband and wife are committed to loving each other regardless of how they are treated in return, they will have a fantastic marriage. Here is a simple principle which has held true in every marriage or dating relationship I have ever observed: if each partner is more concerned about what wrongs the other person has done against them than they are about helping him or her, the marriage or dating relationship is on its way down. Conversely, if each one is more concerned about what to do for the other person and for their relationship than about what that person may have done against them, the relationship is on its way to greater heights. But, you may be thinking, what about the third possibility: that one spouse is honestly trying to overlook the wrongs committed against him or her and focus on how to better love his or her spouse, but the spouse is doing the opposite? Yes, this possibility does exist. In fact, this type of imbalance is essential if a marriage is to turn around, from bad/getting worse, to good/getting better. Quite clearly, if each person is waiting for the other to start loving unconditionally before they will respond, the marriage is stuck in a downward direction. If neither spouse will decide to love and give to the other regardless of whether the initiative will be reciprocated or even appreciated, then they are without hope. **The key is not to love *if* or *because of*, but to love *in spite of*. In-spite-of love cannot fail to make a lasting impact.**

The Memorial

Jesus instituted a memorial feast, while he was on earth, to help the disciples remember the significance of his approaching death. While tradition-based denominations of Christianity today observe many other symbolic rituals, this is the only one which Jesus himself instituted. **He did not intend for his followers to become ritualistic; certainly, his own relationship with God was not based on ritual, and he did not promote religiosity.** Rather, he called people to righteousness. However, this memorial accomplishes a necessary purpose. Eating real bread and drinking real wine helps to remind us of the actual physical reality of Jesus' sacrifice: his flesh was pierced and his blood was poured out. It really happened. The very act of eating involves accepting something and taking it deep inside of us. Similarly, we need to realize that Jesus died for us as individuals as much as he died for us collectively. Because he died for my sins, I share personally in responsibility for his death. If I can accept that Jesus died for me, I can also share personally in what was accomplished through his death—the forgiveness of sins, *my sins*. Thus the symbols of the bread and the wine are effective reminders of the death and resurrection which are the cornerstone of the Christian faith, that which calls us and motivates us to daily deny ourselves and follow Jesus. He knew that we needed help remembering his death for our sins. He made sure that people of his day and of future generations would remember and understand why he died.

So what has this to do with living a life of impact? Simply put, **people need frequent reminders in order to keep on track. We so soon forget what is important; we so easily get distracted by the activities of life, and we so quickly lose our convictions.** However, the fewer different reminders we use, the better. Otherwise we become ritualistic and begin to miss the whole point of what we are doing.

Open Arms

Mark 14:27-31 "You will all fall away," Jesus told them, "for it is written: "'I will strike the shepherd, and the sheep will be scattered.' But after I have risen, I will go ahead of you into Galilee." Peter declared, "Even if all fall away, I will not." "I tell you the truth," Jesus answered, "today—yes, tonight—before the rooster crows twice you yourself will disown me three times." But Peter insisted emphatically, "Even if I have to die with you, I will never disown you." And all the others said the same.

Jesus first gave them the bad news and then the good news. The bad news was that they would all disown him; the good news was that they would come back to him and he would be there to welcome them. On this particular evening their attention was focussed solely on the bad news, which they could not accept. How could any of them turn their backs on their friend and their God? They loved Jesus more than they had ever loved anyone before, even more than they loved their own lives, *or so they thought.* Wanting to prove Jesus wrong just this once, they all in unison rejected this bad news. Later on, they would remember his words. They would bring to mind his promise to remain faithful to them even if they disowned him. They would cling to his declaration that he would be there for them when they came back. He would forgive them, and they would move ahead together.

Imagine how you would react to a supervisor who, after giving you some very challenging instructions, added, "At some point you will fail miserably in what I am asking you to do. However, when you pick yourself up and start over, we can meet again, and I will believe in you then even more strongly than I believe in you now." Our immediate reaction would likely be to emphatically insist that we would make sure not to fail the first time around. But after we did fail, we would be encouraged to remember that our boss had said that he would accept us back with open arms, even if our failure hurt him personally.

Jesus was apparently a better judge of his men's characters and depth of conviction than they were themselves. He also knew that Biblical prophecy backed up his prediction, making it a sure thing. Sometimes, because of our experience or our more objective position, we can better predict how others will handle a situation than they can themselves. It is therefore appropriate that **we should warn others to be ready for failure—not to discourage them, but to assure them that they can bounce back; they can and they must press on.** ___Failure is unavoidable, *defeat* comes when we give up!___ **Our people must know that we will be there for them even after they fail.** People will often react negatively to this type of input, as Jesus' disciples did. However, negative reactions are tolerable, provided our interventions prevent people from later giving up in discouragement.

A Giver of Life

Each of Jesus' men thought that he was prepared to lay down his life for Jesus. To their collective dismay, they were to discover later that very night that they weren't the hero types they thought they were, at least not at that point in their lives. Nevertheless, it is amazing that each of these eleven men would consider Jesus to be more important to him than his own life. Not just one of them or a few of them, but every last one considered Jesus's life worthy of the sacrifice of their own. Part of the reason was surely because they believed him to be the only Son of God, but I believe there was more to it than this. He had become their friend, and they loved him deeply. **He had given each of them *a new life,*** and he had allowed them to play important roles in his plan to turn people back to God. **He**

had **rescued them from lives of** *obscurity,* **and had offered**
them a reason for living. <u>**Anyone who discovers a cause for**</u>
<u>**which he would be willing to die has discovered the reason**</u>
<u>**for which he was born.**</u> **Conversely, if one does not have**
something for which he would die, then for what is he
living? Could your own life be compared to a brief roller
coaster ride with ups and downs, a few brief, thrilling moments,
and then an unavoidable return to where you started—nonexist-
ence? Or perhaps your life could be better described as being
like a merry-go-round or like a bumper car? Jesus had taken
these men out of the amusement park, and they knew it.

Emotional Transformation

Mark 14:32-42 They went to a place called Gethsemane, and Jesus said to
         his disciples, "Sit here while I pray." He took Peter, James and
         John along with him, and he began to be deeply distressed and
         troubled. "My soul is overwhelmed with sorrow to the point of
         death," he said to them. "Stay here and keep watch." Going a
         little farther, he fell to the ground and prayed that if possible the
         hour might pass from him. "Abba, Father," he said, "everything
         is possible for you. Take this cup from me. Yet not what I will,
         but what you will." Then he returned to his disciples and found
         them sleeping. "Simon," he said to Peter, "are you asleep?
         Could you not keep watch for one hour? Watch and pray so that
         you will not fall into temptation. The spirit is willing, but the
         body is weak." Once more he went away and prayed the same
         thing. When he came back, he again found them sleeping, because
         their eyes were heavy. They did not know what to say to him.
         Returning the third time, he said to them, "Are you still sleeping
         and resting? Enough! The hour has come. Look, the Son of Man
         is betrayed into the hands of sinners. Rise! Let us go! Here comes
         my betrayer!"

It would be especially beneficial to read through this passage a
few times. Try to envision Jesus at the beginning of this
passage, and contrast your picture with the Jesus we see at the
end of the passage. Could this be the same man? In just three

hours, Jesus made one of the most dramatic emotional turn-arounds one could imagine. He went from being distressed, troubled and completely overwhelmed with sorrow, to being bold, strong and in complete control, ready for suffering beyond compare; he changed from a pallid, sweat-drenched man with shoulders hunched, back bowed and head held low, to a conqueror, standing erect, chest out, head held high, voice booming, eyes glowing, ready for the battle ahead. Mark makes it very clear that Jesus' friends provided him with absolutely no support at all during this spiritual struggle. Because of their own sorrow, they couldn't even keep awake. Jesus went to God in prayer, initially not wanting to go to the cross, but committed to doing the will of God. And God strengthened him, and transformed him radically. This was not a demonstration of the power of positive thinking; this kind of transforming power can come only from the One who raises the dead.

Unless we are part machine, all of us are overwhelmed at times by family problems, by losses, failures, challenges, frustrations, by life itself. Quite often, these emotionally down times conflict with our plans for personal effectiveness. **If we are leaders, we cannot afford to be "down" for any significant length of time.** Leaders do not have the luxury of "private pity parties." People and projects depend on us. For the Christian leader, souls weigh in the balance. **Therefore, the ability to make a quick and complete emotional turn-around is invaluable for the man or woman who wants to have an impact.** Unfortunately, as leaders we are often forced to face our greatest challenges alone. The mere sight of a leader struggling with something can paralyze the leader's friends and followers. They will continue to be discouraged as long as the leader puts off dealing with his or her emotions and with the situation which provoked an emotional response. The leader must grit his or her teeth, dig down deep, and muster up the courage to face the issues. Indeed, when leaders overcome very real and difficult troubles, their companions gain hope and are encouraged to persevere through the challenges in their own lives.

I thoroughly believe that the man or woman of God is at a distinct advantage when it comes to overcoming negative emotions. According to the Bible, God is "the Father of compassion and the God of all comfort, who comforts us in all our troubles, so that we can comfort those in any trouble with the comfort we ourselves have received from God."† But it is up to each one of us to face up to our feelings, to not accept our downcast hearts, and to wrestle with ourselves until we overcome. For the Christian, this means aligning ourselves, heart and soul, with the will of God.

In Touch With His Feelings

Many of us, particularly the men, would be at a loss if we were asked to complete this sentence: "Right now, I'm feeling... ." Likewise, many of us would never attempt to communicate our feelings, even to someone very close to us. Perhaps our emotional self feels so out of control and unpredictable that we feel compelled to deny its existence. Or perhaps we refuse to accept our emotionally-driven behavior: it is unproductive and irrational, and it certainly doesn't match up to our perfection-conscious self-image. Men often have the socially reinforced misconception that feelings are not masculine. Whatever the reason might be, the conclusion is the same: we are not *complete* people if we are out of touch with our feelings. **The person who is unfamiliar with his or her own emotional nature is a slave to it, while the person who is familiar with his or her emotional weaknesses is in a position to master them.** I was once unable to discern whether I was feeling frustration, impatience, anger, or anxiety. With no handle on what I was feeling, I had no hope to overcome my emotions. I

---

†II Corinthians 1:3-4

used to not be able to admit, even to myself, that I was unhappy, that I wasn't at peace. Part of my problem was that I thought that "spiritual" men were almost always happy, so for me to show how I was really feeling was equivalent to revealing my spiritual immaturity. What I didn't understand was that the spiritual man, through humility, has become acquainted with his own emotional self, and armed with that knowledge, has learned to turn his negative emotions around quickly. Every time I look at the emotional transformation of Jesus in the garden of Gethsemane, I realize that I still have a long way to go to achieving true emotional maturity.

Openness

Most of us fall into one of two personality types: *stoic* **or** *cathartic*. Stoics are those whose feelings and burdens are locked away deep inside of them, never to be shared with even their best of friends; "cathartics" are those who dump their feelings on anybody who will listen, thereby passing their burdens on to others. Neither personality type is conducive to developing deep, emotional bonds with other people. In contrast, Jesus practiced complete openness without making others responsible for his feelings. He made himself vulnerable to the reproach of his three closest friends by expressing to them the depth of his feelings. Yet he maintained his own responsibilty to act upon the situations which were stirring up strong emotions within him. **Jesus leaned on his friends, but he didn't dump on them.** He allowed his closest friends the priviledge of seeing what was going on deep inside of him, even at this time of his greatest inward struggle.

Many of us are so concerned about how others will perceive us that we are unwilling to allow them to know when we are struggling with something. We try to hide it, deny it, or avoid it—often with limited success. The more it hurts, the less likely that we will let others know about it. Jesus was "overwhelmed with sorrow to the point of death!"[†] He was so troubled by what he knew lay before him—the cross—that he was *at risk of death* from the sheer pressure of it. I don't think many of us have been under that kind of pressure. Jesus had the strength of character to talk about it openly with those closest to him, on his own initiative. **Premeditated openness is a key to fostering deep, meaningful relationships.** Such relationships will help us to face the crosses in our own lives. Indeed, the quality and depth of our relationships will to a large degree determine the value of our lives, and the greatness of our impact on others.

Deliberation

Fortunately for all of us, Jesus didn't abandon his decision-making process after just one hour of prayer. Even though he knew that by dying on the cross he would provide us all with forgiveness of sins, thus reconciling us to God, part of him still didn't want to go through with it. He looked desperately for a way of escape. After deliberating at length, he was convinced that there could be no other alternative. After even more wrestling, he was able to rally his heart and soul behind his decision. **Too many of us would be unwilling to persevere through a long and difficult decision-making process. We would like all of our decisions to be quick and easy, and we might think that something is wrong if we have to struggle to get our hearts behind what our heads know to be right.** But tough decisions are an inescapable part of life. We must be willing to put in whatever effort is required to reach the best decision, and to carry through with it.

[†]Matthew 26:38

A Powerful Presence

Mark 14:43-52 Just as he was speaking, Judas, one of the Twelve, appeared. With him was a crowd armed with swords and clubs, sent from the chief priests, the teachers of the law, and the elders. Now the betrayer had arranged a signal with them: "The one I kiss is the man; arrest him and lead him away under guard." Going at once to Jesus, Judas said, "Rabbi!" and kissed him. The men seized Jesus and arrested him. Then one of those standing near drew his sword and struck the servant of the high priest, cutting off his ear. "Am I leading a rebellion," said Jesus, "that you have come out with swords and clubs to capture me? Every day I was with you, teaching in the temple courts, and you did not arrest me. But the Scriptures must be fulfilled." Then everyone deserted him and fled. A young man, wearing nothing but a linen garment, was following Jesus. When they seized him, he fled naked, leaving his garment behind.

Jesus, at the time of his capture, was completely poised and in control. He renounced his captors use of weapons, and their underhanded decision to come in the middle of the night. He chose not to resist capture, and willingly gave himself to them. Apparently this crowd of armed men arriving in the middle of the night was a fearsome spectacle, for all of the disciples eventually fled in fear. One young man didn't even have the presence of mind to grab his robe as he fled.[†] Yet even as swords were raised, Jesus remained undaunted.

John gives us an additional detail about the circumstances of Jesus' capture: "Jesus, knowing all that was going to happen to him, went out and asked them, 'Who is it you want?' 'Jesus of Nazareth,' they replied. 'I am he,' Jesus said. (And Judas the traitor was standing there with them.) When Jesus said, 'I am he,' they drew back and fell to the ground."[‡] Apparently, Jesus was so forceful and so in control that he startled his captors. He had such presence and such fearlessness that they were

[†]Many scholars think this young man was Mark, the author of the gospel.
[‡]John 18:4-6

physically knocked off of their feet. Now that is a powerful presence!

Self-Control

Mark 14:53-65 They took Jesus to the high priest, and all the chief priests, elders and teachers of the law came together. Peter followed him at a distance, right into the courtyard of the high priest. There he sat with the guards and warmed himself at the fire. The chief priests and the whole Sanhedrin were looking for evidence against Jesus so that they could put him to death, but they did not find any. Many testified falsely against him, but their statements did not agree. Then some stood up and gave this false testimony against him: "We heard him say, 'I will destroy this man-made temple and in three days will build another, not made by man.'" Yet even then their testimony did not agree. Then the high priest stood up before them and asked Jesus, "Are you not going to answer? What is this testimony that these men are bringing against you?" But Jesus remained silent and gave no answer. Again the high priest asked him, "Are you the Christ, the Son of the Blessed One?" "I am," said Jesus. "And you will see the Son of Man sitting at the right hand of the Mighty One and coming on the clouds of heaven." The high priest tore his clothes. "Why do we need any more witnesses?" he asked. "You have heard the blasphemy. What do you think?" They all condemned him as worthy of death. Then some began to spit at him; they blindfolded him, struck him with their fists, and said, "Prophesy!" And the guards took him and beat him.

Despite having to face lies, mocking, intimidation, false accusations and the like, Jesus remained calm. Nothing or nobody could cause him to renounce his position. He didn't even lose his cool when he was tried in a mock court of justice. He quietly accepted the abuse which was being poured out on him. When the real issue of contention was brought up by the high priest, he confidently proclaimed his divinity. He was not looking for a safe way out of this situation, and he would not crack or break down under pressure. He was not at all afraid.

After they condemned him to death, they began to treat him quite disgracefully. It is obvious that some of these distinguished and respectable men lost all self-control; anger stored up in their hearts for months and years poured forth in childish cruelty. Remember, for these men to act this way must have seemed completely out of character. After all, they were the religious and community leaders. They liked to walk around in flowing robes and, for a fee, to say lengthy prayers. But they hated Jesus, and this was their hour to humiliate him, as he had so often humiliated them in the past. While they lost their tempers, Jesus maintained his composure. They lashed out at him savagely. All the while, Jesus never retaliated, never cursed them in return. Clearly, Jesus' adversaries were no match for him, even as they led him through the events leading up to his execution.

What is your standard for self-control? Do you allow yourself to fly off the handle if someone makes the mistake of rubbing you the wrong way? Do you justify your own infantile behavior and your childish responses because the other person acted improperly, and do you store up bitterness, rage and envy in your heart, dreaming of the time when you will be able to "get even?" **Take an honest look at yourself and decide whether, if you were present in this situation, you would be more like Jesus or like the religious leaders.** If you find yourself lacking self-control, remember that self-control is a promised fruit of living the Christian life.[†] Before I was a Christian, I personally found it impossible to increase my self-control. The "animal within" often had its way. But I have found that God wields sufficient power to put the "animal"—my sinful nature—to death. I don't believe any of us has the ability to do that on our own. Try it if you like. In the meantime, I will continue to enjoy the freedom that God provides me with in order to do more of what I really want to do, and to do a whole lot less of what I don't really want to do.[‡]

[†]Galatians 5:22-23
[‡]Romans 7:14-25

Unforgettable Words

Mark 14:66-72 While Peter was below in the courtyard, one of the servant
girls of the high priest came by. When she saw Peter warming
himself, she looked closely at him. "You also were with that
Nazarene, Jesus," she said. But he denied it. "I don't know or
understand what you're talking about," he said, and went out into
the entryway. When the servant girl saw him there, she said again
to those standing around, "This fellow is one of them." Again he
denied it. After a little while, those standing near said to Peter,
"Surely you are one of them, for you are a Galilean." He began
to call down curses on himself, and he swore to them, "I don't
know this man you're talking about." Immediately the rooster
crowed the second time. Then Peter remembered the word Jesus
had spoken to him: "Before the rooster crows twice you will
disown me three times." And he broke down and wept.

Jesus' words stuck with people. If they didn't have an
immediate impact, they were able to track down the hearer and,
echoing in the subconscious mind, maintain their power to
challenge and convict. Of course the fact that Jesus was a
prophet helped. The second crowing of the rooster was like a
trigger, and Jesus' words shot back to Peter's mind. Peter
probably never forgot Jesus' words. Even years later, the sound
of a rooster crowing would bring back a flood of memories.
Surely all of his men would have clear memories associated
with Jesus' words, and these memories would always fan into
flame the feelings that they had for him. Their faith and
convictions would be renewed, and their arrogance and pride
would be snuffed out. Jesus' words had—and still have—lasting
impact.

**Leaving behind words that stir people's hearts from
generation to generation is one mark of a man or woman of
impact.** Most of Jesus' recorded words would fall into this
category. H. G. Wells wrote: "The true test of greatness is,
'What did the person leave behind to grow?' By this test Jesus
stands first." Similarly, people of impact will use words which

deeply affect their companions and adversaries alike, words
with latent power to arouse conviction.

An Indomitable Spirit

Mark 15:1-5 Very early in the morning, the chief priests, with the elders,
the teachers of the law and the whole Sanhedrin, reached a
decision. They bound Jesus, led him away and handed him over
to Pilate. "Are you the king of the Jews?" asked Pilate. "Yes, it
is as you say," Jesus replied. The chief priests accused him of
many things. So again Pilate asked him, "Aren't you going to
answer? See how many things they are accusing you of." But
Jesus still made no reply, and Pilate was amazed.

Even facing torture and execution, Jesus refused to renege.
Unlike Pilate, Jesus would not change his story in order to save
his own skin. In fact, he wouldn't even speak up in his own
defence. He was completely composed and did not react to the
false accusations of his accusers. Pilate was amazed at Jesus'
strength of character, and also because Jesus was not afraid of
what was going to happen to him. Jesus would not break down
and he would not retaliate. His courage would not melt under
the fire of his adversaries. He was ready to die.

Mettle

Mark 15:6-32 Now it was the custom at the Feast to release a prisoner
whom the people requested. A man called Barabbas was in prison
with the insurrectionists who had committed murder in the
uprising. The crowd came up and asked Pilate to do for them
what he usually did. "Do you want me to release to you the king
of the Jews?" asked Pilate, knowing it was out of envy that the
chief priests had handed Jesus over to him. But the chief priests
stirred up the crowd to have Pilate release Barabbas instead.
"What shall I do, then, with the one you call the king of the
Jews?" Pilate asked them. "Crucify him!" they shouted. "Why?

What crime has he committed?'' asked Pilate. But they shouted
all the louder, ''Crucify him!'' Wanting to satisfy the crowd,
Pilate released Barabbas to them. He had Jesus flogged, and
handed him over to be crucified. The soldiers led Jesus away into
the palace (that is, the Praetorium) and called together the whole
company of soldiers. They put a purple robe on him, then twisted
together a crown of thorns and set it on him. And they began to
call out to him, ''Hail, king of the Jews!'' Again and again they
struck him on the head with a staff and spit on him. Falling on
their knees, they paid homage to him. And when they had mocked
him, they took off the purple robe and put his own clothes on
him. Then they led him out to crucify him. A certain man from
Cyrene, Simon, the father of Alexander and Rufus, was passing
by on his way in from the country, and they forced him to carry
the cross. They brought Jesus to the place called Golgotha (which
means The Place of the Skull). Then they offered him wine mixed
with myrrh, but he did not take it. And they crucified him.
Dividing up his clothes, they cast lots to see what each would get.
It was the third hour when they crucified him. The written notice
of the charge against him read: THE KING OF THE JEWS. They
crucified two robbers with him, one on his right and one on his
left. Those who passed by hurled insults at him, shaking their
heads and saying, ''So! You who are going to destroy the temple
and build it in three days, come down from the cross and save
yourself!'' In the same way the chief priests and the teachers of
the law mocked him among themselves. ''He saved others,'' they
said, ''but he can't save himself! Let this Christ, this King of
Israel, come down now from the cross, that we may see and
believe.'' Those crucified with him also heaped insults on him. At
the sixth hour darkness came over the whole land until the ninth
hour.

Jesus would simply not turn back. He was determined to
successfully complete his mission—even if success meant
enduring a painful death. Consider all he was to endure
following the abuse he received from the Chief Priests. First, a
murderer was released to the crowd in his stead. Then he was
flogged, probably within an inch of his life, by Romans
soldiers. Then a purple robe was thrown over his back—which
would have been a bloody, shredded mess at this point—and a
crown of thorns was placed on his head, and the soldiers

mocked him. They hit him repeatedly on the head with a staff. They coated him with their spit. Then the robe which had adhered to the blood on his back was ripped off of him, beginning a new flow of blood from the wounds. Finally, they led him out to be crucified. Crucifixion entailed pounding two long heavy nails through his wrists and one through both of his feet. All of his body weight would be supported by these three new centers of pain, not by ropes around his arms as depicted by every product of Hollywood that I've ever seen. Every breath would be agonizing. He would have to push up against the nail in his feet in order to exhale. In the end, his death would be the result of asphyxiation when he was at last drained of the energy to push against the nail any longer. And all the while, the crowd mocked and insulted him.

The nails were not what kept Jesus on the cross. Rather, it was love coupled with determination. Matthew recorded the following words of Jesus at the time of his arrest: "Do you think I cannot call on my Father, and he will at once put at my disposal more than twelve legions of angels?"[†] It is absolutely incredible, but Jesus could have stopped everything at any moment with but one word from his mouth. A single angel was reported to have killed one hundred and eighty five thousand Assyrian soldiers in one night.[‡] I shudder to think what twelve thousand angels could have done to this ungodly world had they been summoned to intercede as the creation endeavored to torture the Creator. Fortunately for us, Jesus refused to summon them.

All too often, we give up on the verge of a great victory. We lose sight of the goal and become overwhelmed by pain and by the obstacles confronting us. Sometimes the apparent cost of victory far exceeds what was expected, and when we find ourselves lacking in stamina, we take the path of least resistance. To have an impact, we must develop the mettle to

[†]Matthew 26:53
[‡]II Kings 19:35

push through obstacles and to take our focus off the pain. We must be those who finish what we start, regardless of the cost. **The human spirit, created in the image of God, is in its glory when tested, as demonstrated in the suffering of Jesus.** When we have given our all, and it seems like our well is dry and there is nothing left to give—at those times, if we do not give up, we will experience a fulfillment unmatched by anything else in life. Only we must not give up!

A Dramatic Death

Mark 15:33-47 At the sixth hour darkness came over the whole land until the ninth hour. And at the ninth hour Jesus cried out in a loud voice, "Eloi, Eloi, lama sabachthani?"—which means, "My God, my God, why have you forsaken me?" When some of those standing near heard this, they said, "Listen, he's calling Elijah." One man ran, filled a sponge with wine vinegar, put it on a stick, and offered it to Jesus to drink. "Now leave him alone. Let's see if Elijah comes to take him down," he said. With a loud cry, Jesus breathed his last. The curtain of the temple was torn in two from top to bottom. And when the centurion, who stood there in front of Jesus, heard his cry and saw how he died, he said, "Surely this man was the Son of God!" Some women were watching from a distance. Among them were Mary Magdalene, Mary the mother of James the younger and of Joses, and Salome. In Galilee these women had followed him and cared for his needs. Many other women who had come up with him to Jerusalem were also there. It was Preparation Day (that is, the day before the Sabbath). So as evening approached, Joseph of Arimathea, a prominent member of the Council, who was himself waiting for the kingdom of God, went boldly to Pilate and asked for Jesus' body. Pilate was surprised to hear that he was already dead. Summoning the centurion, he asked him if Jesus had already died. When he learned from the centurion that it was so, he gave the body to Joseph. So Joseph bought some linen cloth, took down the body, wrapped it in the linen, and placed it in a tomb cut out of rock. Then he rolled a stone against the entrance of the tomb.

> Mary Magdalene and Mary the mother of Joses saw where he was
> laid.

Another characteristic of a life of impact is the ability to make good come from a bad situation. Even in the way he died, Jesus made an impression on the people around him. Mark tells us here about a centurion, a leader over a hundred Roman soldiers and *a man who had probably witnessed many other executions,* who was astounded by watching the final moments of Jesus' agony. Apparently this Roman guard had heard about Jesus' claims, and **in just a few hours of watching him on the cross, he came to believe that Jesus actually was the Son of God.** This is really quite impressive. Imagine: Jesus' head was swimming with pain, blood was dripping from his body, several of his bones had been pulled out of joint.[†] All the while he was surrounded by a hostile crowd of onlookers and had their incessant jeers and taunts ringing in his ears. **His character was exposed to all who watched as he was crushed under the strain and agony of his torture. Nevertheless, he was gaining disciples; he was having an impact.**

Proof

> Mark 16:1-8 When the Sabbath was over, Mary Magdalene, Mary the
> mother of James, and Salome bought spices so that they might go
> to anoint Jesus' body. Very early on the first day of the week, just
> after sunrise, they were on their way to the tomb and they asked
> each other, "Who will roll the stone away from the entrance of
> the tomb?" But when they looked up, they saw that the stone,
> which was very large, had been rolled away. As they entered the
> tomb, they saw a young man dressed in a white robe sitting on the
> right side, and they were alarmed. "Don't be alarmed," he said.
> "You are looking for Jesus the Nazarene, who was crucified. He
> has risen! He is not here. See the place where they laid him. But
> go, tell his disciples and Peter, 'He is going ahead of you into
> Galilee. There you will see him, just as he told you.'" Trembling

[†]Psalm 22:14

> and bewildered, the women went out and fled from the tomb.
> They said nothing to anyone, because they were afraid.

Other men have walked on this planet and proclaimed the way to eternal life, and all of their bones lie rotting in the dust of the earth. **Unquestionably, Jesus' corpse did not remain in the tomb in which he was buried, nor did it turn up somewhere else.** Only about five hundred people in all claimed to see Jesus risen from the dead,[†] however, and all of these witnesses were disciples of his. **Could the Resurrection have been a carefully-planned hoax?** Perhaps Simon the Zealot had led an elite team of disciples—say Rambo son of James, lightfooted Lazarus, and Peter, who may have feigned cowardice just to escape suspicion—to roll back the stone, steal the body of Jesus right from under the noses of the Roman soldiers (who had conveniently fallen asleep while guarding the tomb) and destroy the body to hide all evidence. I personally find this scenario rather hard to believe, yet it seems the most reasonable of all the alternatives that I have heard. **Regardless of whether he was raised from the dead or not, Jesus succeeded after his death in having a greater impact than any of us will have while we are still alive.** This was the beginning of one of the greatest controversies of all time. If Jesus was raised from the dead, his divinity is sure. If he was not, he was perhaps the greatest deceiver who has ever lived. **Did he rise or didn't he? You must examine the evidence and decide.**

One Last Rebuke

Mark 16:9-14 When Jesus rose early on the first day of the week, he appeared first to Mary Magdalene, out of whom he had driven seven demons. She went and told those who had been with him and who were mourning and weeping. When they heard that Jesus was alive and that she had seen him, they did not believe it. Afterward Jesus appeared in a different form to two of them while

[†] I Corinthians 15:6

they were walking in the country. These returned and reported it
to the rest; but they did not believe them either. Later Jesus
appeared to the Eleven as they were eating; he rebuked them for
their lack of faith and their stubborn refusal to believe those who
had seen him after he had risen.

I admit that I have been in the wrong a few times in my life,
(O.K., quite a few times!) and for some of these errors I have
been rebuked. I know from experience how it feels to be
rebuked. However, I still have a hard time imagining just how
bad the disciples must have felt on this occasion. If any of
Jesus' rebukes had a particularly lasting impact on their lives,
this was the one. On any future occasion when they began to
doubt the teachings of Jesus or the Scriptures, they would be
brought back to faith by the memory of Jesus' last stinging
rebuke. They had refused to believe those who had seen Jesus
risen from the dead: "You were merely having a dream";
"You just saw what you were hoping to see"; "I don't blame
you for being fooled by your own wishful thinking, we are all
feeling the great loss of his death." Later, when Jesus walked
into the room where they were all gathered (without even using
the door†), his oft-spoken promise to them that he would rise
from the dead came back into their minds. There were no
"high-fives," no celebration at the beginning of this reunion;
the disciples were rightfully ashamed of their disbelief, and
Jesus was upset about it. He probably didn't need to say a word
to the disciples for them to feel remorse, but he had a few
words with them anyway. They had blown it and they needed to
find true faith. His message was meant to be convicting and
life-changing; by all indications, it was very effective.

His Last Words

Mark 16:15-20 He said to them, "Go into all the world and preach the

†John 20:19,26

good news to all creation. Whoever believes and is baptized will
be saved, but whoever does not believe will be condemned. And
these signs will accompany those who believe: In my name they
will drive out demons; they will speak in new tongues; they will
pick up snakes with their hands; and when they drink deadly
poison, it will not hurt them at all; they will place their hands on
sick people, and they will get well." After the Lord Jesus had
spoken to them, he was taken up into heaven and he sat at the
right hand of God. Then the disciples went out and preached
everywhere, and the Lord worked with them and confirmed his
word by the signs that accompanied it.

As expected, Jesus had a very purposeful final encounter with
his followers. With his last words, he commissioned all who
would come after him to spread the good news of his
resurrection to the rest of the world. He had shown them how to
go about it, and he had already explained why it had to be done.
Now he was simply telling them to go and do it. He told them
that he would be working with them. Amazing signs would
accompany his co-workers for the first couple of generations,[†]
and surely he would continue to accompany and work through
those who remained faithful to him.[‡] He reminded them in the
most simple of terms that theirs was a life and death mission.
Their success meant people being saved from condemnation.
All that he could say or do personally had been said and done.
Now they would have to take the torch and run with it.

[†]For the first generation of Christians, miraculous signs were meant to confirm that
God was with His movement. These signs were not at all like the counterfeit signs
which some religious groups proclaim today. To speak fluently in a language which
you have never studied is miraculous, to babble incoherently is not. To place your
hands on people who have never walked, whose muscles are atrophied and whose
joints are inflexible, and to make them immediately stand up and walk, or to give
sight to those who have been blind from birth is quite different from the dubious
"miracles" performed by some miracle workers (ie. healing backache or asthma).
This is not to say that God no longer answers prayers for miraculous healing. I have
no doubt but that he still does. God answered prayers for healing long before gifts of
healing were given to the apostles. The Bible also teaches that these "miraculous
gifts" were passed on by the laying on of an apostle's hands, but could not be passed
on through those who had received them from an apostle. (Acts 8:12-18) Therefore,
the miraculous signs were to fade away (I Corinthians 13:8-10) over the course of the
first two generations of Christianity.
[‡]Matthew 28:18-20, John 15:4-8

What would your last words be? Think about it. If you could leave those around you with a few thoughts, or with one single admonition, what would you say? Could you pass on to them your drive, your motivation for living? What do they need to hear from you more than anything else, not just for tomorrow, but for all of their tomorrows? If you cannot at this time come up with these answers, then give it some more thought. **Once you know what your last words would be, I give you this charge: Say them today!** Say today what you would say on your last day because you are not guaranteed a tomorrow. **Say it today because then you will have *begun* to fulfill your mission.** Jesus' last words echoed the words he spoke at the very beginning of his ministry: "Repent and believe the good news! Come follow me and I will make you fishers of men."† **Jesus wanted others to join him in saving people out of the world and into the kingdom of God. These were his *first* words and they were also his *last* words.** "... Go into all the world and preach the good news to all creation. Whoever believes and is baptized will be saved, but whoever does not believe will be condemned."‡ Say it today.

†Mark 1:15,17
‡Mark 16:15-16

CONCLUSION

We have just completed our study of, unquestionably, one of the most effective and knowledgeable leaders of all time. Jesus embodies the ideal qualities of a leader. He was both forceful and gentle. He was confident and sensitive. He was fearless and fearsome. He disturbed the comfortable and comforted the disturbed. He was feared by his opponents, and adored by little children. He cleansed the temple and he touched lepers. While claiming to be the King of kings, he lived as the servant of servants. He was a bold dreamer who effectively reproduced his dream in the minds and hearts of his followers. He knew how to move people, how to help them to change and live new lives. He was able to reproduce his personal effectiveness by raising ordinary people to leadership in a relatively brief period of time, people who then raised up other people who would join with them in changing the world.

This book has focussed on Jesus as an impeccable model for our own personal growth. But before concluding this study, I find it necessary to propose and attempt to answer two final questions: **Is it true that Jesus really lived this way? And if indeed he did, does this give us evidence that he is God?**

Consider the first question: Did Jesus really live this way? There are but two possibilities: either Jesus did live the life described in Mark's gospel, a life which epitomizes the ways and traits of an impacting leader, or Mark cleverly synthesized his account of Jesus' life. There are two categorical problems with the second possibility. First of all, if Mark invented stories which revealed such incredible leadership skills of Jesus, then Mark himself was an amazing theoretician of effective leadership skills. It is preposterous to imagine that Mark could weave together hundreds of insights about effective leadership techniques into a fictional life story of Jesus. It is much easier to believe that he merely reported what he saw and heard.

Secondly, all of the parallel accounts of Jesus' life and ministry agree with that of Mark's gospel. Ignorant and unstable people might promote the idea of a grand conspiracy, but the thought is quite absurd, even to those who do not believe Jesus' claims about himself.

On to the second question. Mark's gospel has revealed that Jesus was indeed the very archetype of a great leader. He was much more than a leader who had an astounding and lasting impact; **he was, as far as we can see, *faultless* as a leader.** There have been many great leaders over the course of history. A few of them have risen out of obscurity to effectively lead the masses. Yet not one of them or any of their followers would dare claim that he had known all there was to know about leadership. All have certainly made mistakes, erred in judgement, and made unwise decisions. Some of them have even been merciless, egotistical, or cruel. The impact of most of history's great leaders ended with their death; at best, their impact lasted a generation or two after their death. In contrast, **Jesus seemed to know *exactly* what he was doing from the very beginning.** I find no plausible way to explain his *perfect example* except to say that he was indeed *an example of perfection.* Admittedly, I am very impressed with the lifestyle and teachings of Jesus, and I have not made it a secret that I personally believe him to be the Son of God. But **how else could this unschooled carpenter have known all there is to know about influencing people to change their lives?** The evidence of his effectiveness has already been presented. I encourage you to make your own decision.

An important addendum must be made here. Jesus was a man of impact, but not for the sake of any earthly gain. He was a man of impact to the glory of the Father and for the salvation of the souls of men and women. **He influenced people because he loved people; he didn't love people because he wanted to influence them. What is *your* motivation for being a man or woman of impact?** Perhaps you need to think long and hard on this question. For we have not merely completed a review of the techniques and principles adhered to by an effective leader; we have also learned about the heart and character of this unique man.

On a more personal note, if after looking into the gospel record of Jesus you are eager to learn more about how to become a true disciple of Jesus, I suggest that you send me a letter care of the publisher of this book. Likewise, I would welcome any questions, comments and criticisms you might have.

Can we become men and women of impact? Yes! Can we be more influential than our level of talent and our present course in life might predict? Absolutely! Thanks to the Evangelist Mark, we have had the privilege of personally walking with Jesus, the Master Impacter. We have closely examined his life and character, his way with people. I can honestly say that my own life has already changed as a result of this study. Now it is your turn. **My only admonition to you is this: act upon what you have learned immediately or it will be lost to you.** It is my conviction that you and I were both created to live a life of impact and influence. **We *can* make a difference in this world!** Jesus has set a faultless example for us to follow. Come, let us follow him!

INDEX

CHAPTER SUBHEADINGS

INDEX

CHAPTER SUBHEADINGS